EVERTON'S
FA CUP
100
A CENTURY OF GLORY AND DRAMA

Sport Media

A Trinity Mirror Business

This book is dedicated to Evertonians everywhere who have fought and battled to get tickets for big Cup games and whose passion and pride in the club comes across loud and clear on these pages. They are as much a part of Everton's remarkable FA Cup story as the players themselves. Together they have helped to make history.

Written and researched by:
JAMES CLEARY and WILLIAM HUGHES

Statistics: GAVIN BUCKLAND

Sport Media
A Trinity Mirror Business

Executive Editor: KEN ROGERS Editor: STEVE HANRAHAN
Production Editor: PAUL DOVE Art Editor: RICK COOKE
Sales and Marketing Manager: ELIZABETH MORGAN
Designers: LEE ASHUN, GLEN HIND,
COLIN SUMPTER, BARRY PARKER
Writers: ALAN JEWELL, GAVIN KIRK,
DAVID RANDLES, CHRIS McLOUGHLIN

Published in Great Britain in 2006 by: Trinity Mirror Sport Media,
PO Box 48, Old Hall Street, Liverpool L69 3EB.
ISBN 1905266081

Photographs: Liverpool Daily Post and Echo. Trinity Mirror.
Additional images: Everton Football Club, EMPICS (page 128-129).

Printed by Scotprint, Haddington, Scotland.

Contents

Happy days! Fans gather in
Liverpool city centre to welcome
home the heroes of 1966.

Inset opposite: Bob Howarth's
1897 FA Cup medal

From the moment Everton Football Club enjoyed its first major trophy success – on 20 March 1884 – Blues' fans have been captivated by the magic of Cup football.

They did not win the holy grail of the English game that day, the FA Cup, but rather its Merseyside equivalent – the Liverpool Cup.

But don't under-estimate the prestige locally of this famous old trophy. Don't forget, these were the days when Liverpool FC did not even exist. Everton's city rivals were the likes of St Peter's and the arch-enemy Bootle who were crushed en route to the Liverpool Cup Final where Earlestown were vanquished to take the trophy back to Priory Road and the Sandon pub, the club's headquarters at the time.

This was the year Everton moved grounds – to Anfield!

Having claimed the Liverpool Cup, the fight for more silverware became intense, although it would be 1886/87 before the club entered the FA Cup for the first time. They were drawn against Glasgow Rangers, but on the eve of the tie at Anfield, Everton officials realised they had no chance of winning unless they played men who were ineligible for FA Cup action. They opted to select their strongest team, but formally scratched from the competition – making the game nothing more than a prestige friendly. The Scots won 1-0.

The following season controversy surrounded the Merseysiders again as they sought to make real progress in the competition.

Their opener featured a four-game marathon against Bolton Wanderers who, a year later, would be joining Everton as founder members of the newly formed Football League. The first FA Cup clash, away from home, was lost 1-0 but Everton were granted a replay because Bolton had fielded an ineligible player. Two drawn matches followed before Everton won the fourth clash. This time Bolton appealed, claiming that seven Everton 'amateurs' had been offered money to play.

Before a decision was taken, Everton lost 6-0 in the second round to Preston North End. The FA declared that the Merseysiders had been eliminated anyway because of Bolton's appeal and now Wanderers met Preston in a re-arranged tie. Again, Preston's power showed when they crushed Wanderers 6-0.

The 'Everton Seven' were now declared professionals by the FA and the whole club was suspended for a month from 5 December 1887. Even the Liverpool FA acted against the club, confiscating the Liverpool Cup from its place behind the bar in the Sandon. Everton, frustrated by what should have been a pioneering opening season in the FA Cup, decided not to appear in the competition the following year (1888-89) and they struggled to get beyond the opening stages at the next three attempts.

However, this competition would ultimately prove to be a glorious stage and when the club left Anfield for Goodison in time for the 1892-93 season, Evertonians could celebrate their first appearance in an FA Cup Final, albeit a 1-0 losing experience against Wolves at Fallowfield, Manchester.

The final would be reached again in 1897, but it would be 1906 before the club won its first FA Cup, beating Newcastle 1-0.

This special book marks the 100th anniversary of that success, the Blues claiming the trophy on four further occasions – 1933 (Manchester City 3-0), 1966 (Sheffield Wednesday 3-2), 1984 (Watford 2-0) and 1995 (Manchester United 1-0).

Along the way there have been some incredible moments and this book, marking the centenary of that first success, selects 100 of them. 'Everton's FA Cup 100' has utilised the unmatchable archive of the Liverpool Daily Post & Echo to produce the definitive history of the club's FA Cup achievements.

We salute three legendary FA Cup winning captains – Brian Labone, Kevin Ratcliffe and Dave Watson – who came together to help us produce some fascinating memories from their Wembley triumphs.

We also acknowledge the support of the club, not least Media and Publications Manager Darren Griffiths, while Gavin Buckland's statistical advice was invaluable.

Of course, we acknowledge the fans themselves – the heart of the People's Club. This book is for them.

Ken Rogers

Following the leaders

Everton's three surviving Cup-winning captains relived past glories when they were reunited for a special dinner in the city earlier this year. BRIAN LABONE, KEVIN RATCLIFFE and DAVE WATSON made more than 1,500 appearances for Everton between them but the moment they proudly lifted the famous trophy above their heads at Wembley will always rank among their greatest memories.

What are your own personal memories of the finals? They were all very different.

BL: Yes, ours took place in black-and-white!

DW: Were you expected to win, Brian?

BL: Oh, without doubt and we were lucky to win in the end. It was a relief to beat Sheffield Wednesday especially when you are 2-0 down. Gordon West always says he knew we were going to win but you do start thinking it was not to be.

It had all started off with the team news that Fred Pickering was dropped because he had a bad leg and Mike Trebilcock came in. Trebilcock was like manna from heaven because he only played a few games for us. It was a little bit jammy for Harry (Catterick) but what a time to score a couple of goals!

Then there was Jimmy Gabriel holding the ball up at the corner flag near the end!

KR: Yes, I've seen that footage. He was shielding the ball and when it was finally forced out, he held both hands above his head like a prize fighter who had just scored a knockout.

BL: I think he was trying to waste time because Tommy Wright had a bit of cramp in the back of the calf from

chasing the right winger.

KR: It was interesting watching that game on the DVD. Brian and his defence didn't come off their 18-yard line and their centre-backs wouldn't come off theirs and all you've got is these gaps and Colin Harvey running up and down, up and down!

BL: It was quite defensive for a 3-2 game!

KR: When I watched our match against Watford I found it boring because the referee's whistle didn't stop going. It seemed Mo Johnston (later to play for Everton) was always offside!

BL: As for 1995 Dave, well goodness me!

DW: We were expected to lose against Manchester United. They were the favourites by a long way.

BL: The best Everton performance I've ever seen in my life was at Elland Road in the semi-final. The wrong team got to the final didn't they? It was supposed to be a Tottenham v Manchester United final (Tottenham had originally been suspended from the competition before being re-admitted on appeal) and we murdered them.

KR: 1995 was the first FA Cup final I'd been down to watch as I'd been invited down as a guest and to play in an old boys' match before the game. And you know when you have that

Down memory lane: From left: 1995 skipper Dave Watson, 1966 skipper Brian Labone and captain in 1984, Kevin Ratcliffe

The Captains

'I was the manager of the Everton Old Boys and after the game we were getting changed when Andy King came in. In his cockney accent, he says: 'Flippin' 'eck! Here I am, I've ran my ******** off, I've scored the winning goal and all I can flippin' see when I come off is fans holding up a dirty sheet with 'Bob Latchford Walks On ******* Water' on it!"

BRIAN
LABONE

feeling you're going to get something out of the game? I had that feeling that day. Everything was prominently blue. Littlewoods were sponsoring the game and all their sponsorship boards and so on were in blue. When we played Man United in '85, the majority of the ground was red for some reason. But all around the ground was blue that day. Sometimes when all you see is blue, blue, blue you feel like you've got extra support anyway.

DW: I remember sitting in the hotel in the lead-up to the game and seeing 'On The Ball' and they had clips of all their lads walking around, having a good laugh and they looked over-relaxed. You looked at the faces on our lads and the expressions told you that we all knew we were in for a game and it looked as though United thought they'd

just have to turn up to beat us.

KR: Everyone said that about us in '84. But we were more relaxed because we were all youngsters. We were only 21,22, 23-year-olds. The oldest were Reidy and Andy at 28, 29. I was 23, Trevor Steven would only have been about 21. Gary and Derek 21, Sharpy, Inchy and myself 23, Sheeds 24, Neville was about 25, Kev Rich was 21 or 22.

BL: Neville, Reidy and Andy Gray put the age up. But there's nothing wrong with getting old you know!

DW: I remember the Echo produced all these plastic blue noses before our final and there was a picture of Duncan Ferguson wearing one at the end.

BL: I was working for Littlewoods at the time and the only person who wouldn't wear one was David Johnson,

who said he'd had a falling out with the Echo! The funny thing about that day was the former players game Kev mentioned. It was quite a warmish day anyway and being down at Wembley, well it's always a bit warmer than up here! We beat them 1-0 which was a good omen. I was the manager of the Everton old boys and after the game we were getting changed when Andy King came in. In his Cockney accent, he says: 'Flippin' 'eck! Here I am, I've ran my ******** off, I've scored the winning goal and all I can flippin' see when I come off is fans holding up a dirty sheet with 'Bob Latchford Walks On ******* Water' on it!' Bob was also playing and he came off looking

like a tailor's dummy with not a hair out of place!

KR: I played in the game and the thing I remember about it was that everyone kept knocking balls into the channel for Dave Hickson to run on to! I remember I kept shouting: 'What are you all doing? Are you trying to kill him or what?!'

BL: Before that game, Dave (Hickson) and I were on the bus on the way to our hotel on Park Lane. My wife Pat said to me: 'Why are you and Dave coming all the way into the West End when you've already passed Wembley 500 yards away? You're going to have to come back and there could be a bit of a traffic jam.' So we get out and Dave and I are

'I remember the Echo produced all these plastic blue noses before our final and there was a picture of Duncan Ferguson wearing one at the end'

DAVE WATSON

'If you stepped out of line, you'd be hammered. And not just by Howard Kendall but by every player. You did respond to that responsibility and I think that was a good way of going about it. He wanted you to be a disciplinarian as well. The other lads were with me and I was with them'

KEVIN RATCLIFFE

trying to thumb a lift the last half-mile to Wembley. We've got all our blue-and-white stuff on and all the fans are going past with their blue-and-white scarves and waving at us. They thought we were waving at them but we wanted a bloody lift! One fan eventually stopped and gave us a lift up. We got him a ticket, although I'm sure they'd have got in anyway. But what a day!

KR: Daniel Amokachi scored twice in your semi didn't he Dave?

DW: That's right. That was the substitution where he brought himself on! Paul Rideout went down injured, went off the pitch to get treatment and Amokachi came on without Joe Royle saying so. A great substitution!

BL: Coming back from Elland Road, I remember hearing Leeds had beaten Liverpool at Anfield 1-0 in a league game. So that made the day even better!

All three managers were quite different as well. What was the build-up to the finals like?

KR: Howard was great because even though we were all mainly young lads, the greatest thing was that he still gave everybody responsibility. He didn't really put stipulations on anyone but he gave you the responsibility for looking after yourself and to be professional about things. If you stepped out of line, you'd be hammered. And not just by him but by every player. You did respond to that responsibility and I think that was a good way of going about it. He wanted you to be a disciplinarian as well.

The other lads were with me and I was with them. There were times when people stepped out of line that he didn't know about because the lads rectified it themselves. Whenever someone did

step out of line, they held their hand up and said: 'Sorry, it won't happen again' or accepted a fine and didn't dispute it.

The thing I remember about the build-up to the final was that in those days, before Sky, it was a tradition that the Cup final coverage on television started from eight o'clock in the morning. So when you woke up in bed, there was a camera in your face. The coverage could have been going all day if you had extra-time and then Match of the Day in the evening. I remember growing up watching that FA Cup coverage and wanting to be part of that day.

The captain would go through the team, revealing the lads' nicknames and so on. But Howard got Freddie Starr involved! He was outside the bedroom window doing all his tricks. Out of the window, we could hear Freddie doing all this stuff and we were wondering just what was going on so early in the morning.

I remember we'd just signed Andy Gray a few months before and Freddie went up to him and said: 'Hey Andy, everyone says I look like you but I can't understand that because you're ******* ugly!'

BL: He's a nutcase, Freddie!

KR: It was funny because we always called Reidy 'Fred' because we always thought he looked like Freddie Starr but that was before Andy arrived. The only thing Howard stipulated was that he wouldn't let Freddie come on the team bus. I always remember one interview with him that morning.

As he was covering our side of things, Michael Barrymore was doing the same thing with Watford. So they're at each team's hotels about noon just as we were preparing to head off to the ground.

All these Everton fans were around

Freddie Starr and Michael Barrymore's all alone at the Watford hotel and nobody's there. He says: 'Hey Freddie, how come you've got all those supporters there and I've got none here?' And Freddie says: 'Well I'm a bigger star than you!'

BL: I knew Freddie when he used to go to a place called The Golden Goblet by Castle Street and North John Street. We got to know Freddie very well. He used to live over the water out by Arrowe Park. Me, Colin Harvey, Tommy Wright and some of the other lads used to go to his house. I often used to leave with Freddie playing blow football with Colin Harvey! He was a big Evertonian, Fred. At some Everton away games, Catterick used to get him on the bus and he used to come home with us. But what a nutcase!

KR: He relaxed the lads on the day.

DW: He's a good sort, isn't he?

KR: He sat with us for pre-match and

'Freddie Starr sat with us for pre-match and everything. I remember he was overawed by Nev. He kept looking at Nev and saying: 'You're brilliant.' And you know what Nev's like, he just said: 'Shut up, you *****!''

KEVIN RATCLIFFE

'We have got a good chance today.'

KR: Steve Bruce went off injured as well, didn't he? He was struggling in the first 20 minutes or so.

DW: Yes. Losing their captain was another big thing that went in our favour.

KR: Duncan didn't play either, did he?

DW: No. He came on as a sub.

KR: It was a great header from Paul Rideout for the goal.

DW: It was. The power he got into it coming off the crossbar and everything.

KR: It should have been a goal in the first place, mind you.

DW: Yes, it should. Paul Rideout was something of an unlikely hero wasn't he? Normally centre-forwards at clubs grab the fans' imaginations but Paul, while he was a good footballer, wasn't one who could relate with the supporters and get a good relationship going with them.

He was good at most things without being renowned as a superstar. He had a better touch than a lot of the centre-forwards that Everton have had and he never really got much credit for that but he was a good team player.

He had good touch, his fitness was great, he was a good header of the ball...so he had an awful lot going for him but I don't think he really had the personality to sell himself.

You get some of these centre-forwards scoring goals who are always talking themselves up but Paul would never do anything like that. Maybe that was part of his own doing. But he did a good job for the team and Joe Royle loved him. Joe always played Paul whenever he could.

KR: I think Paul was a better trainer than he was a player. Didn't he play centre-half a couple of times as well?

DW: Yes and in midfield too – but he

'We were like lambs to the slaughter in a lot of people's eyes. Then the team sheets came in and Ryan Giggs was on the bench and there were one or two others missing as well. We thought: 'We have got a good chance today'

DAVE WATSON

everything. I remember he was overawed by Nev. He kept looking at Nev and saying: 'You're brilliant.' And you know what Nev's like, he just said: 'Shut up, you *****!'

BL: I saw Nev at a game a few weeks ago and he said 'hello' to me. I thought that was strange and that he must have lightened up a bit!

DW: He obviously didn't recognise you!

How did it feel going to Wembley as underdogs, Dave?

DW: We were there to go and enjoy it because we'd had another relegation battle and they were going for the double. Really, we were like the lambs to the slaughter in a lot of people's eyes.

Then the team sheets came in and Ryan Giggs was on the bench and there were one or two others missing as well. So when we saw the team we did think:

wasn't that flippin' good!

BL: There are players you play with who the crowd don't have a minute for but when you play with those players you realise what they're doing for you.

You all sampled the other side of the Cup final as well.

BL: We were really odds-on against West Brom at Wembley in 1968 and were beaten 1-0. Joe Royle was great in the air but all the headers went to Jimmy Husband and Alan Whittle that day! Then in 1985, I was in the Main Stand right behind Norman Whiteside when he curled it. He put it in the only place he could have beaten Nev. He bent it round Pat Van den Hauwe and into the only gap and Nev must have seen it very late.

KR: Nev was marking the post. He was so far over. It was bad positioning, but he only just missed it.

BL: I was so cheesed off driving home that day. An Everton coach drove past me as I came to that split in the M6 and I waved to the coach and then went the wrong way! I was heading for the M1. It took me about four hours to get back!

As well as being three cup-winning captains, you were also central defenders and averaged more than 500 games each for the club – a fantastic achievement.

KR: I think the thing is, as someone said to me recently, how many games did you ever actually play when you were 100% fit? These days players don't play because teams have bigger squads. But for a good 80% of the season you were always carrying something or other into a game.

'I was so cheesed off driving home that day. An Everton coach drove past me as I came to that split in the M6 and I waved to the coach and then went the wrong way. It took me four hours to get back!'

BRIAN LABONE

'I ran about 70 yards to kick Gordon McQueen and got the biggest rollicking ever from Colin Harvey. I told him the gaffer had told me to get booked. He said: 'Oh, that's all right then!''

KEVIN RATCLIFFE

BL: When they showed you that needle...well, just the threat of the needle was enough to make you play!

DW: How many subs did you have in your day, Brian?

BL: None for the most part.

KR: We had one.

DW: We had one, then two, then three.

KR: But one had to be a goalkeeper didn't he?

BL: I remember we were playing at Burnley once – it was when I missed the last six games of the 1969-70 Championship season – and Westy and I were staying at the Pack Horse Hotel in Burnley. When we woke up the snow was particularly deep, so me and Westy had double breakfasts.

DW: Double breakfasts!

KR: And it was an 11 o'clock kick-off!

BL: Burnley, thinking they've got a chance of beating us, then get the entire population of the town down to Turf Moor to clear the pitch of snow. So the game goes ahead. And you know how there's a bit of a slope on the pitch at Burnley? Well Steve Kindon is about to go past me – as he would on a flat pitch anyway – and me and Westy both go for the through ball and I get clattered and am out cold for about five minutes. Anyway, there were no subs in those days so I struggled through to the end.

We won 2-1 and I think Martin Dobson scored for them. I went to the toilet after the game and I was passing red wine and I hadn't had a drink the night before. It turned out the collision had ruptured my kidneys. We were like two hippos going against each other!

This all started off with two feet of snow, extra breakfasts, we're not going to play today and next thing I was in Lourdes in Greenbank Road for two weeks and missed the last six games of the season.

Tell us about those final seconds when, as captain, you know you're on the brink of achieving the childhood dream of lifting the cup.

BL: It's not like that, really. That doesn't happen.

DW: It did with me!

BL: Well in my case it just flashes past. In our case, when you've been down 2-0 and win 3-2, well, as I say, it just flashed past.

KR: Maybe Waggy was a little bit different but then I think it's a little bit different when you're expected to win. I've seen that on Waggy's face when he lifted it. But like Labby says, it does tend to pass you by. I think it crosses your mind after the semi more than anything but, even then, Wembley still seems so far away. You want to be playing all the games. The last thing you want to be doing is getting injured. Howard was brilliant. I can't remember whether it was the '84 one or one of the other ones, but he actually used to come to the lads after the semi-final and say: 'Look, you need to get booked today because if you don't you're going to miss the final. So make sure you get booked now.' So we used to have to go out and make sure we got booked. I ran about 70 yards to kick Gordon

McQueen and got the biggest rollicking I ever had from Colin Harvey.

DW: And Gordon wasn't even playing!

KR: Colin had a real go at me and I told him that the gaffer had told me to get booked. He said: 'What for?' When I told him he said: 'Oh, that's all right then.' Howard did other things for the lads as well. You always had to play a certain number of games to get a league winners medal and one season, he made sure that everybody got one. He used to put them sub and put them on in the last minute. He made sure people like Neil Adams and Ian Atkins got their medal. I remember Neil coming on as a sub in a Charity Shield game against Liverpool in 1986 and then coming off again to be replaced by Paul Wilkinson.

Were you ever allowed to take the FA Cup home?

DW: Yes, you could get it off the club and take it around.

KR: I think Adrian Heath had it right after the game.

BL: Harry Catterick was handcuffed to it, as you know, before he got married. Handcuffed to it!

The 1966 final will also be remembered for fan Eddie Cavanagh running on the pitch and there was that famous picture of you pleading with the police not to arrest him, Brian?

BL: He got thrown out of Wembley but reckoned he got back in. Eddie had 14 kids, you know, and I said to him one day: 'I bet you can't name them all, Ed' and he could. He could name them all.

KR: But he did name six of them Simon!

BL: He was a heck of a character, Eddie. He had been a schoolboy player with the club so I used to play against him in training from time-to-time.

What about your collective pride? It must be an incredible thing to be a Cup-winning captain?

BL: Well when you work it out there can only be one every year can't there? Stanley Matthews played until he was 50, but didn't get a Cup winners' medal until 1953 and he must have been around 40 then.

DW: I think winning at Wembley

'We were the Dogs of War, so we were a fighting team as such weren't we? I wouldn't say we had great characters but we were a good, together team. You'd probably have to pick out Duncan Ferguson. Duncan was the man'

DAVE WATSON

'You were
brought up as a
child believing
that the
pinnacle of your
career was to
win the FA
Cup final at
Wembley, not
the league title'

KEVIN
RATCLIFFE

means something more too. Winning the FA Cup's great and it must be fantastic to do that at Cardiff but at Wembley it was special.

BL: Oh yes, headquarters was the place.

KR: The thing with me, later on, was that it annoyed me when they started playing semi-finals there too. The only way to play at Wembley was to be a finalist or to play for your country.

You think of all the players who have played the game but never ever played at Wembley. I always remember Bryan 'Pop' Robson who used to play for Sunderland and Newcastle but never ever played at Wembley. That all made the FA Cup final special.

BL: It did de-value it by playing semi-finals there.

DW: The whole history of the place and the drive down Wembley Way was incredible.

KR: You were brought up as a child believing that the pinnacle of your career was to win the FA Cup final at Wembley, not the league title. It's a bit like saying to horse racing enthusiasts: Cheltenham or Aintree – which is the best? If you ask the jockeys, they'd probably say Cheltenham but for the prestige and everything it would probably be the National and Aintree. It's great to win the league but you were brought up with the FA Cup final because of the focus on the one day with the TV, the radio, everything. I mean you used to have a players' pool just for that one day.

BL: And you only had one chance didn't you really? One bad day and you were out. In the league you could have a couple of bad days and still win the title.

DW: I also remember the record. Did you have a Cup final record?

BL: I think we had one but I can't remember.

KR: Ours was 'Here We Go'!

BL: We did do a few recordings.

DW: We had The Farm song 'All Together Now'. It's a good song.

Each team tends to have a few unusual characters. Who would you pick out as the great characters in yours?

DW: We were the Dogs of War, so we were a fighting team as such weren't we? I wouldn't say we had great characters but we were a good, together team. You'd probably have to pick out Duncan Ferguson. Duncan was the man. He was only sub at Wembley but it was when he first came to the club and he got the crowd going and all that, so Duncan was probably the main character.

KR: In our team, you'd probably say Bails [John Bailey] but you could even make a case for Nev. People would look at him and say he wasn't a funny guy but some of the things he used to say, his one-liners, were unbelievable. But I would say that everyone in the team, even down to the quiet ones like Gary Stevens, would be able to cut you with one sentence. Every time you spoke, you had to think that what you were saying was the right thing, otherwise you'd get slaughtered. Even Trevor Steven at 21 years of age would pick up on something that you'd say. Bails was the joker though. Every day he'd have a joke. He was wearing his masks and so on. I always remember him coming in one day and he'd brought in one of these dogs. You'd clap and it would start walking, you'd clap again and it would stop. Then two claps and it would do a somersault. He'd just make you laugh every day.

Even Howard would join in from time to time and the backroom staff. Mick Heaton wasn't always too serious and the lads could have a bit of banter with him.

BL: Whenever you see documentaries or dramas about football, whatever they do they can never re-create the banter that goes on in the dressing room. We know that because we've been there. It's so phoney when you see it trying to be staged. It's so spontaneous when it happens for real.

KR: I think it's completely different to any other line of work and it's one thing you really do miss after you finish playing. I've just been away with some other British lads and the banter you have is great. Other people see it from other countries and wonder what's going on because there's a completely different sense of humour from what they've got.

BL: We're all kids. Even now me and Westy are playing tricks on each other. You're just like schoolboys, you never grow up and that's brilliant. Westy and I do a bit of after-dinner speaking now and again and he told me he was at a do with Neville at the big marquee at Everton some months ago and they were asked who was the best goalkeeper between the two of them. He said Neville got a bit prickly on occasions and in the end they decided that Westy was the best in black-and-white and Neville was the best in colour. They were both great goalkeepers. I played with Westy all my career and he was very under-rated. He was brilliant. You have to be a nutcase as well to be a goalkeeper don't you?

KR: At the 1984/1985 re-union a few months ago in the marquee, everybody had to get up and do a little bit. It was with Ray Stubbs and he got myself and Derek Mountfield up together, the full-

'Bernie The Bolt (Bernie Wright)! Goodness me! Westy was the only fella who could handle him. He was a nutcase and a big strong fella. He used to come in in the morning with bottles of cheap sherry and he had a pair of jeans and he had them stitched up with string'

BRIAN LABONE

'The bus we came back on looks ancient now! Funnily enough, I remember 1995 quite well as a spectator. Duncan had his kilt on, he was giving us a song and then we had a band on. What a night that was. I didn't even play and I had a cracking time'

BRIAN LABONE

backs together, Neville up on his own and so on. So Nev's the first up and Ray Stubbs says to him: 'Neville, not only were you a great goalkeeper for Everton, for a time you must have been the best goalkeeper in the world.' And he just said: 'Well with this bunch of ****** in front of me, I ******* had to be, didn't I?!' But that's Neville.

BL: Do you remember that occasion when he was sat against the goalposts at half-time. Didn't you think he was out of order doing that?

DW: He was out of order. It was done out of frustration wasn't it?

KR: It was about the time of the change wasn't it? The switch from the old routines to the days of sports scientists and so on. We didn't know Neville had done that. Nobody knew. Nev wasn't one to say things at half-time. He'd be in the bathroom or something like that. So nobody knew anything about it until later.

BL: I don't think Nev would have done that with my old boss Harry Catterick, who was a real disciplinarian. He'd have been out on his ear no matter how good he was!

DW: That was Mick Milligan's debut. He turned up about twenty to three and said: 'I didn't realise it was going to be this busy!' He was used to playing for Oldham where they didn't have quite so much traffic on a match day!

BL: He wasn't the best but then we've had a few haven't we? Bernie The Bolt (Bernie Wright)! Goodness me! Westy was the only fella who could handle him. He was a nutcase and a big strong fella. He used to come in in the morning with bottles of cheap sherry and he had a pair of jeans and he had them stitched up with string. Poor Stewart Imlach who used to put the team up on a Friday came down one day with a black eye because Harry

would never come out of his office. Stewart only put the team up. He didn't pick it but he got a black eye after being belted by Bernie The Bolt when he had been dropped. They always shoot the messenger don't they?

What about the homecomings?

BL: The bus we came back on looks ancient now! Funnily enough, I remember 1995 quite well as a spectator. I've still got photographs of that do at the Royal Lancaster Hotel. It was absolutely tremendous. We had the Seventh Batallion of the Grenadier Guards marching through in amongst the tables playing the trumpet and saxophone and whatever. Duncan had his kilt on, he was giving us a song and then we had a band on and everything. What a night that was! I didn't even play and I had a cracking time!

DW: As soon as you get back and you see the amount of people that have turned out, it's fantastic. Obviously you're still buzzing after the night before and so all the lads are up for it.

KR: I remember going along Queens Drive and there were no toilets on board the bus. So next minute we're all in this house queuing for the toilet and the fella came down and was asking what we were doing. He was a Liverpool fan! Just to see all the people right along the route was a great experience.

BL: In my day we used to get on at Allerton Station and then get the bus through the town.

KR: I think we got on at Goodison.

BL: I'm sure we did in 1995. Before the bus tour, Dave Hickson and I were in the Winslow and we had an imitation FA Cup and took that in there!

Do you get a shiver down the spine when you see captains picking up the trophy now?

KR: You do, but it's different now because they're on the pitch receiving it.
DW: It was great going up the steps.
BL: Yes. Going up the steps and getting those slaps on the back and the back of the head was fantastic!
KR: I was the last captain to go up the original 39 steps. They dropped them down for some reason or other, for the Royal Box I think, after that. But there were originally 39 steps and I was the last one to go up them to receive the cup in 1984.
DW: That may be why your knees are knackered!

BL: When you work it out, we are all very privileged. How many FA Cup finals were there at Wembley before they moved to the Millennium? Whatever way you look at it there are less than 100 people who have done it. When you look at the old Wembley, some of the people who had tickets behind the goal must have been about 60-odd yards away from the game. So how could they have seen what was going on?
DW: I think people were just glad to get in, weren't they?
KR: The whole day is special but the best part about the Wembley experience is probably driving to the ground, getting into the stadium and then leading the team out. That's special.

'As soon as you get back and you see the amount of people that have turned out, it's fantastic. Obviously you're still buzzing after the night before and so all the lads are up for it'

DAVE
WATSON

That walk from behind the goal is something else. The captains lead the team out now at the Millennium and they only have to walk 25 yards on to the pitch. I hope when they unveil the new Wembley the changing rooms are behind the goal because that experience of walking the 100 yards to the centre of the pitch, seeing where your family are – because you've got a good idea because you've been out for the warm-up. Well, to me, that walk is something else.

That build-up and that 100-yard walk, with your tracksuit on, the ball under your arm, looking, waving...you always remember that build-up and it really hits you when you enter the arena. I've been to the Millennium and I honestly believe that it was the best thing that's happened to the FA Cup. I think it had lost its nostalgia at Wembley because people weren't really that bothered about playing in the FA Cup final because the new Premier League had taken off and the Champions League – and the FA Cup had taken a back seat. Moving to the Millennium with the crowd on top of everybody, even though it's maybe not as good as Wembley used to be, helped bring back some of the FA Cup's magic.

BL: Wembley was fantastic. Dennis Stevens used to call it headquarters because he played there for Bolton in 1958. It was like being in the dentist's chair. You may be quite nervous beforehand, but once you're there, you knew you'd relax. You'd see all the people outside the stadium with their pints of beer and they were probably thinking: 'I'd love to be on that bus.' And you're looking at them and

thinking: 'I'd love to be out there swigging that beer.' As an Everton Cup-winning captain I feel very proud. It's funny that all three of us were centre-backs. I was 66 in January and I always say to T.E. Jones, my predecessor, to hang on. He's 74 now and had a bit of heart trouble recently but I've told him that he's got to keep going because T.G. Jones didn't go until he was 84 or 85. We've got to have a strong back line and I'm doing my best!

KR: I remember the song that we played on the way to the ground when we won the FA Cup. That season we had the Bruce Springsteen album 'Born in the USA' on at the time and that was always played every game we went to – probably from just before Christmas and obviously played on the day.

BL: You have to remember that my experience was some 20-odd years earlier. We only had gramophone records then!

KR: Had radios been invented then?!

BL: You get on the Everton coach now and they've got all these big televisions. We had a little table model about six by eight inches stuck up.

DW: We had our cup final song playing. At Norwich in the 1985 Milk Cup final, we had Elvis on...'It's Now Or Never'! That was playing in the background after the game too!

No Evertonian will ever forget the impacts of Messrs Labone, Ratcliffe and Watson. Their Everton pride and passion will be with us forever.

'Wembley was fantastic. It was like being in the dentist's chair. You may be quite nervous beforehand but once you're there, you knew you'd relax'

BRIAN LABONE

The Captains

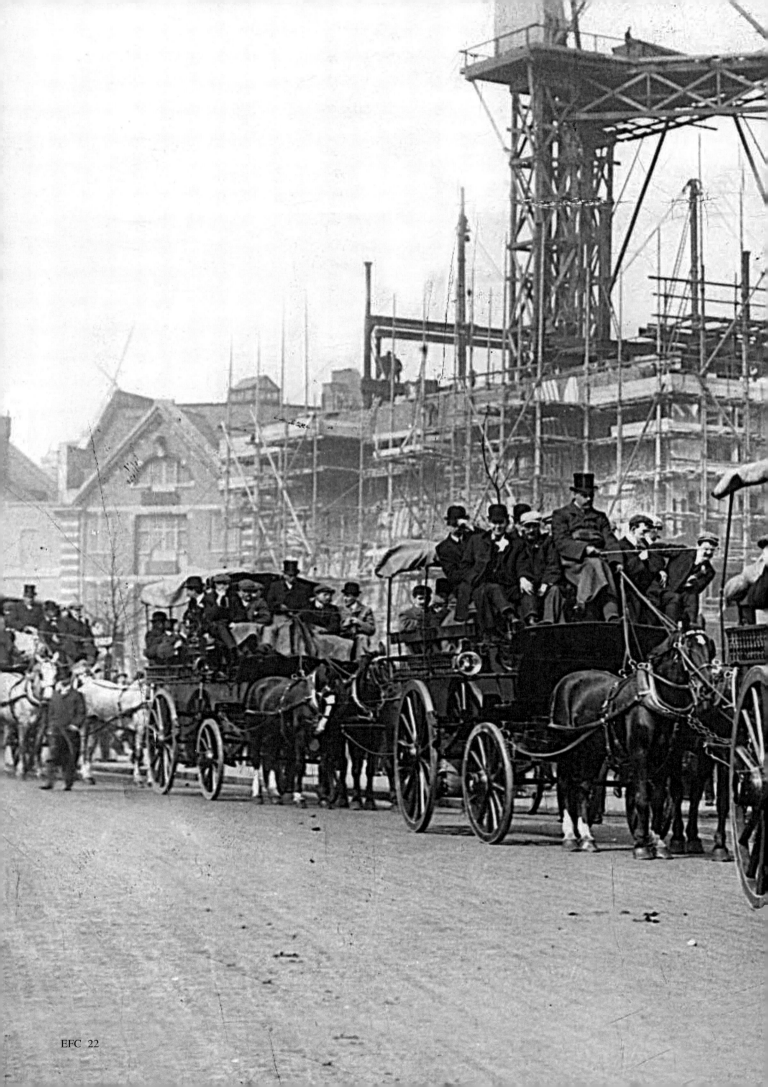

EFC 22

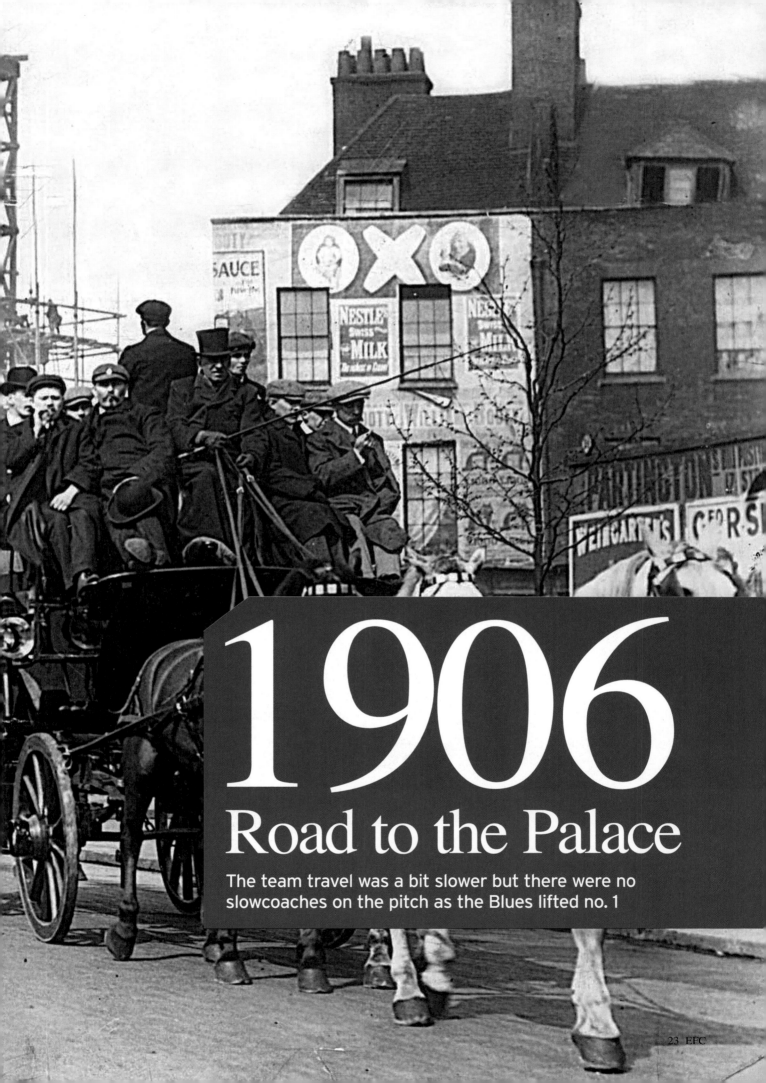

1906
Road to the Palace

The team travel was a bit slower but there were no slowcoaches on the pitch as the Blues lifted no. 1

Against all the odds

Newcastle were favourites but it was Everton who had the lucky charm as they added their name to the illustrious list of teams who had won the famous trophy

Lucky Blue cat

Everton had one thing on their side that Newcastle didn't - a lucky black cat.

In the run-up to the 1906 final, the Echo's reporter observed: '...the famous pussy, with black coat, white socks on fore feet, and white stockings on the hind feet, entered the trainers' room, and Elliott detailed some of its performances. Aged 12, it parades the well-kept Goodison ground more like a hare than a cat, and will follow the trainers just as a dog does the master. She coolly sits and the first bird that comes across her path is quickly made a dainty meal.'

Palace grounds: The Crystal Palace stadium (sketched below in the Echo) was one of the wonders of the age

Brine of the time

Preparing for a major football match like a cup final has certainly changed over the years. These days, the latest technology and modern equipment will ensure professional stars are in tip-top condition ahead of their big moment.

100 years ago, however, the game was not so sophisticated. "Stafford Town Council have offered us some special facilities," Everton trainer Elliott told the Echo. "We have found Stafford brine baths the best we've yet visited. Those at Northwich are good, but Stafford more convenient. The men have been brightened up in their arduous programme by visits there."

Palace fit for royalty

The Liverpool Football Echo preview of April 21, 1906 included a story of the improvements made at 'the Palace' ahead of the FA Cup final.

Around £7,000 had been spent in upgrading the stadium, with 3,000 new seats taking the seating capacity to 17,000 and the standing ground having been raised on all sides to improve the view of the pitch for supporters.

An attendance short of 100,000 was predicted, although the Palace record for a final between two non-southern teams (the 1899 final between Sheffield United and Derby attracted 73,833) was still expected to be beaten.

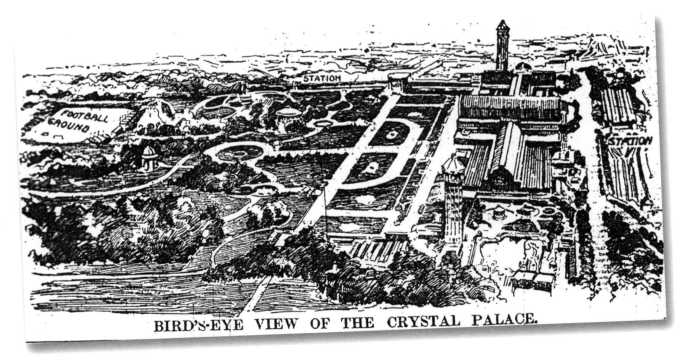

BIRD'S-EYE VIEW OF THE CRYSTAL PALACE.

A feast of football

A rough estimate of the menu on offer for the crowd was as follows:

7,200 rumps of steak
200 chimes of mutton for chops
150 best ends of beef
2,400 pounds of fore ribs of beef
40 whole lambs
500 pounds of soles
400 fowls; 200 ducks
23,000 pounds of potatoes
2,000 cabbages and cauliflowers
6,000 pork pies; 2,000 smoked sausages
25,000 scones
100,000 slices of bread and butter
50,000 pieces of cake
1,000 shortbreads; 1,000 sponge cakes
20,000 French pastries
10,000 Bath buns; 10,000 plain buns
21,000 rolls
20,000 bottles of mineral water
2,000 gallons of milk

PLAYER'S CIGARETTES

BALMER (W)   SCOTT   CRELLY

MAKEPEACE   ABBOTT

TAYLOR

SHARP   HARDMAN (H P.)

BOLTON   YOUNG   SETTLE

Everton 1906: Amongst the line-up are Jack Sharp (back, fourth left) and skipper Jack Taylor (front, third from left)

Cigarette card: Featuring the Everton players

Toon favourites

Newcastle were firm favourites to lift the trophy, having been surprisingly denied the Double 12 months earlier by Aston Villa in the final. Between 1905 and 1911 they'd been champions three times and on five occasions reached the FA Cup final - failing to win any.

The year they did win it, 1910, they drew with Barnsley 1-1 before winning the replay at Goodison Park 2-0.

Everton meanwhile, had done little in the League that season despite reaching their third final (having missed out in 1893 and 1897). According to reports, over 75,000 filled Crystal Palace and both sides were at full strength having been fined for fielding weakened teams the week before.

'Och aye, Sandy scored!'

A closely contested game against Newcastle was decided by a single goal in 1906 - with a famous Goodison Scot the hero

Kicking-off at 3.29pm, the game failed to ignite with both sides cancelling each other out. Jimmy Settle went closest with a header in a drab first half, while John Rutherford had Newcastle's best chance which was deflected for a corner.

Eight minutes into the second half Sandy Young had a goal ruled out for offside from Settle's pass – Jack Sharp's cross having been fumbled by United keeper James Lawrence. But Everton remained the better side with Newcastle needing to be warned by the referee for their 'ungentlemanly conduct'.

Settle had gone close five minutes before the winner came in the 77th minute. Captain Jack Taylor, the sole survivor of the Toffees' previous final appearances in the 19th century, found Jack Sharp. He beat two men before sending in a low centre, which Young converted, striking the goalkeeper on the way in. The reception which greeted the goal was likened by one newspaper to the San Francisco earthquake which happened a week earlier. The song immortalizing Young apparently went: 'Och, aye Sandy scored a goal.'

'Jay CKK' kept tabs of the clock during the match, with some of his comments of the match recorded in the Liverpool Football Echo that night appearing as follows:

'3.35 – Everton all over them. Bolton shoots. His idea is good; his execution rotten.

'3.38 – Everton forwards having a field-day, but they seldom shoot – the importance of the occasion too great

'3.41 – Young is giving great satisfaction.

'4.05 – Pressure by the Blues hot and strong.

'4.30 – Everton still top dog, and visions of the precious bauble loomed in my eye.

'4.34 – Linesman Whittaker examines the ball. He thinks it has gone soft, but it is all right.

'4.35 – Everton press like demons.

'4.36 – Young scores, but Kirkham declares him offside. Great snakes! No matter. Our withers are unwrung.

'4.39 – Only one team in it just now. The other team is Newcastle.

'4.55 – At last a goal, Sandy Young…fireworks and miniature earthquakes galore.'

EVERTON: Scott, Balmer, Crelley, Makepeace, Taylor, Abbott, Sharp, Bolton, Young, Settle, Hardman.

NEWCASTLE UNITED: Lawrence, McCombie, Carr, Gardner, Aitken, McWilliam, Rutherford, Howie, Veitch, Orr, Gosnell.

GOAL: EVERTON Young (77).
ATTENDANCE 75,609.

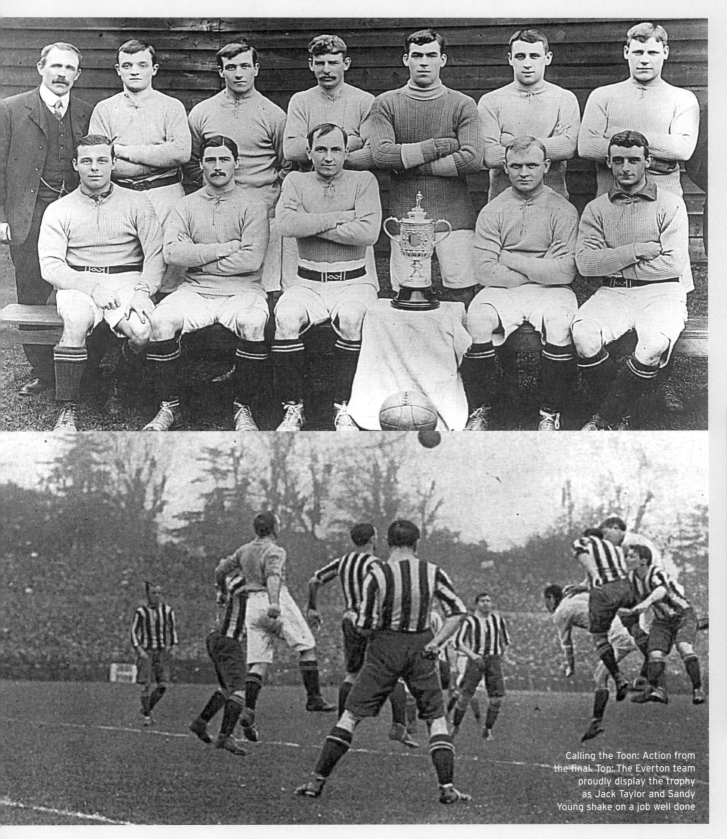

1906

Calling the Toon: Action from the final. Top: The Everton team proudly display the trophy as Jack Taylor and Sandy Young shake on a job well done

Kings of the Palace

Everton's first FA Cup success came a full 59 years before their city rivals achieved the feat. Although not a classic footballing final, it was heartily celebrated at home

Sweet success

Everton's victory was particularly satisfying with a war of words taking place before a ball had even been kicked.

Just like in modern times, comments were made by both camps in the press and Newcastle's highly-rated half-back line had promised to make mincemeat out of the Goodison forwards.

Little wonder

A peculiar fact from the final is that all the players on show were below 6 feet.

First news: Sent by 'special wire' from the game (headline, right)

Below: Everton boss Howard Kendall is presented with a tiled picture, believed to be Cup final hero Sandy Young because of his distinctive snakebelt. It was discovered at the Sandon pub, Everton's former headquarters, in 1985

Conquering Heroes

After the final, the players dined at the Charterhouse Square Hotel. Among the guests was 'Mr J McKenna of Liverpool Football Club'.

Captain Jack Taylor said 'they were naturally proud of winning the "Coop".

'It was an occasion of a lifetime and they were lucky to have won,' he announced.

After the dinner the squad left for the Alhambra, and the day after visited Hampton Court, and dined with the Newcastle United team.

They then headed straight to Sheffield where they played a league match and arrived home via Central Station.

The Echo reported: 'A procession will be formed, headed by a brass band, which will receive the victors by playing 'The Conquering Heroes.' Afterwards the team will journey to Goodison Park via Church Street, Whitechapel, Scotland Road, Walton Road thence to the club offices.

'The 'special Grand Central train' was due to leave Sheffield at 6.05pm, due into Liverpool at 8.20pm.

'The engine was specially decorated with the colours of the Everton club.'

Only a limited number of people were to be allowed on the Central Station platform, with admittance 'ticket only' – while the Lord Mayor was also set to be present to 'add his congratulations on behalf of the city.'

ENGLISH CUP FINAL.

EVERTON v. NEWCASTLE UNITED.

CRYSTAL PALACE BESIEGED.

AN IMMENSE CROWD OF SPECTATORS.

SANDY YOUNG SCORES THE WINNING GOAL.

CUP COMES TO LIVERPOOL AT LAST.

[From Our Own Reporters by Special Wire from the Crystal Palace.]

Blue letter day

Page 3 of the Liverpool Echo on April 23, 1906 offered its congratulations to Everton with an open letter to the team, The letter began:

'Dear John Taylor – Your hand! All Liverpool has respected you for your honourable career, and as you captained the successful side on Saturday in the time-honoured final of the Football Association Cup, may we offer you our warmest congratulations.'

The letter continued in this vein, complimenting each player ('To W. Balmer – One of your best games, William…you had Gosnell in your pocket, and Orr was at least under the flap of the pocket.' 'To Makepeace – Thought you weren't going to play? Glad you did.')

Denying the 'spoilsports'

These were the views of various newspapers after Everton's win . . .

Sporting Chronicle: 'Everton...took off the FA Cup after a hard struggle, in which, whatever their rivals Newcastle United did, they did themselves full justice, and gained a well-merited victory.'

Daily Mirror: 'The tamest final for many years. (Everton) would have done better even had Young, the centre forward, not marred his dashing display with a good many petty tricks, which Mr Kirkham (the referee) generally noticed and always promptly penalized.'

Daily News: 'Everton beat Newcastle United on their merits.'

Morning Post: 'On the run of the game the Lancastrians ought to have been several goals up.'

Liverpool Echo: 'It was a glorious victory.'

Daily Post: 'Thrice has the battle been waged, and twice the victory denied, but the third time pays for all. Bravo the Blues!'

Daily Graphic: 'Sharp – the hero of the match.'

Sheffield Telegraph: 'A poor final.'

Daily Express: 'It was certainly an attraction, but it was not attractive.'

Morning Leader: 'The winners found their feet from the start, and with the exception of a few fitful excursions and alarms of their so-called opponents, they were top-dog all the way.'

Yorkshire Post: 'There were times when, to the onlooker, the men from Tyneside seemed to be suffering from incipient paralysis.'

Manchester Guardian: 'Everton put to confusion that annoying class of person who try to spoil our sport by assuring us beforehand how it will all end.'

Skipper Jack Taylor (standing) takes centre stage as Everton's players and notables pose with the Cup in front of a mock backdrop of Crystal Palace

Celebration drink: A 1906 advert showing a footballer promoting cocoa

No.2

Day a Blues' fan tackled skipper

In 1907, in search of a second successive final appearance, the Blues faced West Brom at Burnden Park, Bolton. The papers made great play of the 'shock news' that the sizeable army even included a 15-strong group who were going by 'motor-car', which was chartered by the Fruiterers Association. The group expected the 60-mile journey to take two-and-a-half hours! Most fans went by train.

Skipper Jack Taylor, who played despite a stomach complaint, was 'tackled' by an over-enthusiastic Evertonian on the pitch before the game. The fan caught the defender round the neck - and was promptly tripped up by the annoyed captain.

Everton still ran out 2-1 winners thanks to George Wilson and Jack Sharp goals either side of the break.

Newspapers didn't name their reporters in those days. They carried pseudynoms and the Echo's reporter was 'Bee.' Bee was actually the highly-respected journalist Ernest Edwards, the Echo sports editor.

He noted how a black cat, in residence at Goodison Park, had been adopted by the Everton players as a mascot. The cat had been ill and the club secretary issued instructions it should be put down. "No fear" said the groundsman, "not until after the Cup final."

Best China: A plate depicting the 1906/1907 season with Everton's 2-1 Wembley defeat recorded in the centre

The absent hero

In the 1907 Final, FA Cup holders Everton would lose 2-1 to Sheffield Wednesday who they had beaten on the way to winning the trophy the previous year. The Blues had dropped semi-final scorer George Wilson after he had hit out at the club's directors. A modern Liverpool Echo feature in May 1995 revealed more:

'Many fans blamed the eventual defeat on George Wilson's absence,' said the Echo 'and the saga continued in the aftermath of the final. Rumours were rife and among the headlines were: 'Why was Wilson dropped?' and 'Mystery of the Wilson case still unsolved'.'

It was suggested the directors' shock selection decision (they named the team in those days) was based on a contract dispute. The rumours were that the board would not play Wilson unless he put pen to paper. The player's anger clearly increased when they refused his demand for a bonus. Player power was stamped on in those days.

When a Liverpool Echo reporter visited Wilson's terraced home in Bardsay Road, Walton, he found the house empty and the furniture on its

Heads we win: Players' faces make up the frame of this 1907 postcard produced for the FA Cup final

No.3

ENGLISH CUP FINAL.

An Echo cartoon on the 1907 game

way back to Scotland.

Wilson was eventually traced and found to have a cup medal in his possession, even though he did not play in the final. Asked where it came from, he said one of the Everton players had given it to him, saying: 'Here, George, take it. If anybody deserves it, you do.'

Wilson revealed he had been offered a final chance to sign on the morning of the match, but refused because of his wife's health. He would have done so had he been able to live in Southport or Hoylake. Clearly he was a player who knew his own mind. The directors would have seen him as a trouble-maker. Wilson said the team was picked on the way to Crystal Palace, but nobody told him he was not included until just before the kick-off.

George Wilson never played for Everton again.

At the Palace: Everton action from the 1907 era – a copy of the picture used for the 1907 final postcard on the opposite page

Above: This goal from Jack Sharp was not enough to prevent a 2-1 reverse

No.4

Sporting fans a credit to city

An FA Cup replay against Middlesbrough at Goodison Park in January 1910 produced an inspired display from visiting goalkeeper Tim Williamson – despite the Blues still progressing 5-3.

The Echo noted how, at the end of the first half, the 'cheers for Williamson were very loud and long and this sportsmanlike conduct cannot be overdone.'

The newspaper added: 'Let us be jealous of the crowd's good name in the Mersey city'.

Indeed, the following day's Liverpool Echo headline summed up the match:

'WILLIAMSON AND THE POSTS AGAINST ATTACK'.

No.6

Taxi for Reds!

The following observation came from a Liverpool Echo reporter in his 'Casual Comments' column in the wake of Everton's 2-1 FA Cup defeat of Liverpool in February 1911.

'Making one's way quietly to Goodison Park today the first thing that struck one was the alarming growth of taxi-cabs and motor-cars. They have become a positive epidemic and unfortunately there seems no likelihood of the disease being stamped out.'

Prophetic words from the Echo scribe. If only he could see County Road before and after a match these days!

No.5

Fall of captain Jack

The FA Cup semi-finals of 1910 saw Second Division Barnsley standing in the way of Everton's path to a third final in five seasons.

The first tie ended goalless at Elland Road, but hopes were high for the replay at Old Trafford, Manchester – described by the Press as 'Cottonopolis.'

But after a lively opening, in which both sides missed spot-kicks, the turning point occurred:

'Out of the blue Jack Taylor, the Everton centre-half, took a kick to the neck. Doubled up in agony, his team-mate White approached him, but Taylor was breathless.

'His pain was only eased when two spectators, who appeared to be 'medical men', came to assist.

'They turned out to be Doctors Whitford and Baxter.'

It's highly likely that the latter was actually Dr. James Clement Baxter who, in 1892, gave Everton an interest-free loan to help them build the new Goodison Park.

Baxter would become a board member.

Medical examination later revealed that Taylor had sustained severe damage to the larynx, an injury which forced him to quit the game.

It was reported that the player could hardly speak after the game.

The eventual 3-0 defeat was inevitable – not least because goalkeeper William Scott was forced off for a spell after tearing the webbing of his second and third finger, a truly nasty and painful injury.

'Breathless': Jack Taylor took a kick to the neck in the FA Cup semi-final of 1910

No.7

Home and away

A 1-1 FA Cup draw with lower division Bury at snow-bound Goodison Park in February 1912 produced a replay at Gigg Lane, or so the fans thought.

In an echo of future meetings between top-flight clubs and traditionally 'smaller' sides, the tie was switched to Goodison.

As a result the Shakers received £750 for keeping the game at Everton, with the Blues losing £100 as a result from lost gate receipts.

And the outcome?

A 6-0 'away' win for Everton (Thomas Browell netting four goals), although they were helped by Bury being without key players.

No.8

Orange 'hooligans'!

A tie with Barnsley in 1915 saw an early show of 'hooliganism' at Goodison Park although it wouldn't have raised an eyebrow in the modern game. At 3-0 up a spectator threw an orange onto the pitch, which hit a Barnsley player. These days it would more likely be an Orange mobile! The Echo reported that the referee called Everton captain Jimmy Galt to address the crowd and 'ask them to be sportsmen'. The report continued: 'Galt did so, and possibly because they feared the Scottish brogue would not be understood, team mates Makepeace and Maconnachie assisted in the lecture.'

No.9

Blues end with seven

Five years after their 1910 semi-final defeat to Barnsley, Everton had their chance of revenge at Goodison in a first-round tie. A Jimmy Galt header put the home side ahead but soon after George Harrison, who had taken the corner to set-up Galt, became the first Everton player to be sent off in an FA Cup tie.

The reason was unclear – Ernest Edwards in the Liverpool Echo claimed to have not seen the incident which also saw Barson dismissed for the Tykes (both had already been cautioned). Edwards viewed how Barson lay injured outside the goalline near the Bullens Road. He then stated: 'The players concerned shook hands as they left the field.' It was later noted that

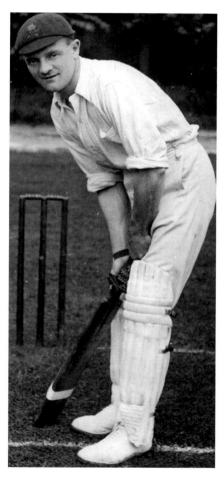

Harry's games: Harry Makepeace – who also played cricket – 'lectured' fans on their bad behaviour in 1915

Barson had swept away Harrison's feet, with Harrison retaliating.

Bobby Parker netted to give Everton a 2-0 lead at the break before he was also sent off in the second half – the only occasion Everton have had two men dismissed in an FA Cup tie. It happened around the hour mark when Parker became the third player to take an early bath for trying to 'rush the goalkeeper'. Cooper then pushed Parker, who kicked him back.

Even so, Jimmy Galt struck a third soon after and Barnsley failed to break through – despite Everton finishing the game with seven men. Joe Clennell came off injured five minutes from time and Tom Fleetwood also went off with an injury problem just before the end.

No.10

Chelsea foil Double bid

Back in 1915 Chelsea were the underdogs, and it was Everton who were pursuing success in both League and Cup. However, it was a feat that seemed impossible to a Liverpool Echo reporter of the day, who made the following observations:

'I have thought all along that Everton would win the Cup this season, but I didn't fancy them for the League as well.

'It is too much to ask any club nowadays to bring off the double. Has it ever been done?

'Oh yes...first to do it was Preston North End, but it wasn't such a feat then, because at that time the Prestonians were in a class by themselves, and had nobody to beat.

'In 1897 it was accomplished by Aston Villa. As you can understand, it was more of a performance, because there was a lot of football talent knocking around in 1897, and among other things, the Villans had to beat Everton in the final of the Cup.'

Controversy raged regarding the continuation of the domestic season despite the beginning of what proved to be World War I but on the day, fears that the double may be beyond Everton proved correct - with Croal and Halse on target for Chelsea (who wore white while Everton sported blue and white stripes) in a 2-0 victory.

At least Everton could console themselves with a League Championship success.

No. 11

Humiliation by the Palace

Struggling in the First Division, Everton would probably not have relished a visit from a mid-table Second Division side in the form of Crystal Palace in January 1922, although league form had improved for the Blues, having recorded three successive wins.

Indeed, the Liverpool Echo match preview for the first-round tie declared: 'Everton is one of the last teams to regard Second Division opponents lightly,' having lost to such opponents the previous two seasons.

Unfortunately an unwanted hat-trick was achieved at Goodison Park, although surely even the most optimistic Palace fan could never have imagined a scoreline of: Everton 0, Crystal Palace 6.

The round-up in Monday's Liverpool Echo would have the final say in this sorry tale:

'The sensation of the day was the complete and humiliating overthrow of Everton.

'It was known that the Londoners were a sturdy lot, but few can have anticipated that they would sweep the Evertonians off their feet in the way they did.

'To be defeated at all was bad enough, but to go under by six clear goals may well give the supporters of the Merseyside club pause.'

That was the nearest the Press went to hammering the team in those days, in what was – and still is – Everton's biggest-ever FA Cup defeat.

Football tips: There were no qualms about sportsmen advertising cigarettes in 1927. Here, Charles Buchan and former Blues star Sam Chedgzoy are used to promote tobacco. Above: Dixie Dean with team-mate Torry Gillick

No. 12

Young Dean signs

A young William Ralph 'Dixie' Dean had signed from Tranmere Rovers in March, 1925 for £3,000. New chairman Will Cuff can hardly have expected the level of impact made by the emerging number nine and he began the 1925/26 season in the reserves. His first FA Cup goal, in a draw against Fulham in January 1926, was one of 33 in all competitions he netted in his first full season at Goodison.

The replay was described as the 'Match of the Century' by the Echo because it was so one-sided but Everton still lost 1-0 – a tie which also saw workmen at the side of the pitch clearing the snow DURING the game. 'THE BLUES OUT OF LUCK' read the Echo headline, while 'Beecham, the young Fulham goalkeeper, was carried shoulder high from the field.' In the years that followed, any goalkeeper who denied Dean deserved such an honour!

No. 13

Tigers burst Cup dreams

An FA Cup fourth-round second replay in February 1927 saw Everton and Hull City forced to travel to Villa Park on a Monday afternoon (decades before television commitments shifted kick-off times on a regular basis). A toss of the coin decided the venue and despite the inconvenience, 1,500 fans travelled from Merseyside, while there were around 200 Hull fans who made the journey in a crowd of about 6,000.

Evern's Cup Battle.—By George Green.

No. 15

Fan helps keep a clean sheet!

The Crystal Palace v Everton tie of 1931 also saw the occasion of Everton goalkeeper Billy Coggins being joined between the posts by a spectator.

The Liverpool Echo's reporter made note of the following occurrence in the second half, with Everton at this stage 4-0 ahead:

'A spectator took off his coat and hat and went from the back of the goal and coolly joined Coggins as a goalkeeper and he would not take his leave. The game was stopped.

'The referee ordered the man off, but he expressed a desire to stay, and finally the police took him out of the ground.'

Whether or not the spectator was a home or away fan is unclear although one thing is certain.

He can lay claim to keeping a clean sheet for Everton!

Everton came back twice to force extra time (Arthur Dominy having made it 2-2 20 seconds from the end of normal time). However, it was Hull City who would progress to round five. After O'Donnell had tried to head away a corner, the ball came to Martin, who hooked home first time, bursting the ball in the process.

The rules stated that a burst ball is a dead ball and possibly a bounce up should have been the decision on the edge of the box, but no one from Everton argued with the referee as keeper Davies retrieved the deflated piece of leather from the net.

No. 14

Sweet revenge

Nine years after the humiliation by Crystal Palace, Everton (on their way to the 1931 Second Division title) had the opportunity to avenge the 6-0 defeat at Goodison Park in the FA Cup.

The Blues were only one goal up at the break, but Dixie Dean went on to claim a four-goal haul, with a Wilde own goal and Johnson's last-minute goal making the final score 6-0. Revenge was sweet!

DEAN'S BAG OF FOUR

EVERTON'S REVENGE AFTER TEN YEARS

PLAYERS WHO STOOD OUT IN ROUT OF THE PALACE

Four star Dixie: An Echo headline of Dean's four-goal haul in the fourth round of 1931

No. 16

Southport derby is no obstacle

A local derby against Southport was the barrier to Everton reaching an FA Cup semi-final for the first time in 16 years in February, 1931.

Interest was high amongst supporters, with £2,000 worth of tickets being sold by the Thursday before the Saturday game, while a broadcast of the game was also to be heard from Liverpool (Lime Street) Station at 6pm that night.

Everton were favourites to progress, with the Liverpool Echo's match previewer also adding that 'if they cannot or do not beat Southport I think it is fair to say the side do not deserve to go any further in the Cup tournament and their defeat will be ignominious.'

As it was there were no such worries.

On a snow-covered mud bath that was the Goodison Park pitch, Everton romped into a 7-0 half-time lead – a club record at the time.

However, the 'Shrimps' as Southport were called at the time, managed to keep the score down in the second half.

The Blues eventually ran out 9-1 winners, with Dixie Dean scoring four of them.

Incidentally, former player Frank Jefferis' post-match verdict claimed that the Blues' front five was 'probably the best forward line that ever represented Everton.'

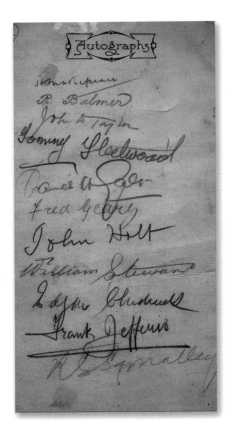

Feast of stars: A rare piece of memorabilia – a signed dinner menu featuring many famous Everton players from the early part of the century. The occasion was the 1929 Jubilee celebration

No. 17

A record crowd

Second Division champions-elect Everton were drawn to face fellow title-contenders West Brom in the 1931 semi-final at Old Trafford.

A crowd of 70,000 yielded record semi-final gate receipts of £7,629 while more than 20,000 fans packed the Old Trafford concourse. In the confusion, over 300 people were injured.

The crowd was such that the match was stopped on several occasions due to spectators spilling onto the pitch.

The Blues had beaten West Brom twice in the League that season (a recurring theme) and missed several chances before gifting the match to the Baggies. Goalkeeper Billy Coggins misjudged a high ball from right winger Tommy Glidden from a wide position just over the halfway line and the ball found the net after bouncing once. West Brom went on to win the trophy.

No. 18

Hats off to Dixie

An FA Cup sixth-round tie with Division Three South Luton Town appeared straightforward opposition for First Division Everton in March 1933. However, the visitors were confident, especially after a scouting mission was made by their manager Harold Wightman and captain Fred Kean.

Train-loads of 'straw-hatted' Luton fans arrived at Lime Street on the morning of the match, reportedly singing: "We'll get Dixie down." The outcome? 6-0 to the home side – and yes, Dean was amongst the scorers.

Packed in: There was major interest in the tie against Southport in 1931 with £2,000 worth of tickets being sold by the Thursday before the Saturday game and a broadcast made from Lime Street

Head master: Dixie Dean leaps to head one of his goals against Southport

1933
In the driving seat

Evertonians already knew they had a genius on their hands – now Dean had a 'full set' of winners' medals to prove it

PETROL

ON   OFF   ON

The numbers game

The 1933 FA Cup final between Everton and Manchester City would prove historic for several reasons – not least being the first time players' shirts were numbered

King's invite

The King ('who is a regular Cup final visitor and understands football with the knowledge of an expert') and Queen were among the many looking forward to the 1933 final.

Also planning to be in attendance were the touring West Indian cricketers and 'many Continental enthusiasts, who have secured tickets for this greatest football fight of the year'.

Recipe for success

Three 'Cooks' were going to be involved for the Blues: Full-back Willie Cook, masseur Harry Cook and trainer Harry Cooke.

Lighting up Wembley: An advert from the Cup final programme in 1933

Cup wish

Before the final, Mr Jack Pagenham of Seaforth, who drove the team coach and horses through the streets of Liverpool 27 years previous, expressed his wish to do the same should Everton be victorious. His recollections included:

'It was getting dark when we neared Spellow Lane and here we were joined by a torch-light procession which remained with us until Goodison Park was reached.

'Would he again like to drive the present team should they succeed next Saturday? Would he? He would jump at the opportunity. Quaint though his idea may at first seem in these days of changed locomotion, it is quite good and may bear fruit. It is this.

'A Liverpool firm has the replica of the coach he used. He would seek permission to use it and the horses could be supplied by Messrs. Thompsons Ltd of County Road, with whom he is employed. He intends to put his suggestion before the Everton FC secretary.'

Let it rain! A fan gets in the mood

Dogs' day

Wembley had literally gone to the dogs before the 1933 FA Cup final.

'When the greyhound racing meeting at Wembley Stadium ends tonight, the concluding preparations for the Cup Final on Saturday between Everton and Manchester City will be set in hand,' reported the Liverpool Echo's own correspondent ahead of Everton's big day in the capital.

'The great lights in the stands will be ablaze all night while workmen tackle the task of installing an extra 20,000 seats.

'Tomorrow morning (Cup final morning) the goal posts will be erected and all the greyhound racing equipment, including the trap, the hurdles, hundreds of electric light globes, miles of cables, and an eight-ton steel girder bridge over the hare escape, will be removed and the pitch will be cut and rolled for the last time.'

Blues pray for rain

According to Liverpool Echo correspondent 'Bee', the Everton players were hoping for wet conditions in the Cup final to suit their style of play.

'Oh it's damp down here – this is the song of the Everton footballers,' wrote Bee. 'And they are charmed with the beautiful rain. It suits their purpose; they feel that every drop of rain adds to their chance of victory over Manchester City in the final tie of the Cup.

'Because there is not one member of the Everton side who does not prefer the 'steady' ball rather than 'the bounder' such as was experienced in recent weeks.'

History game

The 1933 final was described as the most novel game in history by one newspaper for four reasons:
• Neither team will wear its proper colours.
• Every player, for the first time, will have a huge distinguishing number on his back.
• Both teams – Everton and Manchester City – come from Lancashire.
• There will be more foreign soccer enthusiasts than ever before.

More tickets

The total number of tickets sold was 93,513 - nearly 600 more than were admitted the previous year. This was made possible through the removal of two barriers. 1,500 stadium staff were to be on duty, and 400 police.

Replay plans

Plans were finalised for the potential Cup Final replay which would take place at Blackburn.

The prices for the various stands were set out as follows:

Stand A, one guinea; Stands B and C, half a guinea; Riverside stand, centre half, a guinea; Riverside ends, 7s 6d; Enclosures, 3s 6d.

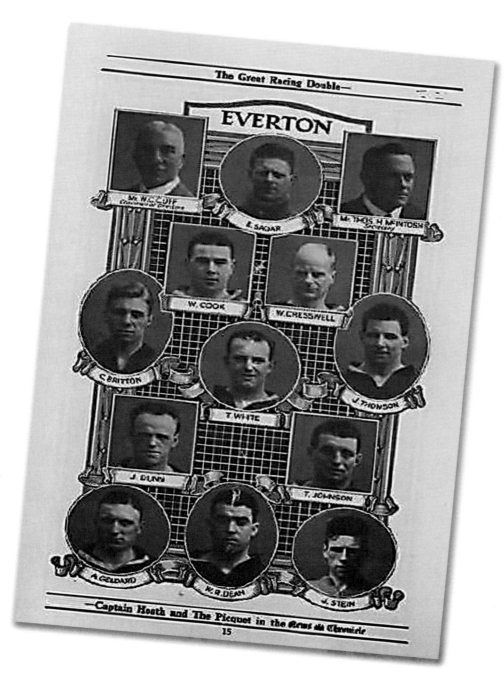

Lining up the Cup: The Everton team pictured ahead of their Wembley encounter

Rail warning

Just like today, the city was keen that the fans going to Wembley upheld the good name of Everton.

With that in mind, reporter 'Bee' issued a warning ahead of the mass exodus to the capital.

He wrote: 'To those who make the journey I would just ask one thing - the railway companies have told me of the wanton destruction that occurred to the railway carriages on a recent trip, and they beg the people to be sporting and behave! It will be a spirited final tie, but that should not make anyone forget the good name of the best game of all.'

'Hey-ho for the South'

Everton opted to prepare for their big final date in the Derbyshire spa town of Buxton. "We have never had such a nice, quiet time as this week at Buxton. You would not have thought it was Cup Final week – just a nice breather, the weather is perfect," Everton secretary Tom McIntosh told the Echo of April 26, 1933.

"Today we are having a sprint or two, then some golf, then hey-ho for the South.

"We are leaving tomorrow, and the boys are going to make this afternoon their last hit with the sticks (golf) before they strike out for the Cup."

We're on the march: Manchester City fans in good spirits

Win it for Buxton!

Everton set off south from Buxton with the best wishes of the Mayor of Buxton and the people of the town.

Mayor Councillor J. Brindley, in the send-off speech at Buxton Station, said: "If you bring back the Cup it will be a credit not only to Merseyside, but also Buxton." Mr J. Hewlitt, the manager of the hotel where the players had stayed, presented each of the team with a blue and white trumpet, while they also wore blue and white enamelled badges which had been sent to them by a Liverpool firm the previous night. Other presents they received were flannel trousers and raincoats.

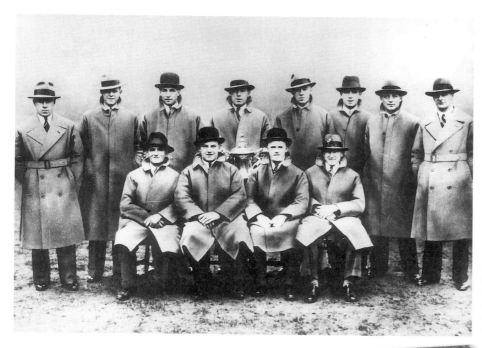

Dressed to kill: The Everton squad look more suited to Chicago than Wembley

Pitch and putt

According to the Echo's special correspondent, the Everton players were continuing to relax as they made a final hotel stop in Dorking.

He reported: 'The Cup Final is likely to be played in typical April-style weather. There will probably be showers, with a good deal of cloud and some sunshine tomorrow according to an Air Ministry expert.'

The word from the Blues' camp was positive: "There is now no need for further intensive training, and we are taking things easily," it was stated.

"The boys are having a quiet, restful day. They are out on the putting green of the hotel at present. It's a nice, mild, restful amusement in preparation for the big event.

"Some of them are very expert at it, too. They can drop the ball like clockwork. If they shoot the way they putt, then the Manchester goalkeeper will be in for a warm time tomorrow."

World class Dixie

Dixie Dean reckoned the Everton side of 1933 had the world at their feet.

"I want just one more trophy to 'make the set'" said Dean.

"It is going to be a great game, and with the changed conditions and our boys in perfect harmony and condition we shall, I feel sure, be successful. We have waited long for this – we made our vow last November – and I am confident we are going to put the world record on the books – First Division championship, Second Division championship, and the Cup in successive years."

Secretary Tom McIntosh added: "I think our boys will show superiority in craft and football skill. May the better side win – and may that be our side."

Record broken

Having witnessed every FA Cup final since 1881-82, Mr W. Brownhill of Prestatyn was disappointed not to see the final because he did not manage to obtain a ticket, reported the Echo.

Golden ticket: The 1933 final ticket so sought after by fans

Lucky dog

Dixie Dean carried his own lucky mascot on arriving with the Everton team.

The hotel staff in Buxton had presented him with a toy dog wearing the Everton colours.

'He declined to discuss his team's chances or to pose for photographers,' noted one newspaper report on his arrival.

The Opposing Cup Final Sides At Wembley Stadium

How they got there

ROUND 3
Leicester City 2-3
Everton
ROUND 4
Everton 3-1 Bury
ROUND 5
Everton 2-0
Leeds United
ROUND 6
Everton 6-0 Luton Town
SEMI-FINAL
Everton 2-1
West Ham United

Referee's fee

The match referee for the final had the choice of a five-guinea fee or a gold medal as payment.

CUP FINAL!
LOOK OUT
FOR THE
FOOTBALL
ECHO
IN LONDON

At all the Stations and principal Hotels; also from newsvendors in

EUSTON ROAD
OXFORD CIRCUS
PICCADILLY CIRCUS
CHARING CROSS
CORNER OF HOLBORN
and KINGSWAY.
LEICESTER SQUARE
CORNER OF OXFORD STREET
and TOTTENHAM COURT RD.

This will be the usual Liverpool edition, with special features relating to the Cup Final. On sale about

10.45 P.M.

Read all about it! Advert for the Football Echo on Cup final night

Going head to head: George Green's Echo cartoon of the two teams ready to do battle

Mass exodus to Wembley

There was an estimated 20,000 Everton fans at Wembley, with 'two hundred thousand Cup-tie trippers from the provinces, it was estimated added to London's millions today.'

A Liverpool Echo reporter who travelled on the first of the special trains, made the following comments: '…shortly after 5am the shock troops from Liverpool and Manchester poured into the Metropolis.

'The invaders were accompanied by a gang of audacious camp followers, who having stowed away on a train, left it near Wembley.

'Thousands disappointed at being unable to go to Wembley, seemed to derive a kind of pained pleasure in watching others depart. Those lucky folk who had tickets started queuing up before 10pm in order to be sure of getting on the 12.30am train.

'The numbered ticket system ensured that every passenger – there were nearly 700 on each train – was provided with a seat.

'More enthusiasts joined us at Allerton and Runcorn and then we 'rattled' along with community singing, and the strumming of ukeleles, guitars, banjos, mouth organs and whistles joining in the concert. As the first exuberance died down, a pair of enterprising 'buskers' did good business.

'A few minutes after passing Wembley we were entertained to a new thrill. The train, with the signal against it, halted and in the twinkling of an eye a carriage door flew open and our friends the buskers were speeding it away.

'They were followed by a gang of youngsters, and before the train officials, or most of the passengers had realised what was happening some nine or ten stowaways – most of them youths in their teens – had made their getaway over a wall bounding the railway.

'"Mugs from the North they call us," said one patriotic Liverpudlian. "Why those kids could buy and sell these fly Cockney blokes."

'The many women folk who accompanied their men folk, true to their sex, could be heard over their early morning refreshments planning a round of the shops – for them these are the sights of London.

'It was in a café that one heard the inevitable word "gradely." It was used by a waitress to a party of Liverpudlians to show she knew the speech of these Lancashire folk; and she wondered at the withering look that greeted her friendly efforts.'

Momentous final

A reported 40 special trains were chartered to take the fans south, with 700 passengers aboard each.

It was a momentous final for many reasons. It was also one of the first matches to be broadcast on radio. Newspapers carried a grid of the pitch divided into a patchwork of numbered squares so that the commentator could describe to listeners where the ball was on the pitch.

Neutral strips had to be found with 7/4 on favourites City choosing red and Everton wearing white. It was also the first final where the shirts were numbered – Everton wearing numbers 1-11, Manchester City 12-22.

It was also Everton's first Wembley final appearance.

There was no Blues manager then so the team selection was made in consultation with skipper Dixie Dean. Indeed, Everton fans were stunned before the game that Albert Geldard (who had just turned 19) started on the right wing instead of Ted Critchley who, despite losing his regular place seven months earlier, had been brought back to score the winning goal against West Ham in the semi-final.

City had their own selection worries with centre-forward Freddie Tilson ruled out, so Marshall came in at inside right, Herd moving to 'No 9'. It was also veteran Jimmy McMullan's last game before retirement.

Everton were not in the best of form as they went into the final, having scored in only two of their previous seven matches.

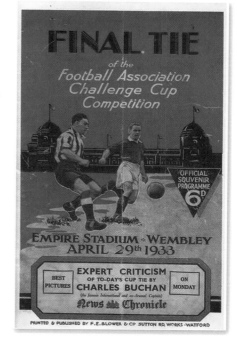

Official souvenir programme: Costing 6d

Trams home

Plans were put in place to deal with the huge numbers of Evertonians arriving back in Liverpool the morning after the Cup final.

An Echo notice before the game read: 'To meet the convenience of train passengers arriving from London between 1.15 and 8 o'clock on Sunday morning, tramcars will be run from Lime Street to Litherland, Black Bull, Carr Lane, Muirhead Avenue, Old Swan, Wavertree, Smithdown Road and Aigburth. The fare will be fourpence for any distance.'

1933

A new era: Everton wear 1-11, Manchester City 12-22 in the first FA Cup final to use numbered shirts

Blues cruise to a record

Everton's players kept their vow and won the 1933 Cup in style – recording the biggest margin of victory in a Wembley final

A lively opening saw Everton survive a scare when veteran Jimmy McMullan ('the old man of Maidstone') and Toseland both saw crosses well fielded by Ted Sagar, while at the other end Langford nearly punched a long ball from Britton into his own goal.

McMullan took minutes to recover having taken a bang to the head while at one point City keeper Langford took the ball to the referee owing to a lace protruding from it.

Dean fired over from distance and Herd and Brook almost combined to head City in front. With Everton stepping up the pressure, City began to feel the heat.

A Geldard corner caused confusion, with Johnson adopting the successful ploy of standing near the keeper, and when the ball was played, making a run in front of him to blot out his view.

The result of this was Dunn shooting just wide before Stein, with the first shot on target on the half-hour mark, saw his effort blocked by Langford.

Dean began to exert more influence and despite missing a golden opportunity from close range having been set-up by White, Everton went in front only a minute later, five minutes before the break.

Winger Jimmy Stein – who had earlier gone close – was the man who broke the deadlock after City keeper Langford had dropped a Cliff Britton cross under challenge from Dean. Brook nearly hit back straight away, forcing Sagar to make a 'clean catch worthy of any cricketer,' but that was as near as City were to come.

Another Langford error after 52 minutes from a Britton centre saw Dean bundle the ball over the line, both keeper and striker ending up in the net before Jimmy Dunn made certain ten minutes from the end heading home Geldard's corner.

The 3-0 scoreline was the biggest-ever margin of victory in a Wembley final at that time – and a thoroughly deserved win.

EVERTON: Sagar, Cook, Cresswell, Britton, White, Thomson, Geldard, Dunn, Dean, Johnson, Stein.

MANCHESTER CITY: Langford, Cann, Dale, Busby, Cowan, Bray, Toseland, Marshall, Herd, McMullen, Brook.

GOALSCORERS: Stein (40), Dean (52), Dunn (80).
ATTENDANCE 92,900.

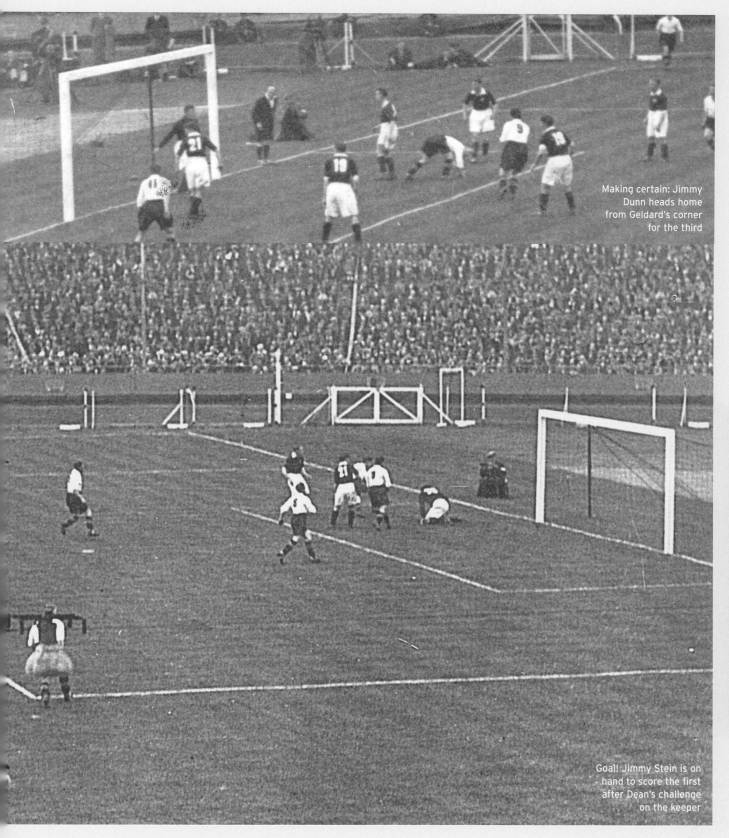

Making certain: Jimmy Dunn heads home from Geldard's corner for the third

1933

Goal! Jimmy Stein is on hand to score the first after Dean's challenge on the keeper

47 EFC

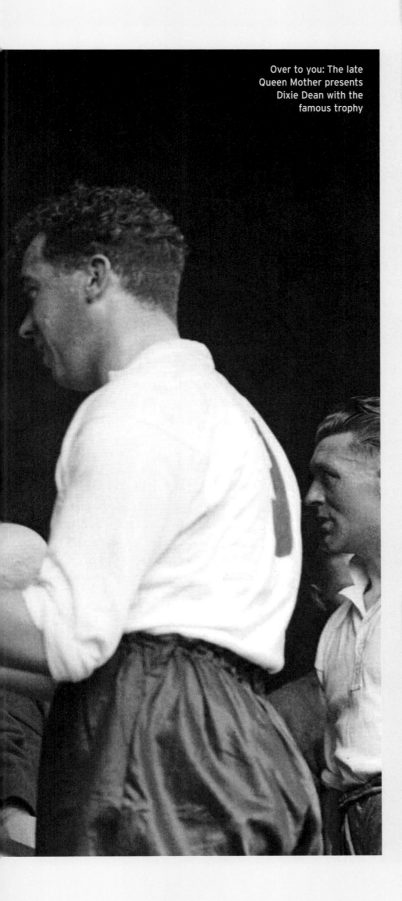

Over to you: The late Queen Mother presents Dixie Dean with the famous trophy

1933

A consummate performance

"One feels it is a grand achievement after forty-one years with the club. I was present at the final in 1897, 1906 and 1907 and today was a happy consummation, as it were.

"I would like to pay a tribute to our doughty opponents, Manchester City. We are delighted at the sporting way in which they have accepted the verdict although one expected nothing but that from such good sportsmen."

**Everton chairman
Will Cuff**

Dixie's royal approval

'The Lord Mayor sat beside the Duchess of York for half the game, and on request indicated the various players.

"That's Dean," said my Lord Mayor. "Ah," said the Duchess, "even I knew of Dean."

'In the next half the Lord Mayor of Manchester sat at the side of the Duchess.'

**From 'Bee's Notes On
Sport Of The Day'**

Dean was an inspiration

"We never really got going except for the first 15 minutes, and I am only sorry that we were all off our game at the same moment.

"That is my only regret; we know that we could have played so much better.

"But we have no quarrel; Dean was an inspiration to his men, and the whole eleven played awfully well."

**Manchester City captain
Sam Cowan**

May Day madness

Dixie Dean and the all conquering Everton team returned to a heroes' welcome as half a million jammed the city streets on a May bank holiday to remember

Crowning joy

Dixie's address to the fans went as follows . . .

"This is the crowning joy of all. Every man deserves a special pat on the back. They played first-class football and won in spite of Manchester City's pace and tactics.

"Everton have taken the Cup home again after 27 years, and there is no prouder man today than yours faithfully.

"My set is complete, as I told you on Friday, and I think every member of the side has fully earned this most coveted medal."

Three Cooks: Full-back Willie Cook, masseur Harry Cook and trainer Harry Cooke with the Cup

Dixie keeps a lid on it

The Duchess of York (the late Queen Mother) congratulated skipper Dean as he went up to the Royal Box to collect the trophy. The success completed Dean's domestic collection.

On the train journey home on the Sunday, in the book 'Dixie – Uncut The Lost Interview', Dean recalls how he nearly lost the lid of the FA Cup.

"When the train was pulling out of Crewe for home there were hundreds of people standing in the fields and lining the track. They had come miles to see the Cup so I opened the window and showed it to them.

"As I showed it through the open window the lid fell off.

"As it happened, Tommy Johnson was standing close to me and he just caught the lid before it dropped on the railway line."

THE HIGHEST SCORE FINAL AT WEMBLEY

Stein, Dean, And Dunn Settle Fate Of Manchester City

EVERTON'S SUPREME FOOTBALL AND TACTICS

Everton Bring Cup Back To L'pool After Twenty-Seven Years

Same coach as 1906

The squad returned to Liverpool on Monday, 1st May to an ecstatic welcome.

In a link to the 1906 triumph, driving an exact replica of the coach and horses bedecked in blue and white that had been at the station 27 years earlier was the same man – Jack Pagendam ('the Pickwickian Pagendam'). The coach, lent for the occasion by Lewis's, was the only one of its kind still in the city.

Dining on success: A rare picture from the 1933 Cup final banquet

'Saving our energy'

The team were due to arrive back at 7.45pm with the trophy, having left Euston at 4pm ('amid heavy rain'). In London on the Monday morning the players 'had a quiet spell, amid still flowing telegrams of congratulation. "We are saving our energy for tonight's reception," said an official.'

On the platform at Euston the party were met by Sir Frederick Wall, secretary of the FA and Lady Wall, and Mr J McKenna, chairman of the Football League ('who by the way is 79 today'), Alec James of the Arsenal, Alec Jackson, Dom Valente and Mr W.C. Cuff.

Homecoming times

'7.45pm – Arrive at Lime Street Station. 7.45pm-8.00pm – Lime Street, Wellington Monument, Ranelagh Street, Church Street, Lord Street, Castle Street. 8pm-8.30pm – Civic reception by the Lord Mayor (Councillor A.Gates).

'The team, with the Cup, will appear on the balcony. From 7.30pm until the appearance of the Lord Mayor and the team with the Cup on the Town Hall balcony, the Liverpool Police Band will play music on Exchange Flags. 8.30pm-9pm – Dale Street, Byrom Street and Scotland Road to Goodison Park' reported the Echo.

Capital gain: Dixie Dean poses for a photo outside the Wembley stadium offices

Liverpool's May King!

May King: A witty Echo cartoon showing Dean in May Day fancy dress - May 1 would have coincided with Everton's celebrations

May Day riot! Thousands packed the streets to welcome their heroes home on May 1, 1933. Above: Cartoonist George Green's take on it all

Too cold for King

At the commemoration dinner held on the Saturday night at the Victoria Hotel in London, Everton chairman W.C. Cuff toasted the King, and expressed his regret that his Majesty had been unable to attend the final due to the cold weather.

Sir Charles Clegg, president of the FA, praised Everton for playing the game with "brains as well as feet".

He said: "We had a good illustration of this in your player Cresswell."

Out of the City

While the fans of both teams enjoyed an evening out in London after the final, for the beaten Manchester City team, the day after was spent in contemplation of what might have been at a more tranquil spot.

'The West-end of London was thronged at night with a crowd as the supporters of Everton and Manchester City blending in a sporting harmony. The Manchester City team spent Sunday at Eastbourne. A number of the players visited Beachy Head, and others enjoyed a walk along the parades,' reported the Liverpool Post and Mercury.

Sunday best: Dixie makes the national news. Below: A young mascot holds on to the FA Cup with Dixie Dean at Lime Street station

Goodison thrown open

The Everton ground was thrown open to the crowds at 8.50pm on the homecoming evening and the trophy put on view at the directors' stand. Admittance for fans was via the 1s enclosure.

The public were requested to keep off the playing pitch and speeches by the directors and the players were due to be made by the aid of loud speakers.

At Goodison Park, 'Bee' estimated that 50,000 were present ('where the field was invaded').

He reported: 'Willie Cook joined in a duo-comedy turn with Dean on the directors' stand, and the crowd there was wondering who was the owner of the straw hat: it was Tom Johnson bearing a Chevalier appearance.'

Bee added: 'At St George's Hall Plateau there would be 50,000 people. Along the route to Goodison Park and from Lime Street to the Town Hall 70,000. And they seemed to fall on me like dew!'

Cup stowaways court

Seven young men who stowed away on excursion trains in London after a desperate effort – fruitless in some cases – to see the Cup Final, appeared at Liverpool Police Court.

The magistrates dealt leniently with the offenders, but the chairman (Mr Harold Lee) gave them a serious warning.

The chairman stated: "We are in a difficulty about you young men. It is no use fining you because probably you have no money. We don't want to send you to prison, lest you have swindled the railway company.

"They offer cheap fares, and you take advantage of the rush and travel without any intention of paying, just on the chance of being able to scramble through. It is a shabby and mean thing to do."

Everton fans appeared to celebrate in moderation as the courts recorded no perceptible increase in 'drunk cases' during the homecoming.

Above: Dixie Dean shows the trophy to the fans on the homecoming parade and the team, in more formal attire, left. Pictured are (back row (left to right): H. Cooke (Trainer), W. Cook, J. Dunn, A. Geldard, T. White, W. Cresswell, J. Stein, C. Britton, T. Johnson. Front row (left to right): T. Sagar, W. Dean (Captain), W. C. Cuff (Chairman), J. Thomsen.

No.20

The 'greatest Goodison game'

Nearly 60,000 crammed into Goodison Park for a FA Cup fourth-round replay against Sunderland in 1935, played on a Wednesday afternoon (they had drawn 1-1 at Sunderland on the Saturday).

It turned out to be a tie that would be dubbed 'the greatest ever at Goodison.' In a game packed with incident, Gurney took the action to extra time for the visitors late on, making the score 3-3 after Everton had led 3-1.

At this point Sunderland manager Johnny Cockrane was ordered off the field before the extra period. He had gone to the middle of the field against the rules to talk to his players. The extra-time period yielded four more goals including the completion of Jackie Coulter's hat-trick as Everton ran out 6-4 winners.

Liverpool Echo columnist Ernest Edwards summised: 'I would like to ask whether there has ever been a greater display of skill in the mud in any league or cup match?'

One big happy family: The 1935 Everton squad in relaxed mood

Thick of the action: Dean competes with two Sunderland players

No.21

People are on the pitch . . .

The interest created by the Sunderland FA Cup tie also yielded some instances of crowd control, which perhaps sums up the lack of attention paid to crowd safety in the 1930s.

The following comments come from the Liverpool Echo's reporter at the match:

'A few minutes before the kick-off the air became dull and ambulance cases numerous, the crush on the angle of Goodison Road and the double-decker stand being severe'

An early Everton chance followed before the following observation: 'At this stage the crowd broke in at the edge of the goal double decker (stand), and the scene was without parallel since Newcastle and Barnsley refought a final tie here. They surged across the pitch while the game was in progress, and the police were well-nigh powerless to stop their inroads around the playing space. The police allowed them to cross the field to the far side of the ground and sit down.'

It's incredible to even consider such a spectacle with crowd safety a major priority these days.

No.22

Dixie out, Lawton in

Everton's 4-3 defeat to Tottenham Hotspur in February 1937 was significant not only for the manner of the Blues' defeat at White Hart Lane – but also due to the final FA Cup appearance of one William Ralph Dean and the first appearance in the competition of Tommy Lawton. Having earned a replay in a scrappy 1-1 Goodison draw courtesy of a last-minute equaliser from Jackie Coulter, the Blues were 3-2 up in the replay with four minutes to go – but somehow contrived to lose in normal time.

Lawton, who had been signed from Burnley only six weeks before, opened the scoring, becoming the youngest-ever Everton Cup scorer aged 17 years, 139 days, and Dean netted the other two, one in each half. Other incidents of note included Everton having a penalty appeal turned down. Torry Gillick was tripped and the referee pointed to the spot although the home players made him consult with a linesman, who had had his flag raised due to the ball going out of play.

John Morrison was the chief tormenter of Everton, netting a hat-trick (his nickname of 'Cag' was inspired because of his apparent likeness to film star James Cagney, famous for his gangster movies).

Former England international-turned journalist Charlie Buchan claimed: "The best team lost", while former Tottenham man Tom Clay noted: "It is shocking luck after playing grand stuff." Dean's record in the FA Cup reads 32 games, 28 goals – an Everton record.

No.23

A thriller in the mist

The visit of Division Three North side Doncaster (who were backed by 1,000 travelling fans) in January 1939 posed few problems for Everton, despite the poor visibility, which according to the Liverpool Echo's match reporter, only cleared once Tommy Lawton had struck the fourth goal four minutes into the second half.

Lawton ended up scoring four goals in the 8-0 victory – including his first hat-trick for Everton.

The Blues eventually went out to Wolves in the quarter-final, but finished this last season before the Second World War as First Division champions.

Class of 1938-39: A picture of the Championship team at Lime Street Station, including Tommy Lawton (fourth from the right)

Salt of the earth: An Echo cartoon depicting the ideal Everton fan - in an era when crowd control was not at its height!

No.24

Shankly pen puts Blues lights out

The 1945/46 season saw the introduction of two-legged FA Cup ties – an experiment which was to prove unsuccessful as it was scrapped for the following season.

Everton were paired with Preston. They lost 2-1 in the first leg at Deepdale with Harry Catterick scoring on his Cup debut for the Blues.

In the return, Everton equalised to take the tie into extra time. A goal apiece in the extra period (Everton had led 2-0 for only one minute in the first half of extra time) saw the tie level on aggregate after 110 minutes (two periods of 10 minutes were played).

The solution? Sudden death, or what has been more commonly known as the 'golden goal.' In what would be a precursor of future occasions, one Bill Shankly proved Everton's nemesis, scoring a penalty nine minutes in after Everton captain Norman Greenhalgh had fisted a Livesey effort off the line. The Liverpool Echo carried the headline: 'PENALTY IN THE DARK'.

The reporter said: 'After the nine minutes of extra time, Preston were awarded a penalty for an offence which, in the failing light, I could not see.'

Ironically, Shankly had been set to miss the first leg, highlighting the selection problems clubs had in the months after the Second World War. As the Echo noted: 'Bill Shankly has written saying he will do his best to get down from Glasgow, where he is stationed with the RAF.'

No.25

Catt's cream

Harry Catterick, later to become one of the club's greatest-ever managers, was the Everton hero in January 1950, as his two goals booked Everton a last 16 berth at the expense of West Ham.

In a 'thrilling match on an icy surface', McGowan had put the home side ahead before Catterick made his mark in a six-minute spell midway through the first half.

The omens appeared to indicate that this could be Everton's year – as the previous two wins against the Hammers (all 2-1 outcomes) in the competition had seen the Blues reach the final (in 1907 and 1933).

Happy as Harry: Future Everton boss Harry Catterick runs out at Goodison. His two goals against West Ham in 1950 inspired a great Cup run

No.26

Liddell punishes Blues

Having seen off Tottenham Hotspur and Derby County following the win at West Ham, only Liverpool stood in the way of Everton reaching Wembley for the first time in 17 years.

Unfortunately, with over 70,000 packed in at Maine Road, Manchester, Everton's 11th FA Cup semi-final ended in defeat.

Bob Paisley and Billy Liddell scored in either half with the clinching goal coming about after Peter Farrell had cleared a corner, but inadvertently gave the ball straight to a Liverpool player – with Liddell punishing them.

However, at least there was some satisfaction for one former Evertonian in 1950 as Joe Mercer captained Arsenal to victory in the final over the Reds.

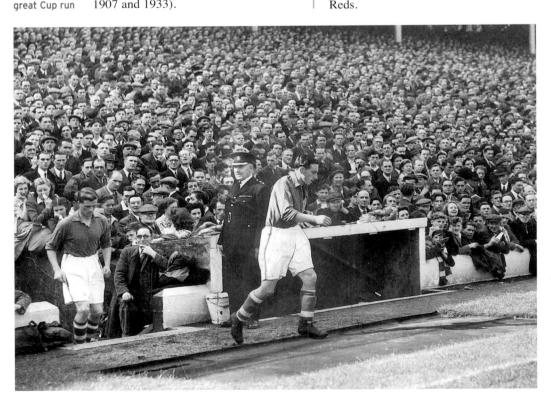

Blue day: Action from the 1950 semi-final and the match programme (right)

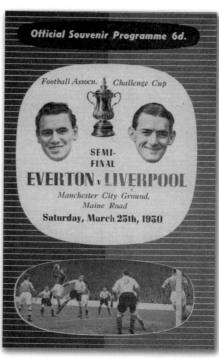

Official Souvenir Programme 6d.

Football Assocn. Challenge Cup

SEMI-FINAL
EVERTON v LIVERPOOL
Manchester City Ground, Maine Road
Saturday, March 25th, 1950

No.27

All white now

A new innovation was tested at the start of the Fifties.

The Liverpool Echo's match reporter, writing under the name 'Stork', made the following observation at Everton's FA Cup tie at Hull City in January 1951:

'An innovation so far as my knowledge in Cup ties is concerned, was the white ball.' However, the Blues failed to adapt to the muddy conditions and went down to a 2-0 defeat to their Second Division opponents. Hull were inspired by Raich Carter, who scored the first. The Tigers made Everton pay for missed chances in the first half while the struggling Blues failed to recover from this setback – being relegated at the end of the season.

Ice cool Blues: Training at Goodison was slowed down to a brisk walk in wintry conditions in this picture from 1951. Peter Farrell leads the way in a depressing season that saw the Blues relegated

No. 28

Hero Hickson defies the pain

Second Division Everton, who had already beaten Ipswich Town and Nottingham Forest in the competition, took on Manchester United in the FA Cup fifth round on Valentine's Day 1953. The Blues were expected to roll over.

Indeed, with Rowley netting for the visitors midway through the first half, all appeared to be going to the script. However, United should have known more about the fighting qualities of one Dave Hickson. With nearly 78,000 packed in at Goodison, the centre-forward inspired the Blues to one of their greatest-ever results in the competition.

Tommy Eglington nipped in to level soon after United opened the scoring and just before half-time, Hickson launched himself headlong in amongst flying boots as he tried to get on the end of a Jack Lindsay cross. He emerged with blood streaming from an eyebrow, having 'connected' with a defender's boot.

Hickson emerged minutes after the second half had begun, dabbing the wound with a handkerchief, although it soon opened up after he courageously headed an effort against the post. Although the referee wanted him to go off again, the 'Cannonball Kid' would have none of it and the Goodison hero stayed on and tormented the First Division defence. Fittingly, he fired home the winner just after the hour mark.

Black and white: The two-tone programme for the Bolton semi-final in 1953

A hero: Dave Hickson (below) receives treatment for a nasty gash – which didn't stop him grabbing a dramatic winner against Manchester United in 1953. Below right: The squad relax before the game

No. 29

Cannonball run

The 1953 final, known universally as the legendary 'Matthews Final', could so easily have been the 'Hickson Final' had the outcome of the semi-final at Maine Road gone Everton's way.

First Division Bolton Wanderers showed their class by racing into a 4-0 lead at the break. Nat Lofthouse, who less than a year earlier had been dubbed the 'Lion of Vienna' after his two goals in Austria had earned England a famous win, struck twice.

Hickson being off the field for 15 minutes – again with a head injury – and Tommy Clinton missing a penalty on the stroke of half-time did not help.

But such was the spirit of the Second Division side that they hit back, through a John Willie Parker double and Peter Farrell. Parker's second, Everton's third, came six minutes from time.

However, the Blues had left themselves with a mountain to climb. They came to within sight of the summit, but Bolton clung on as Maine Road proved an unlucky semi-final venue for the second time in four years. Stanley Matthews' moment of destiny now lay ahead. If only it had been the year of Everton's 'Cannonball Kid'.

David and Goliath: A colourful cartoon poster depicting the FA Cup heroics of Everton's Dave Hickson

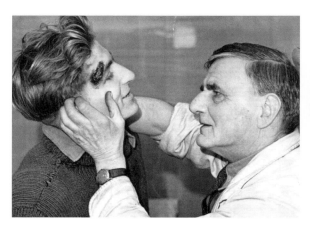

No. 31

With a little help from London

Having taken five attempts to see off Burnley, champions Chelsea visited Everton on February 18, 1956. The 'Pensioners' hardly relished the opportunity to visit Goodison because there had been little chance to rest their players. Indeed, their manager Ted Drake was reportedly quoted as stating that "Everton would not be happy to beat one of the two fine but tired sides which played at Highbury on Monday and at White Hart Lane yesterday, and that there could be little satisfaction for them if they win on Saturday" (Liverpool Echo, 16/2/56).

Everton were lying ninth in the First Division while Chelsea were 13th. One special train carried 600 Chelsea fans although with doubts concerning the state of the pitch, two fans of the Londoners did their best to make sure the tie went ahead. The Echo reported: 'Among those who volunteered to spray sand on the pitch were Reg Parris of Sutton Dwellings, Chelsea and Charlie Vass of Holborn Place, Chelsea. They travelled from London on the midnight train and arrived at the ground at about 6.30am.

"We were in a cafe later when we heard that the ground would have to be sanded so we offered to give a hand," said Reg as he wheeled a barrow load of sand onto the pitch. "We didn't want to come all the way from London after losing a night's sleep and then find the game postponed."'

No. 30

Yellows' long trek

Second Division Everton were drawn to face top-flight Sheffield Wednesday at Hillsborough in February 1954. Both sides sported blue home strips. To make them stand out, Everton wore wasp-like yellow and black hooped stockings.

The visitors, backed by 10,000 fans, suffered an early blow when Shaw gave Wednesday the lead, but from then on Everton dominated. Tommy Eglington, making his 300th appearance for the club, was amongst a host of players who went close before Dave Hickson equalised before the hour mark.

There appeared to be only one winner – with Everton forcing 25 corners – but it did not prove to be Everton. Breakaway goals from Sewell and O'Neill in the last five minutes saw the Blues bow out.

According to the Echo, there was to be further disappointment for over 500 Everton fans. Having been too late for their special trains, they were brought back by an extra train laid on by British Rail although it did not get to the city centre until 2.30am.

They then faced a long walk home as the buses had stopped running.

So near, yet so far: Agony for Tommy Clinton (above) as he sees his spot kick go wide and (top) John Willie Parker scores for the Blues in the 1953 semi-final

No. 32

400-up as Peter edges out Chelsea

Thankfully for Everton, the Chelsea tie did go ahead. Making his 400th appearance for the Blues, it was fitting that Peter Farrell should net the only goal that put Everton into the last eight of the FA Cup - his first goal since Good Friday two years previous.

It seemed luck had been with the home side, as Chelsea saw a late goal disallowed after Leyland, 'harassed by two opponents, had thrown it out to the feet of Bentley.'

Indeed, the visit of Lady Luck could have been due to a female fan, as the Echo reported: 'The first woman to start queuing was Mrs Esther Howard of Harris Drive, Bootle. She arrived at Gwladys Street five hours before the game. In her handbag she carried a crushed rosette, which had been bought at Wembley when Everton last won the Cup in 1933. "I have got it with me today just for luck" she said.'

Another footnote was that it was the last tie that Cliff Britton took charge of, leaving soon after due to a dispute with the board.

Follow the leader: The Toffee Lady greets goal hero Peter Farrell as he runs out at a packed Goodison Park

Below: Cartoon of the Chelsea tie in 1956

No. 33

'175,000' in Goodison

The Liverpool Echo told the off-field story of Everton's FA Cup clash with Blackburn Rovers in January 1958:

'WHEN 75,000 FEELS LIKE 175,000'

The fourth-round tie was staged on a Wednesday night (7.30pm kick-off), having been postponed the previous Saturday due to the state of the Goodison pitch. The on-field action saw Rovers race into a two-goal lead inside 20 minutes. Jimmy Harris pulled a goal back on the half-hour although it was not enough.

Rovers, managed by future Everton boss Johnny Carey, were worthy winners with a certain Roy Vernon catching the eye of Liverpool Echo reporter Leslie Edwards who said: 'This young Rhyl boy showed what a great potential he has.'

Any chances Everton had were all but extinguished too by a first-half injury to Derek Temple, who was forced to hobble through the rest of the game.

The attendance was predicted to have been nearer 80,000 (the official figure given was 75,818).

The crush was such that spectators were allowed to leave the pens and exit via the side of the pitch.

Having been allowed to leave they were then allowed to return although as Edwards noted: 'Thousands of people who had been in the ground when the game started were on their way home long before the interval.'

It later transpired that two crush barriers had broken as a result of the crowd's swaying.

No. 34

Carey joy
New manager Johnny Carey (left) had clearly impressed the Everton hierarchy and had been in charge of the Blues for only three months when Sunderland came to town for a third-round tie in January 1959.

With icy conditions reaping havoc up and down the country, Goodison survived the big freeze due to the installation of undersoil heating and over 57,000 were in attendance to see a comfortable home win.

Dave Hickson struck twice in either half as the Wearsiders' bright start came to nothing.

Jimmy Harris and Eddie Thomas were the other scorers as the Blues marched on to meet Charlton Athletic in round four.

No. 35

What's the score?
In 1959, Everton had earned a fourth-round replay with Charlton after the Blues had hit back from 2-0 down with 15 minutes left at The Valley to earn a replay – the equaliser even prompting a mini pitch invasion from some joyous travelling fans.

Dubbed as 'the most fantastic game never seen' due to fog, the Goodison tie saw the Blues leading 1-0. Dave Hickson was the scorer and many in the 75,000 crowd left near the end thinking this was the final scoreline.

Only one of the five goals was scored at the Gwladys Street End where fans were unaware of the other goalscorers due to the conditions.

Visibility was passable at ground level although even Liverpool Echo & Evening Express reporter Michael Charters confessed: 'The odd thing is that when people come to recall it they will never be able to say they saw it, but merely that they saw a little of it and heard the rest. And I don't mind confessing that too.'

Carey's boys: Action from the 1959 tie against Sunderland at Goodison, as Eddie Thomas nets the third goal

Blues survive late drama
After Hickson had given the Blues a half-time lead, they survived a scare 15 minutes from time when Sam Lawrie side-footed a spot-kick wide of Albert Dunlop's goal.

That relief was short-lived, however, when he hooked home from a corner in the dying minutes to force extra time.

It was told that fans at the other end of the ground thought the score was 2-1 to the visitors, unaware that a penalty had actually been missed.

Bobby Collins took advantage of a mistake by Charlton keeper Duff - who had been sent off late in the first game due to a goalmouth scuffle - to give Everton the lead before the extra time break before Hickson turned in a rebound and Collins lobbed in number four to give the scoreline the emphatic look that Everton's pressure warranted.

Sadly, however, Everton and manager Johnny Carey were later to part company. Chairman John Moores famously broke the news to Carey in the back of a taxi in 1961.

No. 36

Life's a beach for versatile Blues

The big freeze that affected the domestic game in the winter of 1963 failed to disrupt Everton on their march to Championship glory. It also failed to halt their progress into the last 16 of the FA Cup too.

Third Division Swindon Town, who had won 11 of their previous 12 games, hosted the Blues. To beat the freeze they had covered their County Ground pitch with 75 tonnes of sand spread over mud and a layer of ice.

Manager Harry Catterick described the pitch as "impossible" before the game but having trained on Formby beach during the week, his side seemed far from concerned. One Blues fan was also reported to have shouted: "What time does the tide come in?"

Tony Kay made his debut although even before the first whistle, the Liverpool Echo & Evening Express reporter had noted how he was left sprawled on the 'turf' after losing his footing. Running repairs were also needed to the Everton net after the ball found its way there after going through the side netting.

Roy Vernon and Jimmy Gabriel struck in the first 20 minutes to stun the home side before Billy Bingham bulleted home a header.

Johnny Morrissey hooked home before the break to make the second half academic.

Vernon tapped home the fifth before a Smith consolation made it 5-1.

Cold comfort: Mounds of snow are clearly seen piled behind the goal in the 1963 tie at Third Division Swindon

Spot of good luck: Roy Vernon (right) made no mistake with a second spot-kick – but the referee needed a police escort!

No. 37

The 'dirtiest game'

Nearly a year before the infamous 'Battle of Goodison' League match in November 1964, which saw the Everton and Leeds players ordered to the dressing rooms by the referee to let matters cool down, the Blues met Leeds in the fourth round of the FA Cup at Elland Road. These were always bruising encounters.

Leeds were still in the old Second Division, but were clearly a rising force. The champions were fortunate to come away with a Goodison replay after Lawson had

given the home side a half-time lead.

The Blues were awarded a penalty 11 minutes from time when Billy Bremner sent Alex Scott sprawling in the area. Scott's weakly-taken kick was saved by Gary Sprake, only for referee Langdale to order a re-take, adjudging that the goalkeeper had moved too early.

As it was, Roy Vernon made no mistake with the second and an hour after the final whistle the official was given a police escort away from the ground.

After the game Alex Scott admitted to the Liverpool Echo & Evening Express: "It was the dirtiest game I've ever played in."

No. 38

Gabriel answers SOS

With problems in attack for the Leeds replay, including an ankle injury to Alex Young (who had ended the first tie limping), Harry Catterick turned to Jimmy Gabriel for inspiration, and the Scot was not found wanting.

Gabriel (pictured above) converted the opener on the half-hour, latching onto a Roy Vernon through ball and beating Paul Madeley before ramming the ball home past Gary Sprake.

Despite the promptings of former Goodison hero Bobby Collins, Everton always created the better chances and it was skipper Vernon who clinched it late on in front of a crowd of over 66,000.

Thousands more had been locked out while it was reported that St John Ambulance men dealt with more than 50 casualties.

The Blues earned a tie at Sunderland in round five, but went down 2-0, meaning the end of the FA Cup dream for another year – although success was not too far away.

No. 39

Match of the Day debut

January 9, 1965 saw Everton make their *Match of the Day* FA Cup debut. Indeed, their home tie with Sheffield Wednesday was the first-ever FA Cup match televised on the BBC's famous programme. It was unusual for Everton to be featured at Goodison, as boss Harry Catterick did not welcome the TV cameras. This was highlighted by the fact that the next time a Goodison League match was screened was not until August 1967, a 3-1 victory over Manchester United.

It was a tie of high drama, which Everton led at the break thanks to an Andy Burgin own goal on his debut. Lax defending at corners saw Wednesday turn around the deficit to lead 2-1 in the second half (John Quinn, a former Prescot Cables player, netting the second).

The Blues pressed with Alex Scott swapping wings with the limping Sandy Brown but with the visiting fans chanting "easy, easy", Pickering popped up to earn a replay.

Pick it out: Fred Pickering celebrates the late rescue act in front of the TV cameras and heads for goal in the replay

Harvey's delight at first goal

The Blues went on to canter to a replay win at Hillsborough with Colin Harvey scoring his first FA Cup goal. The 3-0 victory was achieved by half-time, and reports suggested it could have been double. Fred Pickering and Derek Temple headers sandwiched Colin Harvey's 20-yarder in front of 50,000.

No.40

'Cattrick out, Young in!'

With his Everton side showing patchy League form, manager Harry Catterick had decided to drop crowd favourite Alex Young the week before and brought in a 16-year-old centre-forward named Joe Royle for his debut at Blackpool.

The change backfired badly on 'The Catt' and resulted in a 2-0 defeat with angry Evertonians confronting the Blues manager outside the ground after the game.

As a result of that disappointment, a fan wielded a placard before the FA Cup third-round tie with Sunderland in 1966 bearing the mis-spelt legend: 'Sack Cattrick, Keep Young.'

Although the fan failed to get his wish, he at least saw the return of the 'Golden Vision'. Young, brought back in for Royle, impressed in the 3-0 victory (claiming the third goal).

With Gordon West, Jimmy Gabriel and Ray Wilson also returning to the side, the XI would be the same all the way through their Cup run that year apart from one notable exception!

A rare colour archive photo from the 1966 semi-final as a young mascot, complete with home-made No. 9 on his shirt shakes hands with Denis Law as Brian Labone looks on

No.41

Third time lucky

The quarter-final against Manchester City in 1966 was forced to go to a third game after goalless draws at both Goodison Park and Maine Road. City, managed by former Everton star Joe Mercer, would win promotion to the First Division only a month later and proved stubborn opponents. Held at Molineux in order to beat the bad weather further north, Everton were boosted by the return of Jimmy Gabriel to the team and, against the run of play, Derek Temple and Fred Pickering finished off City's challenge before half-time.

No.42

White Pele strikes

With a semi-final against Manchester United looming at Burnden Park, Everton fielded a weakened side at Leeds the week before. The team is thought to have been the youngest-ever Blues side, with an average age of 20 years, 11 months. The club were fined £2,000 after the 4-1 defeat.

Hopes were not high for Blues' fans, particularly as Fred Pickering had limped off two weeks earlier against Sheffield United and was deemed unfit while Tommy Wright was also injured. In Pickering's place came Mike Trebilcock, a 21-year-old who Catterick

had signed from Plymouth earlier that season. Sandy Brown came in for Wright.

Interest was fierce and British Rail had laid on extra trains from Liverpool. It was Bolton's biggest crowd since the 1947 disaster, when 33 people had died. Burnden Park was ill-equipped to deal with the attendance and at half-time the fencing gave way in one corner and hundreds watched the second half sitting on the cinder track surround.

It was a scrappy encounter against the reigning league champions until 12 minutes from time when Harvey found the corner off a post after being teed up by Derek Temple. Although United were without the injured George Best, they still included Bobby Charlton, Denis Law and Nobby Stiles.

The smile says it all: Brian Labone leaves the pitch victorious and the Blues are heading back to Wembley

Dream come true

Goalscoring hero Colin Harvey, talking in his autobiography, said later: "The fact I scored the goal in the semi-final at Burnden Park in 1966 was amazing.

"I've heard since that there were supporters close to the pitch in the second half and I suppose that Bolton, at the time, wasn't really big enough for an Everton v Manchester United semi-final, but I was just so wound up in the game and wanting to win that I didn't really notice.

"It was every Everton supporter's dream to score the goal that puts you through to the final."

It was to be Everton's first Wembley appearance for 33 years.

Pele magic: Everton are heading to Wembley and Colin Harvey is the man scoring the all-important goal in the semi-final as these two pictures show

Wembley here we come: Fans invade the Burnden Park pitch after Everton's 1966 semi-final

1966

Comeback kings

Cassius Clay trained in Hyde Park as Harry's heroes
delivered an unforgettable knockout of their own . . .

Catterick's dilemma

Black market ticket rumours were in the Press and Everton boss Harry Catterick had some tough decisions to make as the Blues prepared for the 1966 FA Cup final

Ticket denial

Manager Harry Catterick and secretary Bill Dickinson came out in defence of the Everton players nine days before the final in the Liverpool Echo, denying rumours of black market dealings in Cup Final tickets. A club statement read:

'Everton have received many complaints of Cup Final tickets being sold on the black market which most people are assuming have come from the players. The club wish to emphasise that the players' ticket allocations are in strict accordance with FA rules and no player has yet received any tickets.

'The only tickets issued by the club so far have been to shareholders and season ticket holders, and there are other sources in Liverpool where Cup Final tickets are available.'

Taste of 1966: Bovril was a popular half-time drink - as shown by this advert in the Cup final programme

Question mark over Fred

An exclusive interview with Harry Catterick the day previous by Michael Charters had indicated that Everton had problems at right-back and centre-forward for the final.

Right-back would be either Tommy Wright or Sandy Brown: "I have an open mind on that. Brown has been playing well recently," said Catterick.

'At centre-forward the big question mark hangs over Fred Pickering, whose recent knee injury could be the cause of him missing every footballer's dream – a Wembley Cup Final appearance.

"Fred has had three League games since missing the Cup semi-final. There has been no reaction from his injury but I feel he is not playing with the confidence he was showing in his play before being injured," added Catterick.

'The final choice will not be made until Friday, possibly even on the morning of the match itself.

'Pickering's problem is that he has no further opportunity of proving himself fully match fit. He had his chance in three fixtures, but I believe he showed a mental reaction to his

Knee injury: Fred Pickering

injury which prevented him extending himself.

'The thought must be at the back of his mind that if he stretches and strains, his knee cartilage could go – and what wise manager would take a chance of this happening at Wembley of all places in the showpiece game of the season.'

Charters went on to predict that Mike Trebilcock would start in place of Pickering (who had scored in every round of the Cup he had played), and he also got it right for the right-back berth – Tommy Wright started ahead of Sandy Brown. Leslie Edwards reported the story in the Echo (13/5/66), with Catterick having announced the news from the club's 'secret' headquarters at Selsdon Park, Surrey. Catterick said:

"Wright is preferred to Brown at full-back after considering ground and tactical conditions for this match.

"Whilst Pickering appears to have fully recovered physically from injury, he has had insufficient time to recover his confidence and form for me to risk him in such a vital game as this.

"These decisions were the most difficult I have

On track for Wembley: Harry Catterick waves to the camera as he travels by train down south to prepare for the big day

had to make in my fifteen years of football management.

"Both Pickering and Brown are excellent club men and I have had a particularly difficult duty to inform them of these decisions.

"Trebilcock, Brown, Wright and Pickering were called in to our private lounge at the hotel after training this morning and informed of these decisions."

Former Wednesday manager Catterick had this to say of his former club: "They are a very fit and mobile side and I think they can give us a lot of trouble.

"I think it is very foolish that many people have said that Wembley is a push-over for Everton.

"That is nonsense. Wednesday had to beat Chelsea, a very fine team in the semi-final.

"They have spirit and strength, and above average ability."

Two lucky lads

According to the Liverpool Echo & Evening Express, hordes of fans had been waiting outside Goodison Park since the last of the 15,000 Everton tickets went on sale.

Shareholders and season ticket holders had already received their tickets by post.

Two lucky teenage Everton supporters who were successful in gaining tickets for Wembley were Richard O'Neill, aged 15, of Glover Street, Bootle, and 14-year-old Nelson Mak, of Peel Road, Bootle. They had queued for nine hours.

Each queuer was able to buy one 10s ground ticket in exchange for 13 vouchers from post-Christmas home programmes.

Only one turnstile was in operation, and all vouchers were checked to ensure there were no counterfeits being circulated.

Player protests

Mr Alan Brown, manager of Wednesday, received nationwide publicity and praise for his forthright stand over the allocation of Wembley tickets to his players. After a good deal of public airing of linen the players had been given 12 tickets each as laid down in the laws of the FA.

Everton had done exactly the same thing but without their action being given any notoriety. Mr Catterick said: "There were some protests from the players because they knew how many tickets other Finalists have received in recent years, but they have accepted it now according to the laws of the game.

"I believe that tickets should be available first to club shareholders, season ticket holders and supporters and that is what we have tried to do at Everton."

Mary's wait

According to the Liverpool Echo of May 9, 1966: 'The queue for Cup Final tickets began shortly after 6.30 last night outside the Bullens Road Stand at Goodison Park. One of the first in the queue was 16-year-old Mary Weston, of Andrew Street, Walton, Liverpool.'

Fans' feat of Clay

An unknown Everton fan risked not seeing the Cup Final when he sparred up to world heavyweight champion Cassius Clay in a light-hearted bout in Hyde Park.

The Evertonian was among a group of supporters having an early morning walk through the park when they came across the heavyweight champion during a training run.

Clay was wearing a white tracksuit - the same colour as Sheffield Wednesday's Cup Final strip - so there was an immediate challenge from the Everton group. Cassius obliged and after 30 seconds sparring, in which the Evertonian displayed neat footwork on the retreat, the contest was declared a draw.

2-1 for Everton

The Liverpool Echo's guest writer in the week running up to the big day was Leeds United goalkeeper Gary Sprake. He tipped Everton to bring the Cup home: "I believe that the Cup's new home will be only a stone's throw from Anfield – at Goodison Park, in fact.

"It will be a close thing, for Sheffield Wednesday, Everton's Wembley rivals are not the type of team to be taken lightly. But having played at Wembley last season, and therefore knowing the type of approach and football needed to win there, I cannot see classy Everton losing.

"I have played against both finalists this season and believe that Everton are by far the superior side.

"The Wembley turf should inspire and magnify the superb football they are capable of producing. Every position in the Everton line-up is filled by a craftsman and there is certainly no lack of big match experience throughout the team.

"The two defences are so strong in this instance that only the supreme optimist would hope for a lot of goals. I cannot see more than one goal as the winning margin, so I forecast that the score will be 2-1 for Everton."

Paying the price

Rumours of Cup Final tickets for sale in Manchester led to one desperate Evertonian travelling down the East Lancs Road.

The Echo of May 11 reported: 'There was a board and a man, complete with tickets priced from £8 for a 10s ground ticket to £16 for a 50s stand ticket.'

One to tell the grandkids: Blues watch Cassius Clay - aka Muhammad Ali - training in Hyde Park

Double up for Cup

To celebrate Liverpool's Division One title and Everton's Cup Final appearance, the Spot The Ball prize money in the Liverpool Echo & Evening Express was doubled to £10,000 – with the winner receiving £6,000.

Blues' numbers up

A man, who had never attended a football match, made the newspapers before the final for wondering why the figures '33 33 31' appeared to him in a dream in blue and black. Only when he read next day of Everton's Cup win in 1933 and their appearance in a final 33 years later did he come to the conclusion that the final set of figures (31) represented a score of 3-1 to Everton.

We're all 'mugs'!

The scramble for tickets continued with one irate Evertonian from Southport writing in to suggest that Wembley's capacity should be increased to 150,000 to meet the demand in future finals.

He wrote: 'If the FA Cup Final cannot cater for the many thousands of supporters of the two teams involved as it cannot and never has done since the first final was played at Wembley 43 years ago, why on earth has not Wembley been re-built to house at least 150,000? I believe many true fans would prefer to watch the final on TV if their own team weren't at Wembley.

'What mugs we all are attending match after match in all kinds of weather, queuing for a ticket for this match or that, travelling with our team to away matches hoping, praying that this year it will be Wembley and then to find it is. But then the racket starts.

'It's a rank disgrace. What other country would stand still as we have done with regard to the venue for the Cup Final? Surely the day must come when another ground will have to be built, or the FA Cup Final renamed as 'The tournament attended by the regular fan, until the semi-finals and Final and then by the chosen few.''

Picture this: A special Cup final offer in the Echo giving fans the chance to take a '1966 TV set' on trial for 10 days

Fans at no. 10

'The Prime Minster, Mr Harold Wilson, made an early morning appearance for fans in Downing Street on Cup final morning. Shortly after nine o'clock a large crowd of Everton supporters gathered outside No 10 cheering and waving, and Mr Wilson went into the street and spent a few minutes talking to them.'

Different ball game: The Harlem Globetrotters were also on Wembley duty in 1966

Wembley a piece of cake

'A giant cup-final cake went on show in the window of Cousins Ltd in Lord Street, Liverpool city centre in the days leading up to the final. The cake, decorated to make a copy of the Wembley pitch is three feet long by two feet wide, weighed 57lb and carried goal posts and players. Around it were the names of the Everton players who have played in Cup games.'

It was the work of Mr Ron Freeman, assistant bakery manager. The previous year's Wembley cake was on display at Liverpool Town Hall when the Liverpool team attended the victory reception.

Mr Freeman, who admitted to being an Evertonian, said: "I am still looking for a ticket for the game, but if I don't get one I shall go down to London on spec."

Just the ticket

The clamour of Lime Street Station cafeteria was silenced when a man walked in and asked: "Who wants to buy a 10s ground ticket for Wembley – for 10s."

The first man to reach the ticket seller was Mr J Joseph of 15 Sunnybank Road, Childwall who wanted the ticket for a friend.

After handing over a 10s note in exchange for the ticket, Mr Joseph said: "I am delighted. I am travelling down on the Pullman train and my friend is meeting me. He doesn't have a ticket and was going to try and get one. He will be really surprised when I tell him that it's all fixed up."

Back down to earth

A 15-year-old youth, William Scott of Sparrow Hall Road, Liverpool was taken to a Northwood, Middlesex hospital after falling about 80 feet from a roof at Wembley Stadium.

A hospital spokesman said that Scott punctured his lung in the fall. An emergency operation was performed and his condition regarded as satisfactory.

William, known as Billy, was the eldest of the four boys of Mr and Mrs William Scott. He set off about six o'clock the night before the final with three of his friends to thumb lifts to London.

Said his father, caretaker at Coronation Court, Fazakerley: "Billy has been a keen Everton follower since he was so high, and always went to away matches if he could. On Monday he was to start work at Mintons, the paint shop in Broadway, Norris Green."

Blue fountain

Evertonians were also in the news in the city centre of London. They dyed the fountain water in Trafalgar Square a deep blue.

About 30 of them also queued up outside the Pall Mall offices of Impossibles Limited, the firm which specialises in 'obtaining the unobtainable.'

Singing the Blues: The Swinging Blue Jeans had a plane on standby to fly them to a gig after the 1966 final

Blue Jeans swinging in

Everton had some celebrity fans cheering them on at Wembley in the form of a fab four from Liverpool

It was, however, the Swinging Blue Jeans and not John, Paul, George and Ringo who made the journey down to support Harry Catterick's men.

The group members were 'four of Everton's keenest fans' (Ray Ennis, 23, Les Braid, 24, Terry Sylvester, 19 and Norman Kuhlke, 23) and they paid £60 to watch the game.

The group had to charter a plane to fly them to an engagement at Stamford, in Lincolnshire after the match.

The leader, Ray Ennis, said: "We are shooting off from Wembley to Denham Airport, where a private aircraft will be waiting to fly us to Leicester.

"A car will be standing by there to whip us over to Stamford for the evening's date.

"It will be worth the expense to see Everton win.

"But whether we shall be able to sing after all the cheering we shall put in is another matter!"

1966

Suits you, miss

Wearing a specially-bought blue suit for the Cup final occasion was Hilary Goodwin of Litherland, who finished off the neat two-piece outfit with a striped boater and rosette-trimmed scarf. She was going to Wembley with her fiancé, who had a ticket.

"If I can't get one I'll take a walk around the shops with a friend who lives in London, then go to her home to watch the match on television," said Hilary.

Married to the Blues

Tony Maguire, 23, and his fiancée Miss Barbara Thompson, 20, made their wedding plans before Everton reached Wembley, which forced a re-think. Tony had been working as an electrician in Zambia and due to the amount of leave allowed (seven weeks) the date of the wedding was brought forward so Tony could 'attend' both events. Tony said: "Although I have been in Zambia for the past 12 months I have been following the team closely."

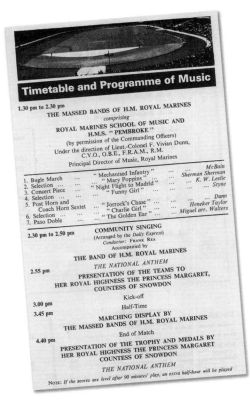

Pickering showdown

The big news in the run-up to the game was Harry Catterick's decision not to risk Fred Pickering in the final.

Understandably, the news didn't go down well with the Everton striker.

The Liverpool Echo of May 14 reported: 'There are strong reports in London today that Pickering is going to reveal his exclusive thoughts on the subject in a newspaper tomorrow.

'He said last night: "I don't want to do anything hasty which might upset the boys in the team, but I feel I have been unfairly treated.

"I have told Mr Catterick that I haven't been given a chance to show whether I was in form or not after my knee injury.

"With the Cup final coming up the lads didn't bother too much about creating opportunities in League games.

"What happens after the final will obviously affect my future."

'The other man omitted from the Cup final team, full-back Sandy Brown, has remained true to character in that he is prepared to accept his bitter disappointment as part of the game and has not rushed to his manager with transfer demands.'

Ready for a 4000-1 winner

Company executive Mr Harold Johnson had 4001 good reasons for fancying Everton for the Cup. One reason was that 57-year-old Mr Johnson had supported the Blues for 45 years. The 4,000 other reasons are the terms of the bet with his bookmaker friend, Mr Billy Vaughan of Lancaster Road, Hindley, near Wigan.

One of the most famous teamsheets in Everton history: Fred Pickering is included in the Blues' line-up in the official match programme but would play no part in the match.

Above: The music and entertainment the fans would have enjoyed before kick-off and during the half-time break

1933 squad at Wembley

The 1933 Cup-winning side were all invited to the post-game banquet, minus Jimmy Dunn who had died

Heads we win: Skipper Brian Labone looks nervously to see if Everton have won the toss ahead of the final

Struggling for Cup final form

One of the most memorable finals of modern times, Everton had gone into it with only one win from their last eight First Division games - although they had not conceded a goal in the competition that season.

For Wednesday, centre-half Vic Mobley was a late concern, with 19-year-old Sam Ellis on standby, while they had reached the final having not once played a tie at home.

Fred Pickering was controversially left out by Harry Catterick with Cornishman Mike Trebilcock, who had been signed the New Year's Eve the previous year and had played in only eight games (including the FA Cup semi-final), in his place.

Just before the third round of the FA Cup he offered Mr Johnson the odds against Everton making the lap of honour at Wembley. Said Mr Vaughan: "£200 for a shilling if Everton win the Cup."

And as he folded his precious 4,000-1 betting slip back in his wallet, Mr Johnson said at his home at Manor Grove, Skelmersdale: "I used to cycle 17 miles to watch Everton when I was a schoolboy.

"They've always been my team. I don't think many people outside Liverpool fancied Everton much for the Cup this year. But Billy has always been one who loves making the unusual bet."

In fact the bet on Everton winning the Cup has been going on for 14 years between the two men.

"So far the bet has cost me 14s over the years, but I have a fancy I've hit the jackpot this time!" added Mr Johnson.

Behind every good team: The wives of the Everton players head for the Cup final

'That's it, Wednesday's Cup!'

Everton were down but not out in one of the greatest FA Cup finals ever at Wembley . . .

A flying start from the Owls saw the Blues a goal down inside five minutes – the first they had conceded in the competition that year, Jim McCalliog's shot deflecting in off Ray Wilson.

Wednesday were on top despite Alex Young first having a goal ruled out for offside, before being brought down by keeper Ron Springett in the area – only for the referee to wave play on. McCalliog had an effort blocked soon after they opened the scoring but they were comfortably ahead at the break.

Young's effort early in the second half was brilliantly saved by Springett while McCalliog again went close before Everton found themselves 2-0 down after 57 minutes, David Ford following up after Gordon West had parried a fierce John Fantham effort. Ford's strike encouraged commentator Kenneth Wolstenholmne to declare: 'That's it, Wednesday's Cup'.

But suddenly the Blues hauled themselves back from the brink with two goals from young Cornishman Mike Trebilcock. The first came on 59 minutes after Derek Temple's header had been blocked, Trebilcock firing home the loose ball from 12 yards before the equaliser stunned Wednesday further five minutes later. Alex Scott's free-kick into the area was half cleared by Sam Ellis, and Trebilcock crashed home as the ball dropped from the edge of the box.

That goal prompted Eddie Cavanagh, a former Everton youth player, to run from the crowd and make a mazy run across the pitch, finally being brought down courtesy of a policeman's rugby tackle just outside West's penalty area.

With 17 minutes left a mistake by Gerry Young, who failed to control a Colin Harvey long ball, let in Temple, who raced from just inside the Wednesday half one-on-one with Springett...and made no mistake to fire home and complete a remarkable triumph.

Again, an Everton supporter on the pitch was chased by policemen.

Trebilcock was denied a hat-trick by Springett soon after while Fantham missed a late chance for Wednesday, but that was it, leaving Brian Labone to collect the Cup from Princess Margaret.

EVERTON: West, Wright, Wilson, Gabriel, Labone, Harris, Scott, Trebilcock, Young, Harvey, Temple.

SHEFFIELD WEDNESDAY: Springett, Smith, Megson, Eustace, Ellis, Young, Pugh, Fantham, McCalliog, Ford, Quinn.

GOALS: McCalliog (5), Ford (57), Trebilcock (59, 64), Temple (73).
ATTENDANCE: 100,000.

Trebil at the double: Mike Trebilcock finds the net a the Blues stage a remarkable comeback.

Top (from left): Harry Catterick leads the team out; Derek Temple scores the winner; England defender Ray Wilson in action with the score at 2-2

1966

'Wembley wizard'

Temple worship: Derek Temple celebrates; Brian Labone looks on as Eddie Cavanagh is finally floored. Left: Mike Trebilcock jumps for joy

Blues' fans in great voice

'...the Everton fans grouped behind the west goal in great voice and certainly louder than the Wednesday contingent at the other end of the ground. The Everton fans drowned the community singing with their own chants and applause. They wanted to sing their own songs.

'When the M.C. called for 'When The Saints Come Marching In', the Everton supporters drowned it with a chorus of boos and whistles.

'Among the many telegrams of good wishes the Everton team received was one from the players of the last Everton Cup winning side of 1933, at the match as guests of the club.

'The attendance was given as the usual 100,000 of course, but the receipts of £109,600 was a record for any match at Wembley.'

From The Liverpool Echo (14/5/66)

Pitch invader's cunning plan

'I was privileged to watch at the stadium and had an unimpeded view of the various pitch-invaders (in the Cup final). I think the intent of the star pitch invader, the lone wolf who had to shed a jacket so adroitly but who was scythed down by a fairly respectable London Irish type tackle, was pretty obvious.

'I understand that this stocky, determined 'Wembley wizard' was some years ago a junior member of the Everton staff and it occurs to me that he selected just the right moment to give the Everton players a breather after Trebilcock's equaliser, a breather designed to recharge the flagging tissues with enough energy to enable them to go all out for the deciding goal. I think this truant had it worked out to the very second when he knew his 'red herring' could be of most use to the Everton players.

'I would conclude by saying that pitch invader No 1 deserves a line or two in the official history of a great sporting triumph.'

(From The Liverpool Echo – 'Looking At Sport with Leslie Edwards'. 23/5/66)

1966

Home are the heroes

Mike Trebilcock and Derek Temple may have been the heroes but the Evertonians at Wembley didn't forget Fred Pickering, cheering the striker's name after the game . . .

Harry's hunch

In the aftermath of the final Harry Catterick said: "Fred (Pickering) was popular and could score goals, but he'd been injured and gone off the boil a bit. Trebilcock was a first-rate goal poacher. I always felt his sharpness would show."

Pick-er-ing!

Michael Charters of the Liverpool Echo wrote: 'The Everton fans spotted him on the pitch, setting up a chant of 'Pick-er-ing' and when he reached the players Jimmy Gabriel shouted: "Come on Fred, get hold of the Cup and come round with us." This was too much for Pickering, who broke down with emotion.'

The Cup that cheers: Brian Labone, Mike Trebilcock and Alex Young have their hands on the Cup as Colin Harvey raises his arms in triumph in the background

Mike left in the dark

Two-goal Wembley hero Mike Trebilcock revealed he had no idea he was going to play in place of Fred Pickering.

"I asked the lads, 'So what happens now?' And they said, 'We go down to Wembley to watch the cup final'. I was looking forward to it because I had never been to Wembley and I would be sitting at Wembley with a new suit. Then, after lunch on the Friday before the game, the manager called me

"I expected to have to help put out the gear. Instead he told me I would be playing in place of the England centre-forward Fred Pickering, who had been injured.

"If ever I had fallen off the back of my seat, that was it.

"Every schoolboy dreams of playing at Wembley and scoring the winner in a cup final," says Trebilcock. "But I didn't score the winner!"

Referee stands firm

Having watched the final twice on film and a slow motion run of the incident when Alex Young and Sheffield Wednesday goalkeeper Ron Springett clashed, Wolverhampton referee Jack Taylor claimed his decision not to give Everton a penalty was correct.

At his butcher's shop, Mr Taylor said: "I have closely studied the film and also pictures of the incident, and if I went back to Wembley today I would still give the same decision. It was obvious to me that Springett was always going for the ball and that Young fell over him. It was definitely not a penalty."

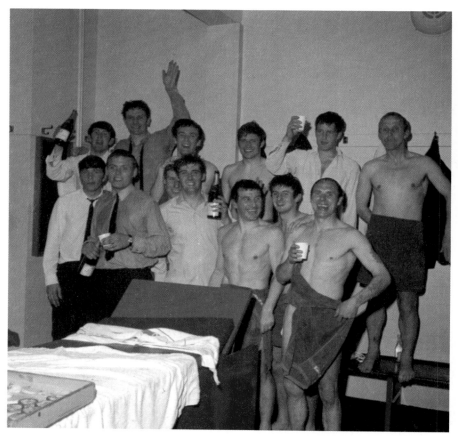

Thanks boss: Harry Catterick is lifted shoulder high with the trophy.

Left: The celebrations start in the dressing room. Below: Brian Labone gets the Cup from Princess Margaret

Dixie impressed

On the match, some of the players from the 1933 team noted:

Dixie Dean: "I thought Alex Young had a great match; he did everything right for me."

Albert Geldard: "Derek Temple's goal was one of the greatest I've ever seen. Those sort of openings can be missed so easily."

Willie Cook: "Ray Wilson was the man of the match for me.

"We were all proud of the Everton team.

"I should also like to pay tribute to the club for the way they looked after us on the day."

Mercer's salute

England and former Blues star Joe Mercer saw the game with his Manchester City players.

He said: "I still can't believe how they got off the floor to win.

"For an hour, an Everton victory was not on, but it was the greatest Wembley recovery ever.

"They didn't play well in that time but what a Final it turned out in the end. Man of the match? Colin Harvey."

Trainer Tommy Eggleston came away with the match ball, which was to be autographed by all the players.

Luck of the black cat

One of the most enduring images to have survived from the 1966 final is that of skipper Brian Labone holding the trophy with a cut-out of a black cat attached to the Cup.

It was a lucky charm adopted by the skipper following the third-round success over Sunderland that stood the Blues in good stead.

History makers

The 1966 final made history for two reasons. Firstly, Mike Trebilcock was the first black player to score in a final.

Secondly, Wednesday were the first losing finalists to acknowledge the crowd with a lap of honour.

Millions thrilled

'The match which no one save the two cities concerned had wanted had become the match which thrilled millions. I congratulate the club, the team and everyone concerned – and especially the scout who 'found' Trebilcock – on a Wembley victory any club will find it hard to equal much less surpass.' Leslie Edwards in the Liverpool Echo.

'Bless Them All'

In Mather Avenue, an Army band alongside the roads played 'See The Conquering Heroes Come'. Outside the main gates of Broadgreen Hospital, patients fit enough were gathered to see the procession go by. 'Everton – Bless Them All', written on one car, captured the spirit of the occasion.

Victory tour: The Everton players wave to the fans

Bringing home the Cup:
Fans throng the streets
as the Blues' victory
cavalcade makes its way
along Scotland Road
towards Goodison Park

Left: The fans bring their
home-made banners on
a day to remember

Champagne memories: Parading the trophy at Wembley (top) and a very cheerful Lord Mayor pours a large bottle of champagne into the FA Cup held by Harry Catterick outside St George's Hall

250,000 line the city streets

About 250,000 turned out on the Sunday to welcome home the team. Behind the players' coach in another coach rode the club directors and behind that a car containing the club's mascot, Bernard Gamble and Mother Noblett Miss Sheila Radcliffe.

This car was later divided from the main party by pedal cyclists, motor-scooterists and car drivers, who gate-crashed the triumphal drive.

Soon after the party left Allerton Station, a group of cyclists tucked themselves in at the back of the police-cyclists following the two coaches.

At one stage there must have been nearly 100 of them and as they were all jockeying for position continual collisions and spills were unavoidable.'

Having left Allerton Station soon after five o'clock, they arrived at St George's Hall two hours later where a crowd of around 20,000 were waiting on Lime Street.

When the players came out on to the steps of St George's Hall a few minutes later to hold up the FA Cup again, Lime Street re-echoed to ear-splitting cheers.

The Lord Mayor (Alderman David Cowley) tried to make a speech - but the roar defeated him.

The team finally disappeared inside the Hall after spending about 15 minutes on the steps, and the satisfied crowd dispersed very quickly with the same good humour there had been throughout.

And if you know your history: Thousands greeted Everton on their homecoming . . .

You bet Sandy is staying

Sandy Brown shrugged off his personal disappointment at missing out on a medal to pledge his future to Goodison.

He said: "Why should I ask to go just because I've missed Wembley?

"I could not go to a better club.

"I'm disappointed of course, but that's how it goes in this game."

Of the other players, Alex Scott (who had a private £1 bet with his manager that Everton would win) said: "This is the greatest football occasion of all.

"Playing at Hampden in the Scottish Cup final or for Scotland has got nothing on playing at Wembley."

Silver service: Fans watch Brian Harris drink from the Cup at St George's Hall (top) and (left) the route the Everton bus took, as printed in the Echo. Above: Lifting the Cup!

A winning team: Back at Bellefield with the trophy taking pride of place

Police praised the way the fans behaved at the homecoming.

Mr Herbert Balmer, Deputy Chief Constable, said: "We had every available policeman on duty in the city centre today. All leave was cancelled."

He added: "The crowd have behaved extremely well especially as so many Liverpool supporters have turned up owing to a rumour that the Liverpool team was coming as well. There have been no clashes.

"Casualties and injuries were well down on the previous year – a total of 395 with just over 30 sent to hospital. Last year 600 were hurt, and 300 sent to hospital."

Fred misses banquet

Everton attended a celebration banquet after the game on Saturday evening in London and then were officially honoured at home.

At the initial dinner, Harry Catterick and each player was presented with a silver tea service and trainer Eggleston with a gold wristlet watch.

Among the principal guests were Mr Denis Howell, the Minister for Sport, the Lord Mayor of Liverpool Alderman David Cowley, Mr Joe Mears, president of the FA and Mrs Bessie Braddock.

In addition, most of the Liverpool directors were there, headed by president Tom Williams and chairman Sidney Reakes.

Mr John Moores replied to the toast of the Everton club, proposed by the Lord Mayor and asked the Everton Cup winning team of 1933 to stand up and take their applause from the guests.

He also gently jibed at the Lord Mayor, who despite protestations to the contrary, is a fervent Anfield fan.

"I'm sure my Lord Mayor would have preferred to see red ribbons on the Cup tonight!"

Meanwhile, St George's Hall hosted a banquet to honour the city's football clubs – Liverpool were also title winners that season – which attracted nearly 500 guests and more than 3,000 who stood in Lime Street and William Brown Street hoping to catch a glimpse of the players.

Liverpool's players arrived just after 10pm minus manager Bill Shankly, who had honoured a previous arrangement to play in a charity game at Tranmere Rovers for Harry Leyland.

The only absentee for Everton was Fred Pickering, who, according to an Echo report, 'could not get a babysitter.'

Sweet success: Brian Labone cuts a specially made Everton celebration cake

1966

No.44

Golden vision shows no mercy

The FA Cup holders faced a tricky task as they launched the defence of the trophy in 1967. Drawn at fellow First Division side Burnley, the Blues earned a 0-0 draw in a rugged affair at Turf Moor.

Mention was made on the morning of the match in the Liverpool Echo (28/01/67) of the mass exodus of fans from Liverpool - second only to 1950 when 55,000 Evertonians and Liverpudlians travelled to Maine Road, Manchester for the FA Cup semi-final. Around 25,000 Everton fans (in a 42,482 crowd) made the journey to Turf Moor, while 10,000 Liverpool supporters trekked south to Watford for their third-round tie.

The Goodison replay was the total opposite in terms of approach, with Everton showing attacking intent although the tough tackling which epitomised the first game was highlighted again. Brian Labone was forced off with a damaged ankle while for the Clarets Irvine went off with a broken leg.

It took the class of Alex Young to see Everton through. He opened the scoring, heading home from a Morrissey corner and despite Burnley hitting back through Irvine, the 'Golden Vision' had the final say.

With Young's cousin Harry Thomson in the visiting goal performing heroics, it took his more famous relative to finally beat him again in the 72nd minute to put the holders through to a date with Wolves.

White Ball: Alan Ball leaves Burnley's Ralph Coates face down in the mud at Turf Moor.
Top left: Alex Young fires home the winner to send Everton through against Burnley in 1967

No.45

Stars of the big screen

Huge interest surrounded the FA Cup fifth-round tie between Everton and Liverpool in March 1967. The first Cup derby for 12 years (the Blues had been humiliated 4-0 at Goodison in 1955) caught the public's imagination. The match was to be screened via closed-circuit cameras at Anfield although it was confirmed that should there be a Tuesday night replay, Goodison Park would not host a screening.

An official of ABC Television, who were operating the TV showing at Anfield, said: "There is not sufficient time to dismantle the screens and projectors which will be in use at Anfield and get them across to Goodison by the Tuesday night" (Liverpool Echo, 1/3/67).

Plans were made for 30 minutes of pre-match entertainment from

Wind threat to the big screen

As it turned out, the big screen at Anfield needed to be reinforced due to 40mph winds although, with over 40,000 in attendance, the experiment proved a success.

A brief review of the spectacle from Anfield reported that the majority in attendance were Reds fans and that pre-match entertainment included film of the 1965 and 1966 final with the "loudest applause of all for the now famous incident when two supporters were removed by policemen."

The four screens set up in a square in the middle of the pitch were hardly sophisticated.

Indeed, they actually looked like giant white sheets, stretched and pinned against a huge scaffolding.

The reception was reported to have been good "although the wind inevitably caused a certain amount of wobbling!"

Stars of the big screens: The scene at Anfield ahead of the Everton v Liverpool fifth-round tie across Stanley Park

Goodison for the benefit of the viewers at Anfield, which would include general pictures of crowd scenes from Goodison and interviews with Harry Catterick and Bill Shankly from their respective dressing rooms. Any first-half goals would then be shown at half-time, with Tommy Lawton summarising alongside two commentators.

Such was the clamour for tickets that a sell-out was announced at Goodison with another 40,500 capacity attendance for the 'TV show' at Anfield.

A Liverpool Echo headline on a Michael Charters story declared: 'TV experiment watched by the League' (2/3/67).

The report said: 'The cost of putting on this giant screen show is so great that if the attendance at Anfield only reached 30,000 instead of the limit of 40,500, there would not be any profit in it at all. The takings would be swallowed up by the cost.'

No.46

Ticket frenzy

The other dominant subject related to the Everton v Liverpool tie of 1967 was the massive demand for tickets. Stories circulated regarding forged tickets for the Lower Bullens Stand. At an early stage it was clear that the remaining tickets for Goodison available for general sale would be nowhere near sufficient to meet demand.

The Liverpool Echo reports from the period give just a taste of the problems.

A headline said: 'Fans begin 34 hours wait for derby day tickets' (6/3/67). The report stated: 'Three Everton fans will have queued outside the ground for a total of 34 hours.

'At 8am this morning, David Dickinson, aged 21; Brian Cooper, aged 16, and Alan Hollis, aged 20 (Billy Cliff, aged 20, of Roderick Road, Walton was an addition in later reports), laid out their groundsheets outside the turnstiles to prepare for the long wait.

"We are certain to be first in the queue when the office opens at 5.30 tomorrow," said Alan, who already has one ticket, but needs another for his girlfriend. But they don't expect to spend the night alone. "I think there will be about 500 people here tonight when they knock off work," said David, of Alexander Street, Everton.

Alan lives in Alexander Street and Brian lives in Malvern Avenue, Bowring Park. Meanwhile, they will be passing the time listening to the radio and playing football - what else!'

Kendall signs: A pre-match boost as Everton beat Liverpool to the signing of Howard Kendall, while below, some of the stories dominating the local press

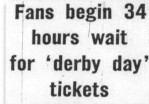

Thumbs up from the first in the cup ticket queue. Left to right: Brian Cooper, David Dickinson and Alan Hollis.

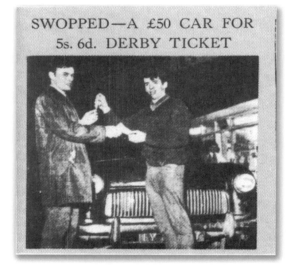

No.47

A good deal

How much was a ticket worth for the derby clash? The Liverpool Echo highlighted the case of one local man:

'SWOPPED – A £50 CAR FOR A 5s 6d DERBY TICKET' (10/3/67)

'Because he did not have a ticket for tomorrow's derby game, 20-year-old Paul Gray decided to put an advertisement in last night's Echo offering to exchange his 1957 Ford Consul car for a ticket.

'A few hours later, Paul had his ticket and a young Bootle man had the car. Paul, of Coronation Avenue, Formby, who is a car salesman, said: "I don't care what sort of ticket it is as long as it gets me into the ground."

'The man who exchanged the 5s 6d ticket for the car was 23-year-old Mr Trevor Roberts of Bootle, a Liverpool supporter. He said: "I jumped off the bus on the off chance that the car was still here." Mr Roberts, who was at night school when he saw the advert, (currently) runs a 1956 Ford Popular.'

No.48

Record crowd sees the ball

"I have never known tickets so hard to get. I am usually an expert at tapping black market sources, but so far I have had no luck. They are like bars of gold, and almost as dear."

The Echo said: 'The above view came from a fan in a city club last night on the eve of the tie.'

Over 250 police would be on duty for the match and to add further spice to the occasion, Everton had signed Howard Kendall from under the noses of Liverpool on the eve of the tie.

Liverpool Echo football reporter Michael Charters noted: 'The ground was full half-an-hour before kick-off and there was crushing in the Stanley Park End, where the majority of the Liverpool fans were.

'Ambulance men had to deal with half-a-dozen casualties, people being pulled out of the densely-packed crowd. The inevitable fan ran on to the pitch while the players were taking position before the kick-off and shook hands with Alex Young.'

With high winds and the tension of the occasion making football difficult,

the action did not hot up until well into the first half.

Indeed, there had been only two efforts at goal in the first 41 minutes, with fouls aplenty, but that was to change just before the break.

Charters continued: 'Milne tried to find Lawrence with a back pass, but Husband was on it like lightning as the ball went past Yeats, and as Lawrence came out Husband and the Liverpool goalkeeper collided, the ball bounced free and Ball, following up quickly, turned it into the net from the narrowest of angles.'

Everton held on for the 1-0 win, with the final whistle seeing 'scores of young fans run on to the pitch.'

Bookies saved!

With nearly 65,000 inside Goodison and 40,500 at Anfield, a combined total of over 105,000 saw the tie - an FA Cup record. It was Liverpool's first FA Cup defeat away from home since 1959.

The result apparently also helped 'save small bookmakers'.

A Willam Hill spokesman said: "That 1-0 win saved many thousands of pounds, but we still have a tremendous number of winners."

Hill's were set to take a 'new long look' before making a decision to carry on issuing coupons after that Saturday when 18 matches were drawn.

No.49

Forest fire

Everton's 'reward' for their derby triumph was a quarter-final trip to Nottingham Forest in April, 1967 (on the day 100-1 shot Foinavon won the Grand National).

Despite the absence of the injured Gordon West all seemed to be going to plan as Jimmy Husband gave the Blues a half-time lead in front of a 47,500 capacity crowd at The City Ground (amongst them FIFA president Sir Stanley Rous and England manager Sir Alf Ramsey).

But having dominated high-flying Forest for an hour, the home side, inspired by former Everton man Frank Wignall, hit back. Wignall had a hand in all of Forest's goals as winger Ian Storey-Moore – only moved inside due to an injury to Joe Baker – took over. The home side's direct approach unsettled the Blues, and Storey-Moore struck twice in a two-minute spell midway through the second half.

Husband hit back for Everton though, and it looked like a Goodison Park quarter-final replay before the final moments. Michael Charters' description in the Liverpool Echo went like this:

'The winner by Moore was fantastically lucky for Forest and disastrous for Everton. Moore actually had four attempts before he put the ball in the net. His first shot struck John Hurst and the ball came back to him; his second shot hit Andy Rankin and the ball came back to him; his third attempt, a header, hit the crossbar and bounced back to him; the fourth time he headed in.'

Moore woe: Ian Storey-Moore ends Everton's Cup hopes while (right) Jimmy Husband opens the scoring at the City Ground

Last-minute agony

It was sweet revenge for Forest's former Blues boss Johnny Carey, and their third win over Everton that season, having twice won 1-0 in the League over the Christmas period. After the game Harry Catterick told the Liverpool Echo: "Well that's what football is all about. I thought the team played really well, but I was disappointed with Young."

It wasn't the first and last time 'The Catt' would express his frustration about the 'Golden Vision', a view that was often in stark contrast with the adulation of the fans. It is also the last time a hat-trick has been scored against Everton in the FA Cup.

No.50

Everton survive Port battle

The rise to prominence of the 'Holy Trinity' coincided with this tie at one of their local rivals (managed by former Blues favourite and future manager Billy Bingham) in January 1968.

A crowd of 18,795 packed into Haig Avenue, yielding gate receipts of £6,175 – a Southport record, although Liverpool Echo reporter Michael Charters would later question the decision of their directors not to switch the game to Goodison.

Their share would be less than £2,000 - while they could have earned four times that amount at Everton.

There was little incident in the first half on a half-sand, half-muddy pitch, except for Southport forward Eric Redrobe twice charging Gordon West in the opening minute while the recalled

Alex Young tested Reeves with a header and Howard Kendall went close.

The injured Ray Wilson was replaced by Sandy Brown at the break while Redrobe was finally yellow-carded for a third charge at West, with the busy Wilf Dixon again forced on to administer treatment.

Everton's class began to show with Young, man-of-the-match Colin Harvey and Joe Royle going close while Kendall had a penalty appeal turned down before Royle headed a glorious winner against the Third Division side 11 minutes from time.

Royle delivers: Alan Ball celebrates as Joe Royle's header (below) dashes Southport's hopes of an upset

Cup romance

Speaking in his autobiography, Colin Harvey recalls: "I also have memories of a couple of potential banana skins in FA Cup ties we played.

"Funnily enough I was at Southport to watch Everton reserves playing there and my thoughts went back to 1968 when we beat Southport.

"Haig Avenue that day was absolutely chokker but there were only a few hundred there for a recent reserve game.

"Of course we went on to play in the Cup final that year only to lose to West Brom at Wembley. While I was at the reserve game, somebody said to me: 'I wonder if this place ever gets full?'

"I didn't say anything but I thought back to that game and the fact that I played there when it was absolutely chokker!

"It's the romance of the cup that there are games like that."

No.51

Computer says ... 9-0 to Rovers!

A bizarre prediction prior to Everton's fifth-round tie against another local side in Tranmere Rovers in 1968 claimed that Tranmere would win 9-0.

The computer, programmed by Rovers chairman Chris Hodgson, had taken into account various corresponding results involving the two teams – plus other relevant fixtures.

Nearly 62,000 crammed into Goodison, although it proved a disappointing one-sided affair – and not in favour of the team that the computer had predicted would end on top.

Indeed, only Tranmere goalkeeper (and the Lancashire pace bowler during the summer) Jim Cumbes prevented an Everton goal spree.

The keeper was cheered for his efforts at the break and at full time by the home support.

Jimmy Husband (twice), Ernie Hunt and Joe Royle were denied although Everton lacked some fluency without Colin Harvey and Alan Ball.

Young Joe Royle maintained his goal-a-game record in the Cup while Johnny Morrissey also netted in the first half as Third Division Tranmere failed to test Gordon West throughout.

Incidentally, it turned out that an Everton fan came nearest to predicting a correct result of 2-0.

He was only one goal out – having dreamt that the Blues would win the tie 3-0.

Howard's way: Howard Kendall volleys home to help Everton regain the lead in the 1968 quarter-final against Leicester

Boys in blue: The Everton v Tranmere match programme and (far right) crowd control at Carlisle v Everton in round 4

EVERTON Football Club
GOODISON PARK · LIVERPOOL

F.A. CHALLENGE CUP — 5th ROUND
EVERTON v.
TRANMERE ROVERS
SATURDAY, 9th MARCH, 1968
Kick-off 3 p.m.   Price 6d

OFFICIAL PROGRAMME

Leicester out-Foxed

'They were a class above the hard-working, hard-running Leicester team, who were always second best in the finer arts of the game.'

Michael Charters summed up Everton's 1968 quarter-final success at Filbert Street, having been impressed with the Blues' style of play.

The Everton team included Roger Kenyon, making only his fourth senior appearance and first in the competition, while Colin Harvey and Sandy Brown were injured.

But against a Foxes side that fielded the famous Peter Shilton in goal, the changes did not affect them – despite Jimmy Husband's opener being

No. 52

cancelled out just before the break (the first goal Everton had conceded in the competition that year).

Indeed, Kenyon and Brian Labone were forced to repel some sustained home pressure before Everton regained the lead midway through the second half, Howard Kendall volleying home.

Leicester's David Nish then saw Gordon West push an effort on to the post soon after before Husband netted the killer third goal, hurting himself in the process with substitute Alex Young coming on to replace him.

The perfect Husband: Jimmy Husband was on target at Filbert Street – but ended up with a badly swollen ankle

Hero off to a nursing home

Taking no chances in his usual thorough way, manager Harry Catterick despatched Husband into a Liverpool nursing home when the party returned home, in order that the youngster could have complete rest to an ankle which was so swollen that he was unable to put his shoe on after the game.

The victory booked Everton's second semi-final in three years.

No.53

Unlucky Ball out

The FA Cup semi-final draw of 1968 saw Everton avoid Liverpool, although the Reds were to eventually lose their sixth-round clash to West Brom in any event.

Instead, it was old rivals Leeds United who stood in the Blues' way of a return to Wembley, while the Baggies took on Second Division Birmingham City in the other semi-final.

Harry Catterick said: "Any semi-final is hard, for only good teams get into the last four. We shall not have to travel any farther than our rivals this time and that's a change. So far as meeting Leeds is concerned we can forget all about League form.

"We have by far the youngest side in the Cup and it is an enormous achievement to get into the last four with so many teenagers and youngsters in the team."

Injury-hit Everton (John Hurst and Sandy Brown missed out) were also without the services of Alan Ball, suspended following his dismissal at Newcastle for disputing a disallowed Jimmy Husband goal (Harry Catterick: "Just how do you go about replacing a player of Ball's quality? All I will say is that whoever goes in must be a player with a high work rate. That is absolutely essential").

However, Tommy Wright, Husband, Howard Kendall and Colin Harvey made it despite little training during the week. Ball meanwhile sang 'The little boy that Santa forgot' for the benefit of the cameras in training in the lead-up to the tie.

Old Trafford glory: Blues fans celebrate on the pitch after seeing Everton defeat Leeds to reach the 1968 FA Cup final courtesy of Johnny Morrissey's penalty (opposite, top)

Royle v Charlton

Despite the problems, Everton had won 10 of their previous 11 games. Indeed, even Liverpool Echo reporter Chris James believed Everton would win, being unimpressed with Leeds despite their successes.

'The result depends largely on Joe Royle's aerial battle with Jack Charlton, and Royle, improving all the time, should gain the advantage. If Everton play to this, they should be appearing at Wembley again.'

This despite Leeds being rated as evens to win, with Everton 2-1.

Everton had been beaten twice in the League that season by United, with Leeds having already won the League

No.54

Cup, being still in the title hunt and in the Fairs Cup.

Everton sold out their allocation to season-ticket holders, so no tickets were available to the general public, while Leeds also sold their 21,000 allocation.

Before the game police had to intervene when scuffles broke out after Everton fans mobbed ticket touts.

Ten-shilling (50p) Paddock tickets were being sold for up to £3 and £2 Stand tickets were costing £5 according to some reports.

'Dirty Leeds . . . '

With John Hurst going down with jaundice, it meant a reshuffle for the Blues with 21-year-old Tommy Jackson making only his second senior appearance, having made his debut five days earlier at Nottingham Forest, while Johnny Giles recovered from injury to take his place for Leeds.

Wright suffered an ankle knock after only two minutes while Colin Harvey was left limping after a challenge from Norman Hunter, prompting chants of 'Dirty Leeds' from Blues fans. But it was a nervy first half with Everton, through Harvey and Howard Kendall, playing the better football of what was played. Gordon West tipped over from Terry Cooper's 30-yarder and from the corner Everton were given a free-kick after Charlton came forward to stand in West's way. But three minutes before the break it was Johnny Morrissey who netted the only goal in Everton's 14th semi-final appearance, holding his nerve to convert a spot-kick having taken over duties from the absent Alan Ball.

The kick was given after Jack Charlton was forced to handle on the line to prevent Husband's shot entering the net, the incident coming about after Sprake completely misjudged a clearance. Before the break Leeds almost hit back, but Cooper's shot struck the crossbar with West beaten.

The game opened up more in the second half with Joe Royle hitting the side-netting while Gary Sprake denied Jackson – Husband fired wide with the rebound. Leeds sub Jimmy Greenhoff went close not long after coming on past the hour mark, while Husband was being left as a lone forward, Royle being required to track Charlton's forward bursts.

West denied Lorimer, but despite the pressure Everton should have added to the scoring. Royle was just a foot away from a Husband cross while Sprake denied Kendall before Royle headed just wide. The final whistle signalled a pitch invasion by Everton fans: 'West was mobbed and Wilson could hardly get off the pitch'. Reporter Michael Charters also noted 'outstanding performances from Labone, Harvey and Kendall.'

Incidentally, it was Leeds' 61st game of the season (including League and Cups), while the £51,000 gate receipts were a record for any game in England outside Wembley.

Big news: Newspapers compete for fans' attention ahead of the 1968 FA Cup semi-final. Below: First headlines of the Blues' success

Everton do it! Wembley bound again

No-one wanted Leeds to win

Michael Charters, summing up in Monday's Echo (29/4/68), indicated the feelings of many:

'Everton's victory will have caused considerable pleasure throughout professional football. Whether they know it or not, Leeds have few admirers among the people who control and play the game and Everton had the support of many more than their own fervent fans.

'Their win, to face Albion in what should be a classic Wembley final, was what most professionals were hoping to see and many of them told Everton officials they wanted it before and after the game.'

Harry Catterick added: "I am delighted that we have got through. I thought that Leeds looked a tired side, but I feel that we did very well when one considers the tremendous blow of being robbed of Alan Ball, Sandy Brown and John Hurst.

"I regard Hurst as the kingpin of our defence. It is the greatest win in my years of management."

Rival boss Don Revie said: "I thought Everton played well defensively, and we wish them the best of luck in the final. I have seen our boys a lot sharper than they were today."

Future Middlesbrough and Republic of Ireland manager Jack Charlton insisted that there wasn't much between the two sides.

"We might have played until the morning without scoring had it not been for the penalty," he joked to the Press.

On the road to Wembley: A fan decorates his car for the 1968 final

Who's for the CUP?

—blunt answers to the BIG question by BRIAN LABONE
Don't miss this great new series!

The People tomorrow!

Let it be: Paul McCartney braves the crowds outside Wembley, 1968

No.55

Astle's sucker punch

Having beaten West Bromwich Albion twice in the League that 1967/68 season (including a 6-2 win in mid-March), in-form Everton started as big favourites to claim their second FA Cup in three years (they had won 11 of their final 16 games) in their seventh FA Cup final.

Not for the first time, tickets – or lack of them – dominated the build-up. There was disappointment for more than 3,000 fans before the game when they were turned away from the turnstiles, having been sold forged tickets that had been introduced to Merseyside by a London gang.

The FA had only allocated Everton 16,000 tickets – despite the Blues averaging 47,000 that season.

In the first FA Cup final to be televised live (it was also the first where a substitute was used – West Brom's Denis Clarke), the Blues could not make the breakthrough despite creating numerous chances, with Jimmy Husband missing the best opportunity four minutes from the end of normal time.

The Blues were then stunned by a sucker-punch three minutes from the end of extra time when Jeff Astle fired home into the top corner from the edge of the area – the last player to score in every round of the competition.

It was a goal that won the Cup for the underdogs and made the Nottingham-born centre-forward an Albion legend – with the club's Astle Gates a lasting reminder of his contribution to the Baggies' cause.

Manager Harry Catterick is introduced to Princess Alexandra by captain Brian Labone and (below) home from home for these Evertonians at the Everton mints van outside Wembley

Fans still make it a capital day out

Everton supporters made the most of their trip to the capital by visiting Trafalgar Square on the morning of the 1968 FA Cup final (right). Below: Edward Ralph misses out on the final as his ticket, for which he paid £7 10s, is found to be a forgery by police.

Our day out: Everton grandmothers pictured at Lime Street before setting out for Wembley; Jo Benbow of Wavertree gets in the Wembley spirit (below, right) and one young fan unveils a good luck message to the players at Lime Street

A rare view from the air as the 1968 bus tour snakes its way around the streets outside Goodion Park

Did we win or lose? A warm reception for the
Everton squad in 1968 as their open-top bus tour
reaches Scotland Road on Everton Valley

No.56

Royle seal

Having scored in every round on the way to the 1969 FA Cup quarter-final with Manchester United at Old Trafford, Joe Royle was on the mark again for Everton in their 1-0 win. In a well-matched battle, the centre-forward struck 12 minutes from the end following Alan Ball's corner to book Everton's place in the semi-finals for the third time in four years. Unfortunately, they were to bow out 1-0 at Villa Park to Manchester City in a dour encounter.

No.57

DJ's first hit

David Johnson, 19, joined the select band of players who have scored on their first appearances in League and FA Cup when he headed the winning goal in Everton's 1-0 victory over Derby County in the fifth round in February 1971. Johnson scored on his debut in the League at Burnley the previous month, and when Johnny Morrissey withdrew injured, he headed the winner from a Howard Kendall centre.

Best team won: Action from the 1969 FA Cup quarter-final at Old Trafford against Manchester United involving Brian Labone and Sandy Brown for the Blues and a young George Best looking on

No.58

Mellow yellows

There was a memorable performance from March 1971 as the yellow-shirted Everton side totally outclassed giantkillers Colchester United at Goodison Park, a side who had knocked Leeds out in the previous round. Four goals in 13 first-half minutes rocked the Fourth Division side, who were backed by 8,000 travelling supporters (and had their own mascot parading around the ground before the game).

Howard Kendall scored twice (23, 32) for the first time in an Everton shirt, Joe Royle lobbed the third a minute later and Jimmy Husband raced through for the fourth on 36.

But for goalkeeper Smith, the visitors could have been facing a double-figure beating, but as it was, Everton only added another goal through Alan Ball in the second half.

Colin Harvey later said: "Leeds were top of the league at the time but were beaten by Colchester, who were probably thinking: 'How easy is this Cup?!' But we beat them 5-0. Fielding weaker teams in the competition was unheard of in my playing days."

No. 59

Derby Blues

Having gone out of the European Cup quarter-final in Greece to Panathinaikos (the final that year was at Wembley), Everton could keep alive their 1971 Wembley dream by defeating Liverpool in the FA Cup semi-final at Old Trafford 72 hours later.

Alan Ball, Colin Harvey, Joe Royle and Johnny Morrissey all played despite not being 100 per cent while Harry Catterick was not well enough to attend

having been taken ill on the plane from Greece. The Blues should have led by more than Ball's strike at half-time, being expertly marshalled by Brian Labone. However, once he was forced off with a thigh strain (Labone's last FA Cup appearance) to be replaced by Sandy Brown early in the second half, the game changed. Liverpool hit back through Alun Evans and Brian Hall won it 18 minutes from time. Everton won only one more League game that season but there was no joy for Liverpool at Wembley either – losing to Double winners Arsenal.

The one that got away: Everton were beaten in 1971 by the old enemy – despite this strike from Alan Ball, above

Ball shock

In December of that year Alan Ball had gone, despite an article in the semi-final programme about Harry Catterick claiming that the Everton manager would never sell the England man.

The piece declared: 'Harry Catterick has said that Everton would expect a transfer fee of £1,000,000 for Ball'.

"We would consider it and then we would say NO," Catterick was quoted as saying.

But Ball did leave in a move that stunned the world of football – heading to Arsenal for a British record fee of £220,000.

Bitter pint to swallow: At least Blues could drown their sorrows after the 1971 semi-final with a glass or two of the local brew

No.60

Sunday best

Everton's first Sunday fixture against West Bromwich Albion in January 1974 came about due to the industrial unrest in the country at the time, which included dwindling coal stocks, street lighting being reduced and the introduction of a three-day working week.

These measures meant many midweek games were played in the afternoon rather than under floodlights. Liverpool were at home to Carlisle and played on the Saturday while Everton's fourth-round game was put back 24 hours for Merseyside's first Sunday FA Cup tie.

A floodlight ban meant a 2.15pm kick-off and 53,509 fans turned up, the third highest of the season at Goodison Park while it was also English football's first 50,000-plus attendance for a Sunday match.

Only Joe Royle and John Hurst played from the team beaten at Wembley in 1968, while Tony Brown was the Baggies' sole survivor. Indeed it

was 'Bomber' Brown who netted a disputed winner in the replay which, as well as seeing the return of skipper Howard Kendall for the first time since September after injury, also saw Archie Styles and West Brom's Willie Johnston sent off.

The tie at Goodison saw Gary Jones twice denied a penalty by referee John Williams, the second time seeing his number 10 shirt torn round the shoulders.

Jones said: "It was just one of 10,000 fouls on me."

Sunday service: The Goodison congregation watches a Mick Buckley effort strike the bar in a historic match against West Brom in 1974

No.61

Non-league struggle

Northern Premier League side Altrincham fancied their chances of an upset when they were drawn at Everton in the FA Cup third round of 1975. The confidence was highlighted by the following Liverpool Echo piece:

'Lifelong Everton supporter Phil Smith is aiming to knock the Blues out of the Cup as an Altrincham player.

'The 25-year-old, a teacher at Quarry Bank School in Allerton, said: "I've been an Evertonian all my life. It's a big treat for me to be playing at Goodison. It really is like a dream come true.

"I happened to see the Carlisle game, but that was the first time I had seen Everton since the time of Kendall, Ball

and Harvey. I don't really think they're in the same class as they were then. They work much harder, but they don't seem to have the same skill."'

Indeed, Everton were forced to come from behind to John Hughes' 36th-minute goal to earn a replay (at Old Trafford) courtesy of a second half Dave Clements penalty. John Connolly was carried off with a broken leg and

Gary Jones was sent off four minutes after Altrincham's opener for striking Ian Morris. There were also claims made by Alty skipper Lennie Dickinson that some Everton players were talking about getting revenge on John Davison, the man whose tackle broke Connolly's leg in two places (pictured above).

Cup scalp:
The resigned
look on Mick
Lyons' face
(top) is in
contrast
with the
Altrincham
players at
Goodison in
1975. Left:
Clements
finds the net
against the
non-leaguers

Mick and Bob get off mark

Mike Bernard, skipper
Roger Kenyon, John Hurst
and Mick Buckley were
amongst the absentees for
the replay with
Altrincham, although the
return of Martin Dobson
was significant.

Bob Latchford and Mick
Lyons' first goals in the
competition eased Everton
home, with Ken McNaught
impressive in only his
second senior appearance.

As for Alty, they were
left with the consolation of
a £15,000 profit from their
FA Cup excursions.

Seeing red:
Gary Jones
is ushered
off the pitch
after being
dismissed

No.62

Blue army

A trip to Plymouth in January is hardly the visit most would relish, but for Everton supporters, that would be the journey they would make in 1975.

The back page headline of the Liverpool Echo (21/1/75) exclaimed:

'Forward the 10,000!'

Over 7,000 fans were set to flock to the south west, while over 3,000 were expected to visit Suffolk for Liverpool's tie at Ipswich Town on the same day.

Forward the 10,000!

The tie at Plymouth was limited to a 38,000 capacity by the local police, while nine trains were set to take many fans south (another five were to take Liverpool fans to Ipswich), with three extra laid on after appeals from Everton. A British Rail spokesman said: "Normally we only get this number travelling for the semi-finals and the final."

Blues secretary Chris Hassell said: "We are going to have a colossal following and it will be tremendous for the team to have all those fans behind them."

Lyons made: Mick Lyons slides the ball home at Plymouth and (right) the players celebrate with the massive away following

Big draw: After watching the Blues in FA Cup action, fans might have gone to see Bond ... James Bond

Billy's reunion

Blues manager Billy Bingham returned to one of his former clubs in Argyle, then second in the Third Division. Although eyeing a title tilt (the Blues were top of the First Division), Bingham said: "I would not say no to a Cup run. And of course, it is an entry into Europe for the following season."

On a heavily-sanded surface, Everton took the lead after only seven minutes when Jim Pearson slid home. Mick Lyons doubled the lead eight minutes before the break, running onto George Telfer's pass and driving home.

Telfer twice went close in the closing moments of the half, but it was the home side who hit back just before the hour. Goalscorer Barry Vassallo headed over unmarked soon after, but it

was Everton who killed off the Argyle threat 14 minutes from time. Having gone close with a header moments earlier, Lyons beat goalkeeper Jim Furnell to slide into an unguarded goal after the ball ran free outside the area to claim his second goal of the game.

Incidentally, with Everton set to meet Nottingham Forest or Fulham (the teams had drawn 0-0 in the first game at Craven Cottage) in round five at Goodison, the Forest manager Brian Clough was already looking forward to the trip. Unbeaten in his four matches in charge since taking over, Clough said: "There would be a 40,000 gate at Goodison and our share could help us in the transfer market."

Unfortunately, it would be Fulham in round five – and a shock defeat.

No.63

Lee hoping to mug Reds

Having not beaten the Reds in over five years and Martin Dobson's strike in an Anfield defeat the previous October being their only goal against Liverpool since then, Bob Paisley's men started as 4/5 on favourites to beat Everton in the 1977 semi-final. The Blues had recently lost agonisingly to Aston Villa in the League Cup final second replay and were offered at 100/30.

On the Wednesday before the tie, manager Gordon Lee suffered an unfortunate incident when he was standing outside the main entrance at Anfield (ahead of their European Cup semi-final, second leg against Zurich). According to the Liverpool Echo (21/4/77), he put his hand to his right-hand side rear pocket and found his cash missing.

He said: "It was a fair sum, considerably more than £10. It included ticket money.

"I suppose the only advice I can give to people is: 'Don't go to a match with any money in your pocket.'

"All that I know is that the person who took this money will be punished. Somewhere along the line he will wind up paying for behaviour like this and then he will want to know what it is he has done to deserve it."

Each club was allocated just under 21,000 tickets for the tie with demand likely to far outstrip supply.

On the march with Gordon's army: The 1977 squad that would come so close to a famous victory over the old foe Liverpool

No Swiss roll-over

Gordon Lee promised Liverpool a tougher tie than they had experienced against the Swiss side FC Zurich in the European Cup.

Liverpool had beaten the Swiss team to reach their first European Cup final and Lee vowed: "We have more skill than Zurich and we'll do better than we did against Liverpool in the League match at Goodison last month. I feel we can do it."

The Reds contingent were also confident, however. The Echo quoted one Liverpool fan, Mally Whetnall, who said: "I respect Everton but we'll win 5-0." When told that Bob Latchford was out, he replied: "Add another five goals to the score then!"

Ticket race

'Red and Blue Fans In Tickets Hunt' was the headline in the Liverpool Echo on April 23, 1977 – on the day Everton went to battle with the old enemy.

The report revealed: 'Some ticketless fans had camped outside the ground overnight hoping that their early bird tactics would pay off with the inevitable arrival of the first touts on the scene.'

Some fans chased touts down streets surrounding the ground in a desperate bid to obtain tickets.

One irate Liverpool fan said: "The spivs were asking £8 to £10 for £1.50 tickets. We just cannot afford that kind of cash. One was battered and another was surrounded by a mob of fans and persuaded to part with his stock at a more reasonable price." Another group of fans were gathered round the players' entrance and one hit lucky when Manchester City manager Tony Book was able to provide a ticket. A group of Liverpudlians even surrounded former Everton centre-forward Joe Royle, but he was unable to assist.

Net gains: A betting advert ahead of the two FA Cup semi-finals between Liverpool, Everton, Manchester United and Leeds featuring the four keepers

The man from Pontypandy

When the action unfolded, with Everton minus the injured 24-goal Bob Latchford and Andy King, there was further gloom early on when Terry McDermott sent a superb chip over David Lawson.

A torrential downpour less than half-an-hour before the kick-off had left the pitch in an awful state and it played a part as Everton hit back just after the half-hour mark. Emlyn Hughes slipped trying to clear to let in Jim Pearson. The forward, who had replaced Latchford, found McKenzie with his cross and he made no mistake.

With the wind at their backs for the second half, the Blues seized control. Michael Charters' Football Echo report indicated the performance of McKenzie. He said: 'McKenzie beat Smith brilliantly and took the ball on a 30-yard run before passing to Pearson, whose half-hit shot was easily saved. McKenzie nearly got through again but Hughes took the ball away with a brilliant interception which McKenzie applauded, a nice touch.'

Despite this it was Liverpool who went back in front with less than 20 minutes left – Jimmy Case heading over the stranded Lawson.

After 81 minutes Everton brought on Bryan Hamilton in place of Martin Dobson and almost instantly it was all square. Again McKenzie had a say, setting up Bruce Rioch for his first goal for the club.

A minute later Ronnie Goodlass cut in from the flank and centred for McKenzie. His flick-on fell for Hamilton who deflected the ball past Ray Clemence and as Everton celebrated, Liverpool's players looked beaten. However, one of the great moments of derby controversy then unfolded.

Charters' Football Echo report noted: 'Hamilton chested the ball past Clemence, but the 'goal' was disallowed, presumably for offside.'

Referee Clive Thomas had stepped in, disallowing the effort and awarding a free-kick to Liverpool, who got on with the game. Thomas later felt that from the angle of Hamilton's contact, there was no way he could have scored without handling the ball.

An astonished Hamilton said: "I could tell that Emlyn Hughes, Ray Clemence and Joey Jones thought it was a goal and it was finished. It hit me on the hip, because it came at a difficult height. It was in between head and foot, and I just turned my side on it and it hit my hip-bone and went in the far corner. Unfortunately it wasn't the winner, but to this day for me it was a goal, and it will always be the one that would have taken Everton to Wembley."

Bryan also noted other explanations on the eve of the 1981 derby (Liverpool Echo, 24/1/81). "I remember someone saying it was an infringement, but I don't really remember an awful lot after that. I met the linesman involved that day quite recently on Merseyside and he said he thought it was for pushing,

Dave's drama

A subsequent Echo headline declared: 'How true blue Dave won his own semi-final' (28/4/77).

The report said: 'Most of the action took place before the kick-off for Evertonian David Cowhig.

'David's night of anguish started when he boarded the 5 o'clock special from Liverpool to Manchester Victoria and discovered moments after the train pulled out that he had left his match ticket at home. Then the drama began for Dave, a 27-year-old meter collector, from Fieldton Road, Norris Green.

• He toured the train on an unsuccessful hunt for spare tickets.

• He asked if he could get off at Huyton, but was told that the train was an express.

• He then explained to a platform inspector at Manchester Victoria and 'Operation Ticket' was hatched.

• The British Rail man phoned Lime Street as Dave called up his wife, Pauline, to explain his dire straits.

• She found the ticket and gave it to a taxi driver who headed Lime Street-wards.

• He just missed the 6.10 pm 'special' – journey time just 35 minutes. Instead it went on the scheduled 6.20 train that made a number of stops before puling into Victoria at 7.25, just 20 minutes before kick-off.

'A second taxi raced Dave to the ground where he entered the Kippax enclosure just as the sides kicked-off. Was it worth it?

'Dave said: "Oh yes. It was better than going out in the third round. I want to thank British Rail for their help and most especially the inspector. He was just the ticket."'

which is a new twist.

"The strange thing was it was the second time it had happened to me, because earlier I had played for Ipswich against West Ham in an FA Cup semi-final. The score was 0-0 when I got the ball in the net. On that occasion, the linesman gave a goal, but the referee disallowed it so I had become quite used to it by the time I joined Everton!"

Thomas said: "I hope no-one thinks that I think I am always right. I have been wrong on occasions and I am the first to admit it. But I still think I was right that time. My linesman disagreed with me, but these are the decisions I am paid to make and I will carry on making such decisions."

Everton, again without Latchford and this time Hamilton, away on international duty (Andy King returned on the bench), went down in the replay 3-0. True Blue Mick Lyons summed up everyone's thoughts: "We are sick."

Thomas would be hated forever by Evertonians. Liverpool knew they had been part of the 'Great Escape'.

Celebrate good times: But ultimately Evertonians were denied Bryan Hamilton's 'winner' (above). Top: Bruce Rioch celebrates his first Everton goal with Jim Pearson and Duncan McKenzie

No. 64

Ken's sad return

Having lost only four times in the League ahead of the third-round home tie with Aston Villa in January 1978, Everton were in good heart and welcomed back Ken McNaught for the first time since the defender moved to Villa Park for £200,000 the previous summer.

McNaught was relishing the chance to play against the country's leading scorer in Bob Latchford but it was to prove a sorry return for the defender. Villa were swept aside at Goodison as a determined Everton side, keen for revenge following the League Cup final defeat the previous season, produced one of their best-ever performances of the 1970s.

An inspired Andy King was amongst the scorers as the Blues raced into a three-goal lead and despite Andy Gray pulling a goal back for Villa in the first half, Bob Latchford, who would go on to hit 30 League goals, added number four in a 4-1 triumph. To complete their misery, Villa also saw Leighton Phillips sent off two minutes from the end.

Amongst the spectators was Scotland manager Ally MacLeod in World Cup year while the controversial Clive Thomas was referee, the first time he had been entrusted with an Everton match since the semi-finals the previous year.

The Blues were drawn away to Middlesbrough in round four in what Gordon Lee described "a terrible draw".

He was not wrong. The Blues lost 3-2 at Ayresome Park.

Eastoe tames Dragons

The visit of Wrexham in February 1980 saw the return to Goodison of Terry Darracott and Dai Davies, while former Liverpool defender Joey Jones also lined up for the Red Dragons. Jones had enjoyed four unbeaten games against the Blues while at Anfield. There was a further threat to Gordon Lee's men, in the form of Dixie McNeil, who was aiming to extend his run of scoring in 10 successive rounds of the FA Cup.

On the eve of the tie defender Darracott, who had spent 13 years at Everton, told the Liverpool Echo: "I hope we win tomorrow. I don't want a replay. I've got a darts match on Tuesday!"

There was no chance of a replay as man-of-the-match Peter Eastoe ended

Losing one of the family: Bob Latchford, Mick Lyons and Brian Labone help to carry Dixie Dean's coffin in 1980

No. 65

his scoring drought with a double, having scored only once in his previous 22 games. The clinical finishing of the Blues proved the difference against the Second Division side. Darracott was made captain for the day and was given a rousing reception by the home faithful.

The tie was also notable for Gary Megson's first goal for the club. He opened the scoring in only his third appearance for the Blues. The only downside of the result was that it booked a quarter-final tie with high-flying Ipswich Town who had beaten Everton 4-0 at Goodison only weeks earlier.

No. 66

Doing it for Dixie

A week after the death of Everton's greatest son William Ralph Dean in the midst of a dramatic Goodison derby day, the March 1980 tie with Ipswich began in a subdued mood.

The day before had been Dean's funeral although motivated by a willingness to remember the great man

Above: Billy Wright.
Top centre: Martin Hodge.
Top right: West Ham's scorer on Saturday Stuart Pearson.
Right: Billy Wright.
Far right: Phil Parkes.
Below: Trevor Brooking, Stuart Pearson (West Ham), Trevor Ross (Everton) at Villa Park on Saturday.

Football Association Challenge Cup
SEMI-FINAL REPLAY
WEST HAM UNITED v EVERTON
ELLAND ROAD, LEEDS
WEDNESDAY 16th APRIL, 1980
Kick-off 7.45 p.m.
OFFICIAL SOUVENIR PROGRAMME **40p**

Hammer time: The alternative cover of the programme for the 1980 semi-final replay

Not to be: Everton fans (below) find missing out on Wembley in 1980 hard to take

Mersey Cup hopes dashed

Having battled through to the last four and with Liverpool facing Arsenal in the other semi-final, there was the opportunity to set-up the first-ever all-Merseyside FA Cup final.

Second Division West Ham were no pushovers though.

They held Everton, for whom Brian Kidd was sent off, having earlier opened the scoring at Villa Park in the first semi-final.

The Blues, with Kevin Ratcliffe making only his second senior appearance in place of the suspended Kidd, dominated the first half of the Elland Road replay backed by 30,000 Evertonians in the ground, but despite their supremacy, they could not break the deadlock.

Both sides had a goal disallowed in the second half before the goals came in the extra period.

Alan Devonshire netted for the Hammers before Bob Latchford equalised with a superb diving header with seven minutes left.

Just as the game was nearing a conclusion with the prospect of a third game at Highfield Road, Frank Lampard's header crept in to stun Gordon Lee's men.

West Ham went on to beat Arsenal in the final and it was to be another six years before the first Merseyside FA Cup final.

Skipper Mick Lyons reportedly told Kevin Ratcliffe: "You've got plenty of time to get to another final.

"The rest won't get another chance."

with a memorable performance, the Blues ran the visitors ragged despite third-placed Town, under the inspired stewardship of future England boss Bobby Robson, being on a 16-match unbeaten run. Full-back John Gidman was moved into midfield and set up Bob Latchford for the opener before Brian Kidd sealed matters late on with a free-kick – Kevin Beattie's goal proving academic. Skipper Mick Lyons said: "The minute's silence for Dixie before kick-off inspired us."

Kids are alright

There was little reason to suspect that Arsenal's impressive FA Cup record in the previous three seasons – three finals, one win – would end in January 1981 against the Toffees, who found themselves on the slide in the First Division table, having began the season so promisingly.

There was the first real blooming of progress in the club's youth policy. Defenders Kevin Ratcliffe (20) and Billy Wright (22) kept quiet 'the best pair of strikers in the business in Alan Sunderland and Frank Stapleton' (as they were described in the Liverpool Echo).

Imre Varadi and Peter Eastoe were a threat up front, with the returning David O'Leary being tested after injury. One of the main features too was the wind swirling around Goodison. At one point an attempted centre by Kenny Sansom went sailing a good 25 yards behind him.

As it was though, and despite being against the wind in the second half, the Blues deservedly claimed the third-round spoils.

Man-of-the-match Steve McMahon was a constant inspiration in midfield, and they made the breakthrough six minutes from time when Joe McBride's hard cross into the box glanced off future Blue Sansom and past Pat Jennings.

With time ticking away, substitute Mick Lyons, on for Varadi, made it 2-0 in the last minute. His shot, cleared off the line by Willie Young, was adjudged by the linesman to have gone in.

Blue derby movie

EVERTON v LIVERPOOL – IT'S A CUP SHOCKER!

So read the Liverpool Echo headline after the 1981 fourth-round draw was made. Everton assistant boss Geoff Nulty said: "It's not the tie we would have picked, but I'm sure the same goes for Liverpool."

At that stage Ladbrokes quoted Everton 2-1 to win with Liverpool 11-8. Liverpool and Ipswich were 5-1 joint favourites to win the trophy with Everton 16-1.

The day before the game a special office in Walton Road received a single bet of £350 on Liverpool and £100 at 10-1 for a 2-0 Reds win. Everton remained 2-1 shots, with Liverpool 6-4 and 15-8 a draw.

Just like all derby matches, particularly in the FA Cup, the build-up provided many a colourful tale.

Hamming it up: Everton's sponsors were right behind the Blues ahead of their clash with the Reds

No. 69

Amongst the talking points was the fact that the FA would allow the tie to be screened on closed circuit viewing in Merseyside cinemas, after the FA turned down a request for an evening kick-off so the match could be screened at Anfield.

The venues showing the match were to be Liverpool Stadium (for 3,500 people), the Odeon and ABC Cinemas in the city centre and the ABC in Southport (a combined capacity of 5,000).

The technicians in Southport were only allowed to install equipment in the early hours of the Saturday morning of January 24th.

The reason? A late-night adults-only bill featured two movies: 'For Men Only' and 'Strip First, Then We Talk.'

The only snag was the price of tickets. It would be £5.50 for a cinema seat, more than for fans at Goodison where a top-price stand seat was £3.20. However, Jarvis Astaire, boss of the London-based Viewsport organisation that handled the screenings, believed in the promise of the venture, having seen success with a similar enterprise weeks earlier for a West Ham v Tottenham League Cup game.

Astaire added in the Liverpool Echo (13/1/81): "Ted Croker, the secretary of the FA, has been in favour of this for a long time.

"But up to now the League have not been so keen.

"There may well be an increased demand for what we offer now that there is a growing trend to discourage people from travelling to away games, although that doesn't apply here."

No. 70

No more reds – and yellows

Liverpool were strong favourites to reach the last 16 and would win their third European Cup at the end of the season. It was the first weekend when the FA scrapped red and yellow cards because they felt they were encouraging over-use by officials, with the referee for the match being one Clive Thomas.

The weekend before the tie, he told the Weekend Echo: "I thought the system was all right. I am disappointed that they have gone."

Fans' stories included Kevin McGuinness, a Liverpool fanatic who flew from Japan (costing £470) without a match ticket. He said: "I will be desperately hoping right up to the kick-off that some kind heart can sell me a ticket." His journey included his flight being delayed for two days in Russia because of bad weather, and a hitchhike home from Heathrow Airport as he hadn't had time to swap his yen into English currency.

Action-packed Echo cartoon ahead of the 1981 Cup derby – with references to the screening of the game, the alcohol ban and Clive Thomas

Derby fever

"I have never known so much interest in a derby," said Liverpool goalkeeper Ray Clemence ahead of the game.

"It is even greater than it was for the semi-finals in 1977.

"The demand for tickets is incredible."

Blues midfielder Trevor Ross, however, was in confident mood that Everton could stage an upset: "It will be won by the odd goal and if we play as well as we have been recently there's no problem. We can pinch it."

A piece of cake

Evertonian DJ Billy Butler, who had reportedly boycotted beer due to price rises, said he would end this drought if Everton won. Also in the Echo ahead of the big game was Aigburth baker Brian Linwood, a keen Blue who had made cakes with the inscriptions: 'EV-ER-TON for the Cup'.

Blue heaven: Ray Clemence tumbles into the net (top picture) as Goodison erupts to Imre Varadi's goal in 1981, right

Imre feasts on Reds

The Football Echo headline told the story: 'BLUE HEAVEN. RISING STAR IMRE SEALS CUP VICTORY'

In front of nearly 53,000 (providing record Goodison gate receipts), Everton created the better chances in the tie even after goals from Peter Eastoe and Imre Varadi. The latter received a meat pie to the face having netted at the Park End where Liverpool fans were congregated. Martin Hodge was given a dramatic call-up, having not played in the first team since the previous April after Jim McDonagh was ruled out with an ankle injury. After only two minutes of the match, McDonagh, (protesting from the bench at the award of a free-kick near the Everton box) would earn a stern talking to from referee Clive Thomas.

Avi Cohen came in for the injured Alan Kennedy on the Liverpool side and referee Thomas was given a torrid reception by the home faithful.

Eastoe's opener, a low shot past the advancing Ray Clemence, prompted Liverpool appeals for offside while in Neal's attempts to clear off the line, the ball struck Cohen and went in (the doubt being whether the ball had already crossed the line before Neal

intervened).

Varadi's second came after good work by Cup debutant Eamonn O'Keefe. Substitute Jimmy Case, on for the injured Kenny Dalglish (who was forced off at half-time with a cut in his left instep that needed stitches) pulled a goal back with 14 minutes left, although Bob Paisley admitted afterwards that his team had been outplayed.

It was the first and only time Mick Lyons had played for the victorious side in 20 derbies and hundreds poured onto the pitch at the end. Lyons declared afterwards: "At the end I didn't want to be on the pitch. I wanted to be on the terraces with the fans."

Reds' boss Bob Paisley admitted: "In all my years at Liverpool I have never known an Everton team that has been stronger than us, but in the first half they were stronger. I hope now that Everton go on and win the Cup."

The final word goes to former chairman and major shareholder Sir John Moores (who had turned 85 on the Sunday): "After years of having our noses rubbed in it, it is some solace to have beaten them at last."

Cheers for souvenirs: The match programme. Below: The two managers, Gordon Lee and Bob Paisley in a heated exchange and the two skippers argue a point with referee Clive Thomas

No.71

McDonagh saves the Saints day

Southampton were seen as one of the toughest possible draws when the Blues were handed a trip to The Dell on Valentine's Day, 1981. It ended Everton's run of six successive home ties while the date of February 14 would be Saints star Kevin Keegan's 30th birthday.

While Everton had lost twice since beating Liverpool, Saints had taken their run to seven straight victories and were unbeaten in 13 games, winning their last nine home matches. They had also scored 28 goals in nine games.

But with Jim McDonagh inspired in the Everton goal, the Blues earned a 0-0 draw on the south coast backed by 6,000 visiting fans in The Dell's 24,000-capacity ground.

Interest was high in the replay, with fans queuing outside Goodison Park for tickets the day before the game, which was not all-ticket. Everton secretary Jim Greenwood said: "We anticipate well over 40,000 for this game."

With all stand seats sold, Southampton sent back 3,000 stand tickets of their 6,000 allocation and as word got round more fans began queuing outside the ground.

Asa Hartford rallied the fans: "If they get behind us as they did against Liverpool it will give us a real lift.

"The atmosphere that day was tremendous. I've played in some big games over the years, but it was an incredible feeling against Liverpool."

Eamonn sinks Keegan hopes

The only change for the Southampton return was John Bailey being ruled out with a hamstring strain picked up in the first game so Steve McMahon, returning after suspension, came into midfield with John Gidman reverting to full-back.

There was little to choose between the sides at a packed Goodison Park (nearly 50,000 crammed in, virtually twice the average League attendance).

But the extra time period saw the Blues edge into the last eight thanks to a player who was playing non-league football for Mossley only months earlier - Eamonn O'Keefe.

Charles Lambert's report began: 'O'Keefe, a man who two years ago was delivering newspapers for a living, last night wrote his name into the headlines.'

In only his 17th first-team game for Everton, the midfielder crashed a rising shot into the roof of the net 13 minutes into extra time after skipper Mick Lyons had headed on a John Gidman centre.

It was also Kevin Keegan's first-ever defeat at the hands of Everton (having limped out of a League game against them earlier that season when Saints were 1-0 up - Everton eventually winning 2-1).

Keegan said: "Good luck to them. I hope they go all the way and win the Cup. The crowd won it for them. There was a tremendous atmosphere . . . and that is what won them the game.

"It's about time they won something.

"They've got a big trophy cabinet and nothing to put in it!"

Seeing red: Kevin Ratcliffe is consoled by Gordon Lee after being sent off. Above: Peter Eastoe scores (top right) and celebrates; Eamonn O'Keefe fires in a shot

Power blow - and out!

The FA Cup quarter-final with Manchester City in 1981 was made an all-ticket affair after the huge demand created by the Southampton replay in the previous round, but Goodison still bulged with a capacity crowd of almost 53,000. With Eamonn O'Keefe and Trevor Ross fully fit, the Blues fielded their strongest team with Garry Stanley named on the bench.

City went close before Peter Eastoe put Everton ahead only for Gerry Gow to equalise. Early in the second half the home side were back in front when Trevor Ross scored from the spot.

Reporter Ian Hargraves then noted: 'One City supporter was so angry that he ran on to the pitch, in spite of all the anti-hooligan precautions, and after waving his fists at several players and the referee he was led away by police.' On the verge of a place in the FA Cup semi-final and with a 2-1 lead, Billy

No.72

Wright had a goal disallowed and five minutes from time future Blues Championship winner Paul Power lobbed the ball home past the outrushing McDonagh. To compound their misery, future Everton captain Kevin Ratcliffe was sent off for a challenge on Tommy Hutchison in the dying seconds, Hutchison claiming he had been butted. There were 50 fouls in the match and four bookings, as well as Ratcliffe's dismissal.

Everton (with John Bailey in for the suspended Ratcliffe and O'Keefe (flu) being replaced by Joe McBride) slumped 3-1 in the replay despite the backing of 13,000 travelling fans among the 52,523 spectators, with City marching onto Wembley where Spurs and Ricardo Villa stood in their way.

No.73

Holders stunned

An FA Cup bonanza was predicted for the city on the weekend of February 19/20 1983, with Everton and Liverpool both drawn at home in the fifth-round. The Blues, who wanted to play on the Sunday, were given a Saturday date as Tottenham club policy deemed they could only play on that day while Liverpool did not want to play on the Sunday.

In the week leading up to the match skipper Billy Wright was put on the transfer list at his own request, having been dropped the previous December for being half-a-stone overweight. Mark Higgins was appointed captain having taken his place in the centre of defence.

FA Cup winners in 1981 and 1982,

Spurs arrived at Goodison with injuries. Glenn Hoddle was only able to take a place as sub due to an ankle problem. Howard Kendall sprung a surprise by including Alan Irvine in place of Peter Reid while Adrian Heath started despite not having trained for two days due to a viral infection.

Visiting boss Keith Burkinshaw said: "It's always a tough game up there. It's a muck and nettles affair."

He was right. Spurs were backed by around 8,000 fans, but Howard Kendall's young side, with Steve McMahon dominant in midfield, won the day. Andy King broke the deadlock, his 11th of the season, early in the second half and Graeme Sharp tapped in Kevin Sheedy's free-kick for number two, after Ray Clemence had collided with King. Next up was Old Trafford.

So near: Adrian Heath and Graeme Sharp attempt to break down United in 1983

No.74

Late show sinks Howard's battlers

The young Blues were rated as clear underdogs when they travelled to Manchester United. The home side were third in the table (Everton were 10th) while United had already won the corresponding League meeting that season 2-1.

But roared on by 15,000 Evertonians in a 58,000 plus crowd – the biggest attendance anywhere in England so far that season – the Blues more than held their own. Spectators included Andy King, recovering from his recent knee ligament operation. He declared: "It will take more than a pair of crutches to keep me away."

Although United created more chances in the first half, Everton had the better of things in the second half, Graeme Sharp (twice) and Adrian Heath going close. But with time ticking, there was to be no happy end for Howard Kendall's men.

Sub Lou Macari headed a Ray Wilkins corner into the path of Frank Stapleton, who shot into the roof of the net two minutes into injury time. The Cup favourites eventually went on to win the trophy, while it was to be Everton's last defeat in the competition, excluding finals, for nearly four years.

Howard Kendall said: "It was disappointing to lose after playing so well, but I was proud of the team. We are trying to build something big at Goodison." Roll on 1984.

No.75

'Do it for them!' says Kendall

Signalled by some as one of the key turning points in the club's history, the Toffees were struggling at the wrong end of the old First Division when they began their 1984 Cup campaign against Stoke City at the Victoria Ground.

Howard Kendall opened the dressing room window before the game to let the players hear the backing of the fans in a bid to inspire his men.

Such was the noise generated by more than 10,000 fans, he told his players: "That's how much they want you to win.

"If you can't do it for them today you'll never do it for anybody."

On a wet and windy day it seemed to work as the Blues came through 2-0 (with Adrian Heath returning to his old club) after some earlier scares.

Andy Gray's superb diving header from a free-kick broke the deadlock, with Alan Irvine's fierce left-footer doing the trick.

'Andy Gray: Leather Seeking Missile' was a famous banner from the 1980s and here's why – diving to score against Stoke in 1984

Andy dives to sink Notts

Having continued their run to the quarter-finals courtesy of wins over Gillingham (in a second replay) and Shrewsbury Town, Everton were drawn at First Division strugglers Notts County. But a grim afternoon in Nottingham ended on a high note, with the Blues battling to a 2-1 victory, to the delight of the 10,000 travelling Evertonians.

Kevin Richardson – complete with plaster cast on his arm – headed the first before John Chiedozie hit back, the only goal Everton conceded in that season's competition. Neville Southall showed why he was rated one of the best in the country with a string of saves and it was Andy Gray who headed home the winner from a Kevin

No.76

Sheedy free-kick, a remarkable diving header literally inches off the ground.

Howard Kendall later joked: "Andy rotivated the ground with his nose as he slid in to meet the ball!"

In the aftermath of the tie, Andy Gray said: "I couldn't believe some of the reports which said I fell over. It was nothing like that at all. Kevin's kick came over the head of Graeme Sharp and I saw it late.

"I didn't think I was going to reach it. It was a split second decision to dive.

"It took the keeper by surprise and was just a case of improvisation."

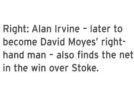

Right: Alan Irvine – later to become David Moyes' right-hand man – also finds the net in the win over Stoke.

Far right: Kevin Richardson heads home against Notts County

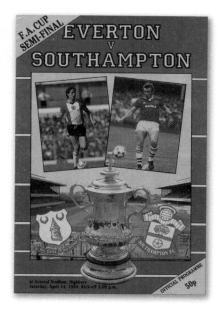

No. 77

Inchy nicks it

Although not a classic game, the 1984 FA Cup semi-final against Southampton will never be forgotten by Evertonians. It was a match that could have gone either way, with both goalkeepers Neville Southall and Peter Shilton in top form.

Danny Wallace was a constant threat but it was left to Adrian Heath to head home the only goal with three minutes left of extra time (the first time a semi-final had gone to the extra period), after Peter Reid's free-kick had been touched on by Derek Mountfield.

Blues' boss Howard Kendall later explained: "Frank Worthington was playing for Southampton, and we tried to target his 'area' because we thought he wouldn't want to go back and defend. Adrian Heath finished it off, in Frank's area. It's down to a little bit of planning or a bit of luck. Who knows?"

Flying the flag: Ten-year-old Everton fan John Smalley gets ready to travel down to London for the Blues' 1984 semi-final at Highbury

Wembley here we come: The Blues fans celebrate as Adrian Heath's late winner finds the net. Above and right: Action from a closely contested match. Opposite page: Police deal with a fans' invasion and (far right) Adrian Heath holds a picture of his winning goal

1984
Kendall's revival

Elton cried and we had smiles as big as the Watford gap.
Howard's heroes had done it – and this was just the start

Elton plays the Blues

Watford's chairman was making the headlines ahead of the FA Cup final - but it was Howard's Blues that were tipped to hit the right notes on the day

Big day nerves

Although set to play a live concert before a sell-out audience at Wembley on June 30, Watford's chairman - a certain Elton John - was more nervous about the forthcoming FA Cup final.

The entertainer had been in Montserrat earlier in the Hornets' cup run on holiday, and in Paris after a concert performance the previous night for the semi-final.

"I shall be a bag of nerves but this is one match I must see.

"Nothing at all would keep me away from Wembley on the club's most glamorous day in cup football," he said.

"I nearly died during the second half of the semi-final against Plymouth, when the Third Division side was doing so well against us.

"I had never known a match last so long."

Back in the summer of '84: Elton John, Paul Young, Kool and the Gang and Nik Kershaw play Wembley (below)

Howard signs on

There was a boost for the backroom team that had steered the Blues to Wembley as the club prepared for their first FA Cup final since 1968.

'Everton have rewarded manager Howard Kendall and coaches Mick Heaton and Colin Harvey, by giving them new contracts,' reported the Liverpool Echo on May 17, 1984.

Kendall signed on for a further four years and said: "Obviously I'm delighted, and I hope it's not the last contract I get at Everton because I would never want to leave.

"I don't see my future as being anywhere else.

"Even when the team had some problems earlier in the season I believed I was doing the right thing, and the chairman and the board have been tremendous, because they have supported me during that difficult period."

Baby Blues for Len

Proud dad and keen Evertonian Len Bethel started his FA Cup celebrations a week early.

He and his wife Irene had notched up their own personal triumph in the shape of a new baby girl – but the special delivery was also a bit of a relief for the father!

Sub post-master Len (39) was so pleased by the marvellous news that he posted up the announcement with paint on the window of his Allerton store.

"Obviously I am absolutely delighted about having a daughter, and so is my wife," said Len, of Homefield Road.

"But I must admit I was getting twice as nervous because it was so overdue that I don't think I would have been able to go down to Wembley!"

"The doctor is a keen Everton supporter as well so I think the wife will not be coming out of hospital until Sunday."

Len and Irene (33) have had so many requests about when the baby was due from customers in the store he has put a message on the window – 'It's a girl! Karen, 8lbs 14ozs.'

"I reckon 4,000 people have asked me how she is over the last month. Now they can all share in our happiness," he said.

Billy stuck at home

One of the three survivors from the 1933 Cup-winning side Billy Cook was forced to watch the game on TV at his Bootle home after missing out on a ticket.

However, Billy (74) was not too upset to let it put him off supporting the Blues.

He said: "I don't bear any grudge against the club."

A club spokesman said that had Billy contacted the club he would have received a ticket.

He felt sure there would have been no problem, but it seemed as though he had left it too late.

Prize guy

Bootle plumber Fred Smith, a true-blue Evertonian, won an FA Cup weekend in London - courtesy of the Echo.

Mr Smith (50) and wife Ann (42) won a weekend stay in a plush hotel during the Wembley weekend.

He won the prize following his success in the Echo's Cup final competition, which involved supplying a caption for the cartoon of Andy Gray, John Bailey and Adrian Heath next to a chocolate machine (above).

His winning caption read: 'Right Adrian! We want 12 toffee cups and a trophy for the boss.'

Final plea

Cup Final fever reached court when a bail application was made so that a defendant could go to the FA Cup final!

A condition of a 19-year-old Evertonian's bail was that he reported to Admiral Street police station each Saturday at 7pm. Magistrates agreed to change the date to Sunday so the defendant could attend the Everton game at Wembley.

Presiding magistrate Mr Henry Gilbert said the request might be thought frivolous, but he added: "Conditions of bail were not intended to infringe on a defendant's liberty or to be a punishment."

One for all: Watford chairman with Hornets stars John Barnes and Maurice Johnston - who would go on to play for the Blues under Howard Kendall

Born Blue: Evertonian dad Len Bethel lets his customers know about the new arrival

Hatton's spot of bad luck

'Councillor Derek Hatton missed out on a chance to score against Watford at Wembley. Instead, he was at Westminster trying to score a political 'goal' for Liverpool against the Government.

Hatton (above) and the Mayor of Watford were to have taken part in a penalty shoot-out at the Cup Final in front of TV cameras. The match before 'The Match' had to be cancelled when the Labour group of Liverpool City Council were called to meet Environment Secretary Patrick Jenkin for talks on the city's financial crisis.

A disappointed Hatton said: "The times clashed - and that was that. It would have been nice to score a goal - and do the 'double' over Watford!"'

Ready for the off: Two young Blues at Lime Street en route to Wembley. Below: A British Rail advert

Here we go!

'Howie's happy army marches back to Wembley' was the front page headline of the Liverpool Echo on May 19, 1984.

The report read: 'Up to 25,000 Everton fans poured out of the city in thousands of cars, soccer specials and 500 coaches.

'British Rail laid on a dozen trains for 6,000 supporters – with two of them stopping at rival Watford to ferry the London team's fans to the stadium.

'True blue skies greeted the 5,000 Evertonians who travelled yesterday to spend the night. They mingled in good humour with Watford fans in the West End and for the police it was just another night.'

Ticket hitch for Peter

Ticketless Peter Shaw (21), spent two days hitch-hiking 800 miles from Marseilles to be at Wembley – and picked up a cost-price ticket within minutes of arriving.

Peter, a French student, whose family live in Sandrock Road, New Brighton revealed that his friend Dave Wilson (22), from Hoylake, was even more determined to see the game than him.

Peter said: "The French are one of the few countries not showing the match on TV. So Dave's hitch-hiking from France to Italy and heading to the nearest bar to watch the match."

Other fans were paying up to £40 for a ticket outside the stadium with touts complaining that business was down on previous years.

2.30pm KO

Blues fan Terry Fearnehough (24, of Wellstead Road, Wavertree), a cellar man in the Everton 300 club and his Liverpool-supporting bride Christine Lamb (26) were due to be married at 2.30pm on the day of the final.

'Christine, of Score Lane, Childwall has persuaded her family of Reds fans to venture into rival ground for the occasion,' reported the Echo.

She said: "We're solid Anfield through and through. But today we're making a few concessions. Even my page boy is dressed in blue and white."

Terry's mother Eileen was a season-ticket holder and his twin brother John was staying away from Wembley to be the best man.

"We've avoided football arguments in the four years we've been going out," said secretary Christine. "I've kept his mind off the Cup Final by decorating our new house most nights."

Stumped

Despite the good weather, local cricket clubs were finding problems in fulfilling early-season fixtures over the Cup final weekend – as the Blue army headed for London.

Liverpool, who were set to face St Helens at Aigburth, were without three of their regular XI – the previous season's captain Steve Phillips, David Dunkley and Mike Mather.

Chester Broughton Hall were forced to bring in Andy Myers for Jeremy Jordan, while three others were unavailable for their William Young tie at Winnington Park.

Good luck!

Everton left for Wembley with a powerful good luck message from the Liverpool Echo on behalf of the city.

It read: 'To Howard Kendall and his merry men, not forgetting coaches Colin Harvey and Mick Heaton and those unfortunate players like skipper Mark Higgins who have been sidelined by injury, the Echo says . . . good luck. Go out and win for Merseyside in style. We know your players will be a credit and that your fans will enhance their reputation for sportsmanship.' Bookies made Everton the 8-11 favourites, with Watford 11-10.

Milking it

Soccer pundit Lawrie McMenemy tipped the Blues to put their Milk Cup disappointment behind them.

McMenemy said: "I would be inclined to plump for Everton, if only because of their recent experience of taking part in a Wembley Cup final. They were unlucky not to win their Wembley tussle with Liverpool. I'm convinced that a repeat of that performance on Saturday will be too much for Watford to handle."

Cup final line-up: Excited fans pose for a picture ahead of their trip. Left: Echo ads for coach travel to Wembley

Hard man Terry up for the fight

Watford hard man Steve Terry said he wouldn't be holding back in the FA Cup final - despite getting sent off in his last game against Everton.

The 21-year-old was dismissed at Goodison Park the previous October, the first time it had happened in his career. He earned a booking for a pull-back, before being booked again and consequently sent off following a challenge.

"I won't be thinking of the sending off," said Terry, whose competitiveness had earned him around 50 stitches that season.

"I'll be going in as hard as I normally do. I won't be holding anything back.'"

Aiming to make history: The Everton v QPR match programme (below) carried a good luck message and a picture of the squad with Howard Kendall and Colin Harvey holding a picture of Mike Trebilcock with the FA Cup in 1966

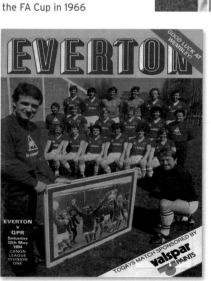

Howard's army

It was 14 years since Everton's last piece of silverware – a period in which rivals Liverpool were dominating at home and abroad with the Blues having endured disappointment in the Milk Cup at the hands of their neighbours only weeks earlier.

The final proved a rarity in that every player appeared in an FA Cup final for the first time, while the Blues started as favourites although the last meeting between the sides in the League that February had ended in a remarkable 4-4 draw at Vicarage Road.

Kevin Sheedy, Alan Irvine, Terry Curran and Mark Higgins were all absent through injury while Alan Harper was preferred to Andy King on the bench. John Bailey returned from suspension into a team that was unbeaten in their last six League games to finish seventh in the table.

Manager Howard Kendall said: "The lads are ready. I couldn't have asked for more in recent weeks in terms of attitude and effort. When a team gets to a final it is easy for their form to dip,

The road to Wembley

Pictured getting ready to board the coach bound for the Twin Towers are (back row, from left): Howard Kendall (manager), Peter Reid, Andy Gray, Derek Mountfield, Graeme Sharp, Alan Irvine, Alan Harper, Mark Higgins, Jim Arnold, Neville Southall. Front row, from left are: Gary Stevens, Kevin Ratcliffe, Adrian Heath, Kevin Richardson, John Bailey, Trevor Steven.

Yellow peril

Skipper Kevin Ratcliffe revealed that manager Howard Kendall had told his players to play dirty – so they avoided missing out on the biggest match of their lives.

Ratcliffe said: "Howard was a big believer once we'd reached a final, that we should get booked as soon as we could if we were near a suspension."

1984

but it is a compliment to the professionalism of the players that we have finished our League programme so well.

"We are not complacent. There is nothing much between the sides. Last time we met, it was a 4-4 draw.

"We're going not just to play our part, but to bring back the Cup.

"We've got players who can settle people down and inspire confidence. You can look to Andy Gray and Peter Reid to do that and what a character John Bailey is in the dressing room.

"Reid has been very important. We had a spell this season when people didn't want the ball, waiting for other people to do it. Peter came in and couldn't wait to get involved, and that was a key factor in our revival."

Reid added: "We're not that different a team now than earlier in the season.

"What we had around January was a change in confidence, not in attitude or style.

"A good team playing without confidence can look a bad side even though they're not."

On the right road: How some Blues fans might have travelled to the final

Freddie stars

One of the most memorable images from the Cup final is Elton John in tears . . . before the final.

The entertainer was so moved by the fans' rendition of traditional Wembley song 'Abide With Me' that he was captured in emotional mood by the TV cameras.

The Echo reported: 'The fans united to give a memorable rendering of the hymn Abide with Me, which used to be such a highlight of the Cup Final. In recent years irreverent fans have often spoilt this particular piece of entertainment but it was most enjoyable to hear it thundering out over the ground from 100,000 throats.'

Comedian Freddie Starr came out before the kick-off with the Everton squad to conduct thousands of fans in their singing. The comedian had been with Everton for the whole day entertaining the squad. Watford, meanwhile, had Michael Barrymore as their 'entertainer'.

Police reported just five arrests before the game, all for minor charges not for trouble in the town. Two were arrested for drunkenness, two for obstruction and one for theft.

Starr of the show: Freddie Starr conducted the Wembley sing-a-long for the Evertonians. Michael Barrymore was the Watford entertainer

Reserve a box for the Cup Final for only £8·22

Get a grandstand view of the Cup Final with this 20" remote control colour TV for only £8.22 per month with one month down.

DER

Come in and choose a bargain.

Cup final box: An Echo advert in 1984

Taylor on alert

Watford were in patchy form following their semi-final victory over Plymouth, with results having included a 5-1 defeat at Nottingham Forest. Captain Wilf Rostron was ruled out due to suspension while Steve Sims missed out through injury.

"We must forget Wilf and I mean that not in a nasty sense because it is a tragedy such a good professional and nice man is going to miss the greatest day of his career, but because we cannot do ourselves any good to mope about it," said Graham Taylor.

The Hornets boss was well briefed on the threats posed by Kendall's Blues.

Taylor picked out Kevin Richardson, Peter Reid and Andy Gray for special comment.

Speaking of Gray, he said: "Everyone remembers his goal against Notts County when he virtually nosed the ball in. He's had a new lease of life at Everton."

Way to go

Among the vast contingent of Evertonians who made Wembley Way a sea of blue and white were a party of 32 who arrived on the official Liverpool team coach which was available because the Liverpool party were away in Israel.

Elton claps the Blues

Elton John shook the hand of every Everton player when the rival squads made their traditional stroll out onto the Wembley turf, while rival Scottish strikers Mo Johnston and Andy Gray posed together for pictures. Elton later applauded the stand holding the main body of Everton fans.

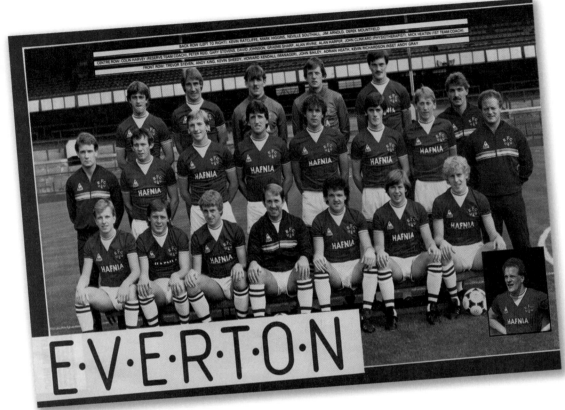

Air we go

Other pre-match entertainment for fans arriving early into the ground featured an aerial combat between radio-controlled model aircraft in the colours of the respective clubs and a small parade of vintage cars, one of them carrying the FA Cup.

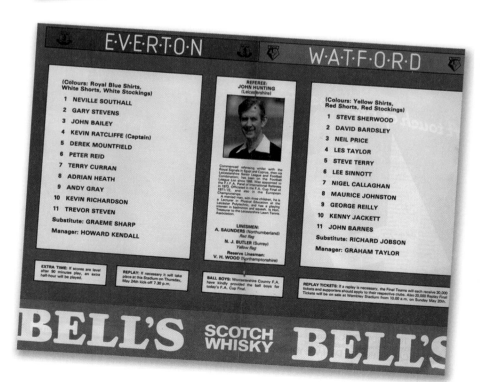

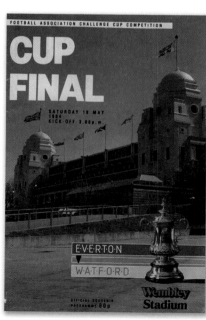

Programmed for success: Pages from the 1984 FA Cup final programme

'Sherwood didn't collect...'

Sharpy got us the first and when Andy Gray jumped with Watford keeper Steve Sherwood, we were heading for a memorable victory

Graham Taylor's side went close inside the first minute when a Watford long throw was headed on by George Reilly for John Barnes, only for the winger to miscue his close-range effort.

Everton dominated possession without being able to create too much, and Les Taylor saw an effort deflected wide by John Bailey while Mo Johnston was close with a header for the Hornets. But after Graeme Sharp and Kevin Richardson had gone close for the Blues, it was the former who gave them the lead before the break. Richardson's centre was cleared as far as Gary Stevens, who drove the ball back towards the Watford area. Sharp pounced on it in an instant, controlling the ball before firing a crisp finish in off the post after 37 minutes. Richardson fired just over four minutes later as Everton threatened again.

The final was all but over six minutes into the second half. Trevor Steven's right-wing centre was headed home by Andy Gray, who beat keeper Steve Sherwood in the aerial challenge. Sherwood had come out to claim but could only throw his hands towards the ball and Gray's head. The Watford players and Sherwood appealed to the referee for a foul but the goal was given.

From then on it was one-way traffic, with demoralised Watford always second best. They brought on sub Paul Atkinson for Neil Price soon after the second goal, but it made little difference. Man-of-the-match Trevor Steven continued to torment while at the other end Johnston found the net – only for it to be chalked off for offside.

The final whistle signalled joyous Everton scenes and their first silverware for 14 years – bringing tears to Watford chairman Elton John's eyes for a second time. Incidentally, the win also completed a unique treble. Like Tottenham Hotspur (1982) and Manchester United (1983), the Blues lost to Liverpool in the Milk Cup final before going on to capture the FA Cup.

EVERTON: Southall, Stevens, Bailey, Ratcliffe, Mountfield, Reid, Steven, Heath, Sharp, Gray, Richardson. Sub not used: Harper.

WATFORD: Sherwood, Bardsley, Price (Atkinson), Taylor, Terry, Sinnott, Callaghan, Johnston, Reilly, Jackett, Barnes.

GOALSCORERS: EVERTON Sharp (37), Gray (51).
ATTENDANCE: 100,000.

The cup that cheers: Graeme Sharp opens the scoring (main pic) while the Blues celebrate Andy Gray's clinching second goal

1984

'Now for the cake'

'Crisis? What crisis!'

"It just shows that when people talk about a crisis at a football club, they should think in terms of the whole season.

"Fortunately the chairman and the board had faith. I am delighted for everyone that we have taken a major trophy back to Merseyside that belongs to Everton for a change.

"It was important to win it and now we can look forward to European football next season.

"We didn't get hold of the midfield early on but after Andy Gray's goal we were always in command. You've got to give your opponents credit sometime. We are a young side and hopefully we can now go on from here.

"To win the FA Cup is fantastic, but in the long run it is the championship, achieved over 42 games, that has to be the main objective. The Cup was the icing, now we want the cake."

Everton manager Howard Kendall

Save a thought for Mark

"It is a marvellous feeling to be captain of an Everton side who have won the FA Cup. I also feel sorry for Mark Higgins, who might have had that honour if he hadn't been injured."

Everton captain Kevin Ratcliffe

Goal was fairly scored

"Steve Sherwood never had the ball under control when I went in. He was stretching and I headed the back of the keeper's hands. That was enough to send the ball in. I made contact only with my head and there was no bodily contact."

Andy Gray (on the second goal)

Keeper crying foul

"That goal would have been disallowed 99 times out of 100. Sherwood is upset because he feels he was fouled."

Watford manager Graham Taylor

1984

Rebirth of the Blues

Everton's 1984 FA Cup final success over Watford was to prove the catalyst to the most successful period in the club's history under the inspirational Howard Kendall

Start of an era: Howard Kendall's team celebrates with the Cup

Launch-pad to success

Ian Hargraves made the following observations in the Liverpool Echo (21/5/84). Concerning the potential for new contracts for Kendall's squad: 'The winning of the FA Cup, which generated gate receipts of £915,000 alone and the club presence in two Milk Cup Finals, which generated even more money, may well tempt the players to take a harder line.

'This was further hinted at on Saturday, when the players and their wives celebrated separately away from manager Kendall, coaches Heaton and Harvey and the club directors, in order to boost their final perks.

'Kendall was at pains to emphasise afterwards that the two party celebrations had no particular significance, but many fans must have felt sorry for him on Saturday night, when he confessed to *Match of the Day* presenter Jimmy Hill that he would have liked to have been celebrating with his players – and with the FA Cup.'

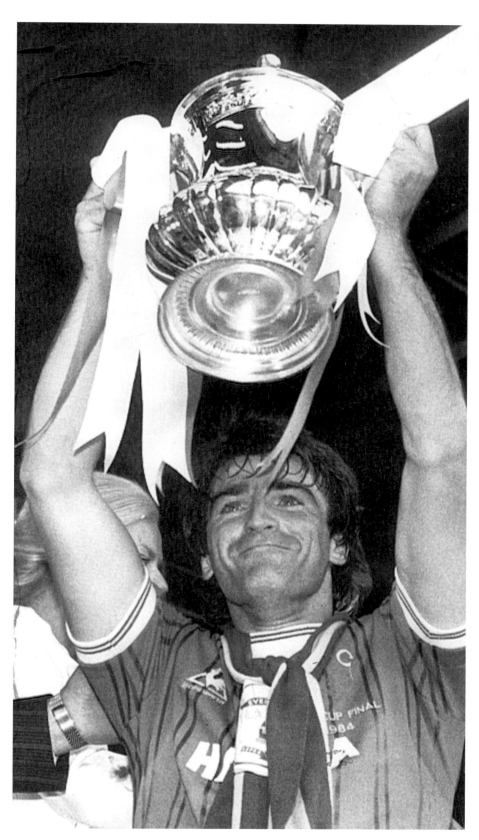

Silver service: Skipper Kevin Ratcliffe with the Duchess of York and (left) lifting the famous trophy to the delight of Blues

Youngest captain

At 23, Kevin Ratcliffe was the youngest winning captain since Bobby Moore 20 years earlier.

But he revealed that he was struggling with an injury when his big moment to lift the Cup came. "I had injured my shoulder in the game so when it came to getting the cup I couldn't lift it properly. It was straight up and down - I was struggling to hold it."

Fans repaid

Midfielder Peter Reid paid tribute to the Evertonians who managed to find enough tickets to out-number Watford fans at Wembley. "I am delighted for the fans because they have been magnificent all season."

Meanwhile skipper Ratcliffe was already looking ahead, telling the Daily Post: "This means so much to us and the supporters and maybe we can make the next step - the League Championship."

Sharp's the word

Graeme Sharp's Wembley goal was his fourth in Everton's last three matches, and he told the Daily Post: "I am just pleased to have been part of this triumph. Every player dreams of hitting one in a Cup final."

1984

It takes two: A famous picture from the day as scorers Andy Gray and Graeme Sharp salute the camera holding their winners medals

Right: Neville Southall and Graeme Sharp on the lap of honour

Below: The FA Cup base is in safe hands . . .

1984

BLUE HEAVEN! MAGIC SHOW WINS THE CUP

Blue Heaven: Football Echo headline following Everton's victory, while (right) Howard Kendall shows Bob Paisley the FA Cup on the journey back to Liverpool. Bob had been an interested spectator

Hole-in-heart Robbie's treat

Tiny hole-in-the-heart patient Robbie Poole was too unwell to attend Everton's Wembley cup final.

But Robbie, aged 9, whose hero was Adrian 'Inchy' Heath made up for it when he found himself a star for the day on the club's victory parade.

Echo photographer Eddie Barford heard that Robbie - who was born with a hole the size of an old sixpenny piece in his heart - was due to be admitted into Alder Hey hospital for a vital operation.

And he went into the crowd to invite the Page Moss youngster and his dad Brian on to the open deck bus carrying the world's Press.

"I was waving my scarf at the crowd and it was just like they were cheering me," he said.

Singing the Blues: Misery for Watford chairman Elton John in this Echo cutting

Pop goes Elton's dream

Elton John's greeting to the Everton fans before the match.

I guess that's why they call it the Blues . . .

Glory! Glory!

More than 200,000 people turned out to give a magnificent Mersey welcome to Everton when they came home with the FA Cup.

A Merseyside police spokesman said that the day had passed off without a single problem, despite the 'unbelievable' crowd which he estimated at up to 250,000.

"It was an excellent turnout and everyone was so well behaved. God bless them all," he said.

Thumbs up: John Bailey, Andy Gray and Peter Reid show off the Cup
Left: FA Cup T-shirt from 1984

Young Blues double up

There was double cause for celebration in 1984 - thanks to Goodison's young Blues.

The FA Youth Cup also made its way into the club trophy cabinet thanks to a 4-2 defeat of Stoke City in the final.

Ian Marshall skippered the young Everton side to victory before leaving the Blues in 1988, going on to play for a host of clubs.

Cup returns: Kevin Ratcliffe and Mark Higgins are welcomed at Broadgreen Station

Fans pitch in

Stadium police chief, Commander Alan Gibson was full of praise for the Evertonians at Wembley.

He said: "Some things which happened on Saturday I have never seen before.

"For example, when a few spectators ran on to the pitch at the end . . . when the crowd began chanting to them to get off, they turned and went.

"That was incredible. If supporters have been on the pitch in the past we have a heck of a job getting them off. But the Everton fans - and the Watford people - made it a well behaved final."

5,000 sang and cheered

The special trains carrying the Everton party arrived at Broadgreen Station at 3.45pm on the Sunday – more than 30 minutes late. 5,000 sang and cheered as the team boarded their open deck bus.

Banners on the journey included: 'Everton give Elton the blues' and 'Howie's got more hair than Elton'.

The siren-blasting motorcade included 16 police motorcycles, and was led by an official car carrying city council chairman Hugh Dalton.

The coach was almost brought to a halt outside Goodison Park and nearby Spellow Lane where at least 20,000 more supporters were waiting…then

came a faster section down Scotland Road – chased for more than a mile by a black and white mongrel – before the team arrived in the city centre.

In Lime Street, where it all began for so many Evertonians on Saturday morning, at least 50,000 supporters waved and cheered.

Some over-enthusiastic fans even tried to kneel down in front of the players' bus – a move discouraged by police.

The crowd there had been among the most patient all afternoon, and were given some free entertainment as a reward when a group of Scottish pipers turned up and performed a lively jig.

The hat that made history

Speaking in The Evertonian in January 1995, left-back John Bailey had the following recollections: "I wish I'd had a pound for every time someone asked me about that hat and those glasses! I was walking down the stairs from the royal box after collecting my medal. I already had a scarf on, but the next thing I knew someone had plonked this big top hat on my head. I suppose it's part of history now, but that day was the highest point of my Everton career."

Welcome back: John Bailey, Andy Gray and Peter Reid parade the FA Cup on the open top bus tour in 1984 (left). Right: The first home match league programme after the win

No. 79

Twice is nice for free-kick king Kev

Less than five minutes of the sixth-round tie had been played when Everton were awarded a direct free-kick against Ipswich Town in March 1985.

As was common, a buzz of anticipation reverberated around Goodison Park with Kevin Sheedy poised to prepare to test the opposition keeper. He struck the ball to Paul Cooper's right, but it had been taken too quickly for the ref's liking. This earned Sheedy a berating from Peter Reid.

It didn't matter. Sheedy stepped up and curled the second over the wall, beating Cooper to his other side. Sheedy later said: "I still fancied it. I think after putting the first one in that Paul Cooper had over compensated to stop me doing the same again. It was a good feeling."

Indeed, Everton had the ball in the net three times in the first five minutes (an Andy Gray header adding to Sheedy's free-kicks), but only one goal counted.

Lowly Town hit back to lead 2-1 at half-time thanks to Kevin Wilson and Romeo Zondervan and were holding on with 10 men after Steve McCall had been dismissed. But with four minutes left, Pat Van den Hauwe crossed from the right and defender Mountfield slid in for his ninth of the season to earn a quarter-final replay and maintain the record of not having been beaten at home in the FA Cup since 1975. They won at Portman Road in the replay thanks to a Graeme Sharp penalty.

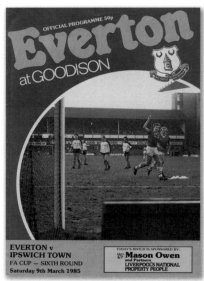

Action replay: Kevin Sheedy takes his controversial free-kick against Ipswich (top) and right, Graeme Sharp celebrates his penalty in the replay at Portman Road

Tributes to Harry

The match against Ipswich at Goodison was all the more poignant as afterwards it was announced that Harry Catterick, who was attending, had died of a heart attack.

In the Liverpool Echo tributes flooded in from both sides of Stanley Park.

Liverpool manager Joe Fagan said: "I shall be forever grateful to Harry for all he taught me about the coaching side of the game.

"I learned more about that from him than from any other person and he gave me an invaluable insight into what is a very tricky business. He gave me my first job as a coach with Rochdale and later on he recommended me to Liverpool. 'H' was a really good manager."

Former Everton captain Roy Vernon said: "Everton came before everything else with him. At times he seemed to do certain things that the players – and sometimes the supporters – didn't like.

"But in his heart it was always the best for the club. If you played well for him you got the credit. If you didn't then he made sure you knew about it."

Unfancied Luton, with the wind at their backs, proved stubborn opposition at Villa Park, and having gone close on a number of occasions, deservedly went into the interval a goal to the good thanks to Ricky Hill's superb strike.

Everton came back into the game after half-time and Paul Bracewell saw a volley hit the upright.

At the other end Neville Southall saved one-handed from Hill and also kept out Mick Harford. Kevin Sheedy blazed over and Derek Mountfield headed straight at Les Sealey.

The Blues' grip on the trophy seemed to be slipping as well as the end of their 20-match unbeaten run. But with five minutes remaining Everton were handed a lifeline. They were awarded

Degsy heads for Wembley: Derek Mountfield climbs higher than Steve Foster and Ricky Hill to register the winner

a free-kick for a foul on Mountfield 20 yards out.

Kevin Sheedy stepped up and somehow the ball bobbled into the corner. The Hatters looked a beaten side and Derek Mountfield, so prolific from set pieces, headed the winner (his 10th goal of the season) seven minutes from the end of extra time from a Sheedy ball. Cue pitch invasion.

Mountfield said: "It was fantastic to win the Cup last year, but it feels even better to be back at Wembley again."

No. 80

Fan-power

Having been on the receiving end of crowd trouble from Millwall fans at their own Kenilworth Road in the previous round, Luton fans were promised a more civilised reception from Evertonians for the 1985 FA Cup semi-final.

Supporters club chairman Mike McNally said: "We are going to Villa Park for a good day out and we don't want to think about losing. But at the end of the day, come what may, I hope that both sets of fans will be able to shake hands and help to show that not all football supporters behave like animals."

Luton player Ricky Hill said: "We all fancy our chances of causing a bit of an upset. We know Everton are favourites but we have been playing well lately. And there will be more pressure on them than on us."

Howard Kendall was cautious. He said: "Their league position is totally false. They won 4-0 away in their last match so they will have no fears about going into a semi-final."

Under the headline 'Fans a step ahead' (12/4/85), the Echo reported: 'It is expected the Blues will have over 10,000 more fans than Luton cheering them on, hopefully to Wembley.

'Luton are sending about 1,000 match tickets to Villa Park for general sale. They will have 18,000 fans at the game, which is about double their average home gate. But the club is disappointed that it was unable to sell its full allocation, of 19,200.

'Everton, on the other hand, estimate they will have 27,000 supporters.'

No.81

Tickets 'pieces of paper gold'

On the verge of a unique treble in 1985, favourites Everton had added the European Cup Winners' Cup to their first Championship success in 15 years only three days earlier, courtesy of a 3-1 triumph over Austrian side Rapid Vienna in Rotterdam.

Defender Derek Mountfield had recently been rewarded for his outstanding goalscoring form with a sponsored Toyota car, while Everton supporter Stephen Bullen of Sefton Park was travelling to Wembley on foot to raise money for the Gigs and Kids anti-heroin campaign. Bill Devine (62) made the same journey, raising money for the N.S.P.C.C.

Black market ticket prices were ten times the face value, with the best seats reportedly fetching between £250-£400. "They're like pieces of paper gold," one supporter claimed, while over 35,000 Blues fans were also expected at Wembley.

Here we go: Brookside actors get in the Cup final spirit in 1985 – as do the players' wives before their trip to Wembley (top)

The Class of '85!

Danish Cooked Meats

HAFNIA

JAKA FOODS GROUP LIMITED

Tasty game: Hafnia backs the Blues ahead of their Wembley date

Two out of three . . .

Unfortunately, Everton's exertions in Holland seemed to have taken their toll on the players, even allowing for Kevin Moran's sending off by referee Peter Willis for a foul on Peter Reid in the second half – the first such instance in 105 years of FA Cup finals.

The Blues continued to huff and puff before United's Northern Ireland midfielder Norman Whiteside – later to join Everton – curled home a goal worthy to win any final in extra time.

This gave United a first win in four attempts that season against the Blues.

It was the first instance of a match in Britain generating gate receipts exceeding £1 million.

Despite the disappointment, an estimated 250,000 people welcomed the team home on their open-top bus tour of the city.

One banner proclaimed: 'Two out of three is Scouse poetry.'

On the bus tour, Derek Mountfield said: "Our name just wasn't on the FA Cup yesterday afternoon. But it has been a tremendous season for everybody connected with Everton. This welcome home is wonderful."

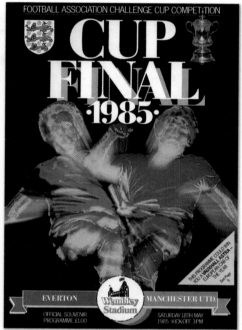

A step away from the Treble: The 1985 final programme, the dismissed Kevin Moran with Peter Reid and Neville Southall dives in vain for the extra time winner - scored by future Blue Norman Whiteside

Here We Go - on Wogan

United's Cup final song 'We All Follow Man United' reached No 10 in the UK charts, with Everton's 'Here We Go' making No 14 (one place higher than 'She Sells Sanctuary' by The Cult). This is how the Liverpool Echo reported the story on May 3rd, 1985:

'Everton's incredible winning run may soon come to an end – in the pop charts!

'Pundits in the pop world have already voted Everton's single as the better of the two, but because of United's vast following all over Britain, they look likely to put one over the Blues in the charts.

'Advance sales for Everton's record on Merseyside would be enough to give it a high placing. The United single looks like picking up lots of sales based on returns from all over the country,' said a spokesman for EMI Records who recorded both songs. The Everton squad were featured singing 'Here We Go' on The Wogan Show.

Gray day: A famous Andy Gray banner – referring to his diving headers; a Cup final song and a homecoming with three trophies on display

Andy's blue letter day

The 1985 FA Cup final proved to be the last Everton appearance of Andy Gray, who had made such a positive impact with the club since joining in November 1983.

Such was Gray's relationship with the Everton faithful that he felt compelled to write a letter to the Liverpool Echo in order to pass on his thanks to the fans. The following extracts are taken from that letter, dated June 22nd, 1985:

'My dear friends...I have never felt so moved or humble as I did when your cards started to arrive.

'I have so much to thank you all for over the last two seasons and am proud to have been part of The Everton Revival.

'Everton will always be a special place for me as it gave me two of the happiest years of my life. God bless you all and may your amazing success continue."

'Your mate forever, Andy Gray'

Pride of Britain: Despite the 1985 FA Cup final, the Blues were the kings of the country and also won their first European trophy - the Cup Winners' Cup. Below: One fan's own hen party

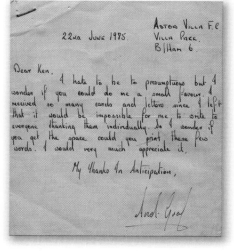

Thank you letter: Andy Gray's letter to the Liverpool Echo's Merseyside soccer correspondent Ken Rogers - who he asked to thank the Everton fans on his behalf

No. 82

White Hart gain

Although their challenge for the First Division title was dwindling, Tottenham were tricky fifth-round opposition in 1986, particularly on their home ground where Everton have always found it tough.

Howard Kendall said: "Nothing is taken for granted. It is a big Cup atmosphere and everyone will be wound up."

Paul Bracewell returned after a shin injury although Gary Stevens failed a late fitness test. Indeed, with a scratch back four and skipper Kevin Ratcliffe limping off through injury in the first half, the Blues were up against it in the pouring rain.

The reshuffle saw Alan Harper partner Pat Van den Hauwe in the centre of defence with Kevin Richardson moving to right-back and Neil Pointon at left-back.

But the changes did nothing to diminish Everton's spirit against an aggressive Spurs side. Early in the second half substitute Adrian Heath opened the scoring, squeezing the ball in from a Peter Reid cross.

Gary Lineker's diving header seemed to have ended matters but Mark Falco headed home 11 minutes from time.

Kendall's men were forced to hold on with Southall, in one of his final games of that season before injury intervened, in inspired form. A late scramble with Glenn Hoddle claiming the ball had crossed the line followed, but the Blues deservedly went through.

Kendall declared: "They were all heroes."

And he's buried it: Gary Lineker heads what proved to be the winner in the fifth-round tie at White Hart Lane in 1986

No. 83

Sharpy's volley

Due to mounting tension between football fans in Manchester and Liverpool (illustrated by a spray incident when United visited Anfield), the 1986 FA Cup semi-final was switched from Old Trafford to Villa Park. The Blues were in confident mood, chasing the Double and a third victory over the Owls that season.

Top scorer Gary Lineker was ruled out through injury while former Blues keeper Martin Hodge survived a late injury scare to take his place in the Wednesday side.

Boss Kendall said: "Most of our team have been through what can be a very tough experience on two previous occasions and hopefully they will be all the better for it.

"We have done well against Wednesday in the past, mainly because we have been prepared to take them on at what they do best. We shall go out prepared to do that again."

Wednesday chief Howard Wilkinson

said: "We're confident we can win. When we turn in one of our best performances, as we are capable of doing, we are a match for anyone."

Keeper Martin Hodge said: "I don't think anyone relishes playing against Sharp and Lineker, with their record. Everton would not only hold their own in this country, but all over the world."

Wednesday's uncompromising style caused problems throughout for injury-ravaged Everton, who saw Trevor Steven limp off in the first half to be replaced by Alan Harper. But after the break it was the unlikely figure of utility man, sub Harper, to open the scoring with a cool lob over Hodge.

The Owls equalised soon after though, Carl Shutt forcing home from close range to take the tie into extra time. Seven minutes into the extra period Sharp's superb volley from a Paul Bracewell pass saw the Blues to Wembley for a third successive year.

WEMBLEY BOUND

Sharp shooter: Graeme Sharp salutes the Evertonians after volleying the winner in the 1986 FA Cup semi-final against Sheffield Wednesday at Villa Park

Howard's salute

Howard Kendall was full of praise for two stand-ins after Everton's triumph.

"Look at Alan Harper. I have talked about him as a full-back, a central defender and a midfielder. Suddenly, I'm talking about his goal scoring ability as well.

"Bobby Mimms has played in three very big games for us since Neville Southall was injured and he has been excellent."

Liverpool's win over Southampton meant the first all-Merseyside FA Cup final was set up.

The road to Wembley: The match programmes from the 1986 FA Cup run – culminating in the semi-final against Sheffield Wednesday

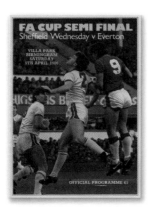

Ticket woe: One frustrated Everton fan shows how many letters he has sent in a quest to get a Wembley ticket. Top: Rival fans prepare for the big day – with a new hair cut

No. 84

Mersey fever

As expected for such an occasion, the Liverpool Echo went into overdrive in the build-up to the 1986 FA Cup.

Both teams were recording their Cup final songs on the same EMI label, but in separate studios.

Liverpool would record 'Sitting on Top of the World' and the B-side 'Running Like The Wind' at Stockport, while the Blues stayed closer to home, recording their songs 'Only 90 Minutes Away' and 'Everyone is Cheering the Blues' at the Amazon Studios at Simonswood, Kirkby. Both records were due to be released on April 21.

One gran predicted an epic clash. Liverpool psychic and medium, Mrs Ivylea Turner had predicted that Liverpool would meet Everton in the FA Cup final. The 66-year-old grandmother said she had a number of other predictions for that year. Tantalisingly, she added: "These will remain under wraps for the time being."

The local papers were full of Cup Final headlines and stories . . .

'A gift for the touts'

Everton secretary Jim Greenwood said: "We could easily sell the full 100,000. We will have major problems but it would be pointless to ask the FA for more. The tickets have already been

allocated and they take the view that it is a national occasion."

One desperate Everton fan had his own solution to the ticket crisis. He said: "You should be forced to produce a birth certificate to prove you're a true Merseysider."

Ticket concerns dominated the local news, with both clubs only being given 25,000 tickets each, the other 50,000 being distributed to other clubs and the FA.

Wives' saucy leg-pull

Cup crazy Scouse husbands were being

set up for a saucy leg-pull by their fed-up footballing wives! A local firm offering a revealing Cup Final kiss-o-gram was being inundated with inquiries.

Demand was so great for the £22 sexy stunt that more gorgeous girls were being taken on.

Scores of wives booked the one-off kiss-o-grams, which involved their husbands being surprised by a model dressed in football kit.

Sick as a parrot!

'Mad Max, the true Blue macaw, has been given the red card by pet shop boss George Roberts. Liverpool fan George is as sick as a parrot over Max's Cup Final prediction of a soaraway Everton victory,' read one Echo story.

George, 75, from City Pets, said: "He never stops squawking how Everton will pulverise Liverpool at Wembley. He sits on his perch all day saying 'Everton for the Cup'.

Double misery

Having lost out to Liverpool in their bid to retain the Championship, Everton were hoping for some consolation at Wembley, while denying Liverpool their first-ever League and Cup double.

Amongst the considerations in the lead-up to the final included the need for extra vigilance from police amid fears of a terrorist backlash due to the recent Libya bombings, while an estimated 30,000 fans travelled without a ticket.

The Liverpool Echo reported tales of singing into the small hours by both sets of fans in Covent Garden and Trafalgar Square.

At more than 50 Scouse-run pubs and clubs beer flowed throughout the night at 50p a pint.

With Bobby Mimms deputising for Neville Southall, who broke his ankle on Wales duty, veteran Northern Ireland keeper Pat Jennings was drafted in as cover.

The match started well enough for the Blues, with Gary Lineker setting Everton on their way in the first half – his 40th goal of the season – and they were looking dominant, before Liverpool hit back early in the second half with Ian Rush and Craig Johnston turning the game on its head.

Graeme Sharp had an effort brilliantly saved by Bruce Grobbelaar after Alan Hansen's mistake but after Gary Stevens was sacrificed for Adrian Heath, Rush took advantage in space to fire home the third and heap more misery on the Blues.

"In the end I was getting so many complaints from Liverpool fans I had to act." But until the game is played, George is staying at the back of the shop. His owner said: "I have even tried dressing him up in a Liverpool rosette, but he still backs Everton. He must be the daftest parrot around."'

Macca's black market blues

The Echo reported that Paul McCartney was forced to splash out more than £1,000 on the black market to ensure seven family members could attend the game.

A friend claimed the millionaire musician had paid £1,050 after a deal with an agency, which demanded £150 for tickets with a face value of £25.

Back on Merseyside the ex-Beatle's brother, Mike, said: "Paul was speaking to me last night about the arrangements for taking the clan down to the match, but he did not mention how much he had paid. The older members of the family were from Everton originally, so they will be supporting the Blues."

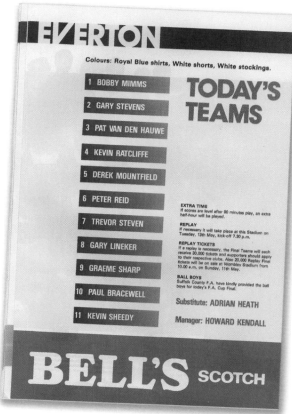

Everton 1986: The team line-up from the programme.
Above: A good luck kiss for Peter Reid ahead of the Blues' trip to Wembley, as Kevin Ratcliffe and Adrian Heath look on!

Reidy: No tour

Prior to the 1986 final both sides had agreed to do an open-top bus tour of the city on their return. The one man who missed it? Peter Reid. He said: "I shook hands with every Liverpool player, but there was no way I was getting on that bus for the drive round the city. I just couldn't have handled it. Instead, I was well away from it all in a pub in Manchester."

Margie Reid (Peter's mum) said: "It was a complete misunderstanding. He was so upset, completely gutted by the defeat, that he simply couldn't face up to the tour of the city.

"Peter was one of only two Scousers out there on the pitch. He was physically sick at losing, but he was still the one who rounded up the players at Wembley to salute the fans. You can only drive yourself so far and after the game he just went under.

"The players had their banquet in London on Saturday night and we all worked very hard at trying to enjoy it. Just before he went to bed, Peter came to me and said 'Mum, it's just a nightmare.'

"The lad was absolutely shattered. There is no truth in the stories that he snubbed the fans yesterday, nor the rumours that he had flown out to meet Cologne officials. He loves the supporters and desperately wanted to win the Cup for them.

"He would have been facing all those fans, in his eyes, as a failure. He doesn't like to be second best. He's a winner and that is why he is such a good player.

"I hope people understand why he was missing from that parade."

Long player: Two of the programmes from the four-game tie against Sheffield Wednesday in 1988. Right: Graeme Sharp on target in the first replay at Goodison

No.86

Wednesday marathon

One of the longest ties in FA Cup history occurred in January 1988 between Sheffield Wednesday and Everton. Little could separate the sides after the first third-round game at Hillsborough and two games at Goodison.

The first Goodison replay needed a Graeme Sharp volleyed equaliser 15 minutes from time to earn a 1-1 draw. The third game saw Everton go ahead for the first time in the tie through Trevor Steven's 58th-minute header, while in the third replay in South Yorkshire, Everton took advantage of a pre-match injury to Owls defender Lawrie Madden, who had been a rock for Wednesday in the previous games.

Colin West missed a good opening for the home side after only 15 seconds but then the visitors in all yellow took

charge. An impressive hat-trick from Graeme Sharp – which many visiting fans missed having been caught in heavy traffic – helped the Blues to a 5-0 romp, with Adrian Heath and Ian Snodin also on target before the break.

The visitors cruised through the second half with Paul Bracewell coming on in the second half, his first senior appearance since the 1986 FA Cup final due to injury.

Incidentally, between January 1 and January 27, Everton played Wednesday five times and discounting the tie against Bolton in 1887-88, it is the longest FA Cup marathon in Everton history.

No.87

Rats v Vinny: The revenge

Having drawn 1-1 in a stormy League encounter a month earlier (which had seen Vinny Jones sent off for clashing with Kevin Ratcliffe), a lively quarter-final tie was expected in March 1989, against the Wimbledon 'Crazy Gang'.

Stuart McCall's goal from close range, only his second in Everton colours settled the tie and Jones was brought on soon after.

Years later, Ratcliffe recalled the game on a fans' website. He said: "It was billed as the Ratcliffe and Jones

refight type of thing. It had us side-by-side in the papers with height, reach, weight, and it was ridiculous. I took stick for supposedly taking a dive! He was upset, I think it cost him a boot deal!

"Vinny was a sub and when he came on he got the biggest boo you've ever heard. He ran on past Sheeds, who thought he was going to chin him. Sheeds had his fists up!"

Football doesn't matter

With Norwich riding high in the First Division (despite having lost four out of their last five matches) under the stewardship of Dave Stringer and his assistant David Williams, Everton faced a tough task in their bid to reach their fourth final in six years in what was their 22nd semi-final.

Backed by 25,000 fans, Everton sneaked through thanks to Pat Nevin's scrambled effort after 26 minutes. Ian Crook deflected a Trevor Steven cross onto his own crossbar, and after Kevin Sheedy could only mishit the rebound against the left-hand post, Nevin pounced.

Referee George Courtney blew the final whistle at around 4.42pm, signalling a pitch invasion. Harvey punched the air before moving along the touchline, stopping only to wave to family and friends in the crowd.

Pat Nevin also took an age to reach the dressing room, having been carried shoulder high from one side of the pitch to the other. But within 20 minutes of the final whistle, Everton's celebrations had ended because of the realisation of what had happened in the match between Liverpool and Nottingham Forest in the other semi-final. Radio and television reports revealed a shocking tragedy had unfolded in Sheffield.

The Liverpool Echo's Paul Byrne reported: 'News of the Hillsborough disaster left Evertonians stunned, shocked and numb as they filed away from their semi-final victory over Norwich. Instead of cheers there were tears, as the full extent of the tragedy hit home.'

Pat's day: Pat Nevin scores the semi-final winner in 1989, celebrates and Tony Cottee is mobbed (below) by the fans ... all before the devastating news had filtered through from Hillsborough

Just one family

Blues boss Harvey echoed everyone's thoughts. He said: "It's terrible. Everyone is very sad in the dressing room. We came off feeling full of the joys of spring and then we heard about Hillsborough. Our thoughts are with all the families of the people who have died over there."

The next day Harvey widened his thoughts when he said: "We are not a divided city. There are Evertonians and Liverpudlians in the same family.

"It was always going to be an occasion when we would come together and help each other.

"We reached Wembley on Saturday, but our feelings went from absolute elation to the very opposite when we heard what had happened.

"It wasn't until we got home and saw the TV that we realised the full implications of the disaster."

No. 89

The city unites

The spectre of the Hillsborough disaster loomed large as Merseyside united at Wembley for the FA Cup final, which was scheduled a week later than planned, after Liverpool's replayed semi-final with Nottingham Forest on May 7.

Much of the Liverpool Echo coverage centred on the fact that touts were again cashing in on a big Wembley final.

Reporter Paul Byrne noted how, having answered an advertisement in The Times, he was quoted £100 for an £8 standing ticket, while stand seats were £225 for a £32 ticket.

Liverpool manager Kenny Dalglish said: "You can't pick and choose your opponents, but if we could have chosen it would have to be Everton. They have made their own contribution to the city of Liverpool and they have helped a lot of people. Everton have brought a lot of joy here during the 1980s and are there on merit. They have our total respect as a club and as a team.

"The fans here are unique in that they get on so well together. They mingle freely, and respect each other.

"That's not just important for Saturday, it's important for football."

The Liverpool Echo reported: 'Thousands of red and blue scarves left on Anfield's Kop, in memory of the 95 who died at Hillsborough, are to be sold off tomorrow to Cup Final fans.'

The money was to go to the Hillsborough families.

Top men: Tony Cottee and Kevin Ratcliffe wear it well; rival fans arm in arm on Wembley Way and the fans stick together. Right: Graeme Sharp is mobbed

Harvey's heroes edged out

It was to be Everton's 11th Wembley appearance in only five years (their last being just three weeks previous, a 4-3 Simod Cup final defeat to Nottingham Forest), and unlike previous finals, each side was allocated more tickets than normal – in this case 37,000 each.

Kevin Sheedy and Pat Van den Hauwe overcame injury scares to take their place while Ian Wilson was preferred on the bench to Wayne Clarke.

Liverpool were strong favourites, having won 19 of 22 games in an unbeaten run which had taken them to within reach of a second double.

Colin Harvey said: "Our cup campaigns this season have been very good and while we haven't been able to turn it on in the league, we have been able to divorce one from the other and we just hope we keep it that way on Saturday."

Adrian Heath said: "I've got a sneaking feeling for Everton. I certainly hope the Blues win, especially for Colin Harvey.

"He deserves it because nobody cares more about the club than him. The day when he was going to get all the headlines, the tragedy happened."

The right spirit

Speaking after the match, Blues boss Harvey said: "The game was very competitive. What both teams wanted was a game played in the right spirit, and the crowd to watch it in the right spirit, which they did.

"The barriers were down, and people came on the pitch but I don't think that meant a thing on the day."

Stuart McCall said: "It was beyond my wildest dreams to get two goals at Wembley. But it was a real sickener for the supporters who have backed us through our cup campaign."

Tony Cottee added: "I didn't do myself justice and felt very tired after the first 15 minutes. When I put my foot on the accelerator there was nothing there. The whole day was a very tiring experience."

Ticket but no seat!

It appeared that at least 100 fans at Wembley bought tickets for seats that did not exist.

The blunder came about because of building work at the stadium, which was due to become all seated by the end of that year.

Euro MP Andrew Pearce was astonished to find his £26 seat had been removed to create a wider stairway. He said: "This is our national stadium. They ought to be able to get these things right."

Liverpool band The Spinners took centre stage with Gerry Marsden before the match.

There was also a minute's silence observed in memory of the people who died at Hillsborough.

Everton kicked-off, wearing their new home kit, but for much of the game it was Liverpool who were the ones to watch.

They dominated the midfield early on, opened the scoring, and missed further chances before the introduction of Stuart McCall for Paul Bracewell. Ian Wilson later came on for Kevin Sheedy.

It was John Aldridge who got the fourth-minute opener. But that was the only goal separating the teams as the final entered injury time.

Then a break from Pat Nevin set up Dave Watson whose shot was parried into the path of sub McCall to take the tie into extra time.

Fellow sub Ian Rush put the Reds ahead again early in the extra period (a record 20th goal in a derby), but it was McCall again who hit back, volleying home from 20 yards before Rush struck again just before the end of the first half of extra time.

This time it was the winner.

No.90

Woking scare

Having won 4-2 at First Division West Brom in the FA Cup third round in 1991 courtesy of a Tim Buzaglo hat-trick, Vauxhall Conference side Woking were rewarded with a home tie against the Blues. However, due to ground restrictions they decided to revert the game to Goodison, but took a sizeable following including many neutrals.

Over 8,000 were expected to attend including four coach loads from West Brom. There was also a Rochdale contingent who had seen the Baggies tie after their League game was called off.

Woking were quoted at 20-1 to beat Everton but the team six divisions below the Blues restricted Everton's chances, with even the visiting fans chanting: "Are you West Brom in disguise?"

It took the second half before Kevin Sheedy volleyed home but it was the only goal the Blues could muster. As well as being given a standing ovation, the Cards also left Merseyside over £80,000 richer from their share of the gate receipts paid by the 34,000-plus crowd.

Huyton-born Woking striker Paul Mulvaney wrote a letter to the Echo after the game. He said: "I must congratulate the people of Liverpool. You have given Woking players and fans a fabulous day to remember. It made me proud of my home town."

No.91

Spot of derby controversy

There was another all-Merseyside affair in the FA Cup in 1991 – a tie that would go down in history for many reasons.

Everton had lost 3-1 in the League eight days earlier. This live *Match of the Day* fifth-round tie of February 17th was a much closer affair.

Record derby goalscorer Ian Rush returned to the Liverpool side, but another returnee, Steve McMahon, suffered serious knee tendon damage in a tackle on John Ebbrell while the Blues were denied a penalty by referee Neil Midgeley when Gary Ablett appeared to bring down Pat Nevin in the area. The 0-0 draw meant Everton

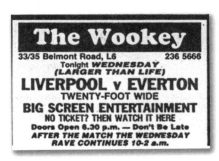

No.92

4-4 and all that

In the build-up to the replay, stories ranged from the clamour for replay tickets to Everton assistant groundsman Wally Stone and his 'little' secret.

Boss Kendall said: "It's shaping up to be a rather special evening which makes you think back to the last time our fans really raised the roof here. That Bayern game was very special."

had ended a run of five successive derby defeats.

Everton boss Howard Kendall, now back at Goodison for a second time, said: "My immediate reaction was that Pat Nevin got the first touch and was brought down in the area. He doesn't feign it, but he's been down twice at Anfield within two games. The vocal support was unbelievable, just like derby games as I used to remember."

Not surprisingly, Reds boss Dalglish replied: "It didn't look like a penalty to me."

Former Goodison favourite Andy King, having picked up the gauntlet in the shape of a pre-match bet with Tommy Smith, said it all. "Tell him he should pay out", chirped Kingy, "because surely we won on points!"

"No way", said the Anfield Iron. "The money rides on to Wednesday."

There was a lot of banter at Bellefield when it was revealed that assistant groundsman Wally Stone had been a closet Liverpudlian for years. He was only found out when the BBC went into their archives in the build-up to the FA Cup clash at Anfield and broadcast some black and white footage from the Sixties.

It showed the pipe-smoking Bellefield man in a street interview, extolling the virtues of his beloved Reds!

Howard Kendall & Co. recognised

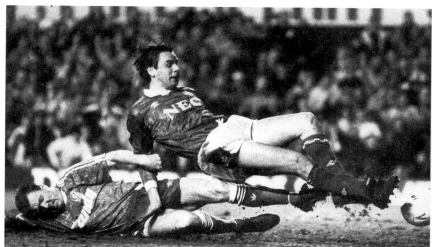

Wally straight away and insisted he prove his allegiance by holding a banner: 'Wally – A True Blue.'

Pat Nevin said: "It's going to be a brilliant atmosphere. I feel more geared up and excited about this game than the FA Cup final itself in 1989 which is a strange thing."

Similar to the first game at Anfield, Everton started with five men in defence – except they went for a 5-3-2 formation with Andy Hinchcliffe back in the side, while Liverpool, due to injuries, saw David Burrows partner

Jan Molby in central midfield. Peter Beardsley started his first game since December 15.

Four times Everton were behind, yet four times they hit back to earn a second replay. Graeme Sharp struck twice after Peter Beardsley's double had twice given Liverpool the lead and Ian Rush's header looked to have won it for the Reds. But up popped 85th-minute sub Tony Cottee to take it to extra time. John Barnes curled a beauty past Neville Southall, but late on Cottee made it 4-4.

Night of pure drama: The Blues refused to be beaten and came back time and time again. Top: Tony Cottee beats Gary Ablett to score; above left Graeme Sharp scrambles the ball home and scores again, right

The greatest ...

After the game, Blues boss Kendall said: "It was one of the greatest cup ties of all time - and one of the greatest derbies. I am proud to have been involved."

Graeme Sharp said: "It was the greatest game I have ever played in. I don't think you will ever see a game like that again."

An Echo report, under the headline 'A Knockout Show,' declared: 'It was a night that touched on all the emotions.'

No.93

Waggy's winner

Kenny Dalglish had shocked the red half of Merseyside by resigning as manager following the 4-4 draw. Both sides had lost the weekend after the epic replay – Everton at home to Sheffield United and Liverpool at Luton. It was little surprise that the second replay at Goodison (Everton having won the toss of a coin to stage the game) failed to live up to expectation.

A match of few chances was won when Dave Watson (a 33-1 bet to score the first goal) scrambled the ball home after Martin Keown's effort was parried by Bruce Grobbelaar on 12 minutes to send managerless Liverpool to their first derby defeat since March 1988. Having taken the lead for the first time in 222 minutes in the tie, Everton fought a rearguard action for the rest of the match and could thank Neville Southall for a string of fine saves, most notably from Ian Rush, Ray Houghton and Steve Nicol.

Hero Watson said: "I thought we defended very well. Liverpool threw everything they had at us but our back line held. We just hung on in there."

Agony and ecstasy: Liverpool keeper Bruce Grobbelaar is in despair but it's all smiles after the 4-4 in 1991 for Graeme Sharp and Pat Nevin

Home and dry: Match programme from the third derby game of the tie. Right: The 1990s saw the launch of Radio Everton

No.94

Canaries grounded

Just over three months into Joe Royle's Everton reign, the Blues found themselves in a more positive state of mind in February 1995. Out of the bottom three in the League, they welcomed a Norwich City side in freefall to Goodison Park in the FA Cup fifth round, having despatched Derby County and Bristol City in the earlier rounds.

It proved to be one of the most memorable games of Royle's reign. Norwich were pummelled 5-0 and had Jon Newsome sent off. On-loan goalkeeper Simon Tracey had a nightmare afternoon (getting his hands to each of Everton's first three goals) as the Canaries fell to defeat at Goodison for a second time in as many weeks.

Everton were ruthless with on-song Duncan Ferguson's run though the middle and arrogant finish off the underside of the bar probably the pick of the goals.

The result also left Canaries fans chanting for the dismissal of their manager John Deehan.

Watson sinks Geordies

Matt Jackson returned to the Everton starting XI for the home quarter-final with Kevin Keegan's Newcastle United, having lost his place to Earl Barrett. He had made 20 successive appearances before the Aston Villa defender joined the Blues and had played only once since then –

against Norwich in the fifth round, with Barrett ineligible.

He said: "It's a strange position. My last appearance came in a 5-0 victory and I've not been involved since. I have only played two reserve games, so it's difficult to adjust."

Andy Hinchcliffe was ruled out and Joe Royle decided to move Gary Ablett to centre-half with David

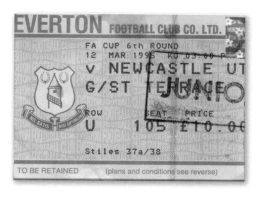

Unsworth moving to left-back while John Ebbrell was available after suspension, and expected to replace Vinny Samways. For Newcastle, Peter Beardsley returned after injury although defender Steve Howey was suspended.

On the eve of the tie the Liverpool Echo carried the following story: 'BBC radio commentator Mike Ingham has reportedly quit in protest from the selection panel which chose Everton's

Duncan Ferguson as Carling February Player of the Month.'

Newcastle were favourites against an Everton side who were still in a relegation battle. Chances were missed at either end. Paul Kitson, Lee Clark and Ruel Fox were denied by Neville Southall in the first half, while Stuart Barlow, when clean through, saw an effort turned onto the bar by Pavel Srnicek. It was left to Everton skipper Dave Watson to head the only goal midway through the second half.

Unsworth's free-kick from near the dugouts caused defensive confusion with future Blue Marc Hottiger only able to head Ferguson's header up into the air. This allowed Watson to head home despite the efforts of Srnicek.

Watson was 33-1 to score first. He won all three man-of-the-match awards from the sponsors' lounges, having booked the Blues a place in a record 23rd semi-final. The team had yet to concede a goal in the competition and the last time this had happened was a famous Cup year – 1966.

Afterwards, Watson remarked: "I believe Gary Lineker has tipped us to go out in the last two rounds so when I spoke to him after the match I told him he has to back Spurs for Wembley!"

Blues go marching on: Dave Watson climbs to head home and send the Blues through to a semi-final against Spurs

'Not worth turning up ...'

All the talk was of Tottenham in the lead-up to the FA Cup semi-final of 1995.

An FA charge the previous summer, relating to the mishandling of financial affairs, had not only seen Tottenham fined £1.5m, but docked 12 points and banned from that season's FA Cup - the latter two charges later being quashed on appeal.

There was, so it seemed, more sympathy for Spurs in the Press - a point not missed by Blues boss Joe Royle, who believed the overwhelming wish of the country was for a Manchester United v Tottenham final.

"I have read the papers and seen what they all say. There's really no point in us turning up," he said cheekily.

Midfielder Barry Horne, was happy for Spurs to be favourites. "There's certainly nothing to be nervous about," he said. "The media has already decided on Manchester United v Spurs, but that's probably because it hands them a story on a plate with the team that shouldn't even be in the competition making it to Wembley."

So much for the 'dream final'

It proved to be one of Everton's most complete performances ever, in terms of pre-match expectations and the fact that Joe Royle's so-called 'Dogs of War' were expected to roll over with Spurs set to take their place in a 'Dream final' with Manchester United.

The Blues were backed by 18,000 Evertonians on three sides of the ground with two giant 80 feet x 40 feet flags, bought by the club, being shown off beforehand while Spurs fans took up the huge East Stand at Elland Road for the 1.30pm kick-off.

Once Matt Jackson had headed the Blues in front from an Andy Hinchcliffe corner, it was one-way traffic with Horne and Joe Parkinson in particular dominant in midfield.

Paul Rideout saw a goal chalked off early in the second half and straight from the free-kick, Everton did indeed double their advantage. Graham Stuart struck after Ian Walker could only parry Rideout's effort, and it all looked plain-sailing before Spurs were handed a lifeline when Teddy Sheringham was adjudged to have been leaned on by Dave Watson in the area and Jurgen Klinsmann fired home from the spot.

But it was to be the day Daniel Amokachi re-ignited his Everton career in remarkable and famous circumstances. Rideout suffered an injury and was receiving treatment. He could have carried on, but the eager Amokachi rushed on the pitch with the action resuming.

Any panic was soon brushed to one side as the Nigerian netted two goals in the final eight minutes to book Everton's passage.

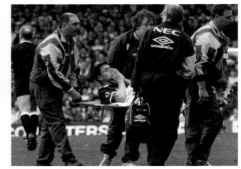

Elland heaven: Paul Rideout is carried off the Elland Road pitch (right); 'Amo' dives to score past Ian Walker and a North Stand ticket from the game

Best sub that never was

Manager Joe Royle laughed about Daniel Amokachi afterwards and said: "It was the best substitution I never made."

He added: "I shouldn't be here, should I? Sorry about the dream final lads. We played a lot of good football, which is perhaps surprising to one or two of you having read the previews. So ******s to you. And that's double 'L'. Only joking lads.

"Daniel took his goals well, but to be honest he shouldn't have even been on the pitch.

"The signs from Rideout and the physio were that Paul would be ready to carry on. Daniel had misinterpreted it and walked onto the pitch. He was desperate to get on. It was a great mistake, wasn't it?

"I want to hear 'dogs of war' for the last time today. We went out there as underdogs of war, and outplayed them. That's the last time I want to hear that phrase."

David Prentice in the Liverpool Echo added: 'Everton upset everybody. The media tipsters, the Spurs supporters who invaded the pitch two minutes before the final whistle and tried to break Neville Southall's crossbar, even fate.'

Incidentally, it was only Everton's second victory at Elland Road in any competition since 1951.

Dan is the man: Daniel Amokachi celebrates and (above right) is presented with the photo by the Echo. A fan in party mood and (below) Matt Jackson is mobbed after his goal

EFC 170

1995
The Bluenose final

'All Together Now', Mystic Meg, Amo's beret - all were in evidence as the 'Dogs of War' claimed Wembley glory . . .

Blues stand together

Ticket troubles dominated the build-up to Everton's first FA Cup final appearance in six years, although for once, a club released a Cup final record to be proud of . . .

No expense spared

One group of Evertonians were determined to enjoy the 1995 final in style. Joseph Clay and his friends blazed the Wembley trail in two 23-foot long stretch limousines.

The 12-strong bunch decided to blow the expense and travel first-class.

Record signing

The Everton squad signed copies of their FA Cup final release 'All Together Now' at Virgin Records in Liverpool city centre in the build-up to the big game.

Wash out for fan

Everton fan Patrick Gill faced a Wembley washout after being hit by a double whammy.

The 11-year-old left one of his ticket stubs – which had to be saved to qualify for a cup final ticket – and another belonging to his dad in a shirt pocket.

But his mum put the shirt in the wash.

When they realised the blunder it was too late anyway – thieves had stripped the clothes line.

As a result Patrick and his dad Derek Hutson, of Fonthill Close, Kirkdale, had just three Everton match stubs and were left sweating on FA Cup final tickets when queuing began.

Mum Margaret Gill said: "After the match last Wednesday I told him to take the tickets out of his shirt, but he obviously forgot.

"The shirt went in the wash and was hung out to dry.

"On Saturday morning all the washing was stolen and it was only later we realised the ticket stubs were in the shirt.

"They may have been worse for wear, but at least it might have been some proof they had been to the game.

"Now it means that with only three stubs they will have less chance of getting Wembley tickets."

Clothes worth £190, including underwear, were taken from the line, Merseyside Police confirmed.

Everton fans attending the last four home games had a chance of a Wembley ticket on a first come, first served basis by presenting used ticket stubs.

Prepare for queues

Hundreds of Blues fans were expected to start queuing at Goodison Park for the chance of grabbing a precious Cup Final ticket.

Some were intent on lining up at 9pm – 10 hours before the ticket office opened at 7am.

Police and club stewards were on hand to keep order and make sure residents were not disturbed.

Refreshment facilities and portable toilets were made available for the overnight vigil.

Inspector Ray Johnston, of the Merseyside Police football unit, said beforehand: "We will be keeping a low profile, but if anyone does get out of hand they can expect to be arrested."

Pray for victory

Everton had God on their side as they set out for the Twin Towers of Wembley... in the shape of true blue vicar Harry Ross.

Mr Ross, vicar of St Luke's at the corner of Goodison Park, went to Wembley dressed as he always is on match day, in blue and white - a clerical blue shirt and white dog collar.

Mr Ross, unofficial Everton chaplain, who never misses a home match if he can help it, said as he set out: "I'm praying for victory.

"I've a feeling it will be a very tight game and one goal will make the difference.

"I prefer being the underdogs like we are and I think even Liverpool supporters want us to beat Manchester United!"

Mr Ross was on his knees when Everton were bottom of the Carling Premier League in October, the only team in the country without a win.

He said at the time: "Prayers can raise the dead - I'm just hoping we are not dead and gone!"

Now he said: "My prayers were answered and now we're at Wembley."

1995

All together now and forever: Reverend Harry Ross at St Luke's Church

EVERTON F.C. MERCHANDISE

Have your favourite players name and number printed on your shirt.
Call at the club shop for details.

■ KANGOL BERET £5.99

NOW OPEN
Merchandise Kiosks in the Park Stand and Gwladys Street Concourses

Beware of street traders. These people have no connection with Everton FC. Only purchase items from the official club shop.

■ SALE OF MANY T-SHIRTS REDUCED TO £7.99

Blue berets: The queues build at Goodison (below). Left: Official products at the time included an Amo beret

'We're sorry' say Everton

Everton apologised for the ticket fiasco that shattered the Wembley dream of thousands of fans.

Director Cliff Finch admitted the club had got it wrong in the way it organised the distribution of Cup Final tickets.

The chaotic scenes outside Goodison Park were top of the agenda as club bosses and police held an inquiry into what happened.

Mr Finch said: "I am deeply disappointed that arrangements were not handled better.

"This is something that will not be allowed to occur again."

Fans were disappointed and angry at the ticket allocation.

Many blasted the arrangements which led to people panicking as massive queues built up on Saturday night and Sunday morning.

Police reinforcements were drafted in as it became clear demand was going to exceed supply. Some supporters came away without a ticket despite queuing for 16 hours.

Inspector Tom King, of Merseyside Police's football unit, said: "We intend to ask the club for some answers. It was

never made clear how many tickets were available and it became quite obvious at the outset that not everybody was going to be satisfied.

"Most of the fans were responsible and well behaved.

"However, there was an element of queue jumping which caused problems. Panic set in when supporters realised they may be disappointed."

Everton secretary Michael Dunford said: "Clearly when you have 31,000 people regularly attending games and only 26,000 tickets to distribute some people are going to miss out."

Fan Paul Allison said: "The club knew how many tickets they had.

"Why didn't they tell us on Saturday night that there was no point queuing beyond a certain number?"

Furious supporter Alfy Hicks said: "I am surprised no-one was seriously injured.

"It was a disgraceful way to organise things.

"I would like the club to break down exactly where all the tickets have gone.

"Many fans were conned into going to the last four home games only to become involved in a free-for-all fight for a ticket."

Bill's final frontier

Wembley workaholic Bill 'Dad' Devine was preparing for his 10th trip to watch the Blues at the Twin Towers in 1995 – on foot!

Bill, a sprightly 72, had made the solo trek to Wembley nine times before, starting with Everton's historic meeting with Liverpool in the 1984 Milk Cup final.

The Blues season-ticket holder walked to the big matches to raise money for the Royal School for the Blind.

He said: "It usually takes me about a

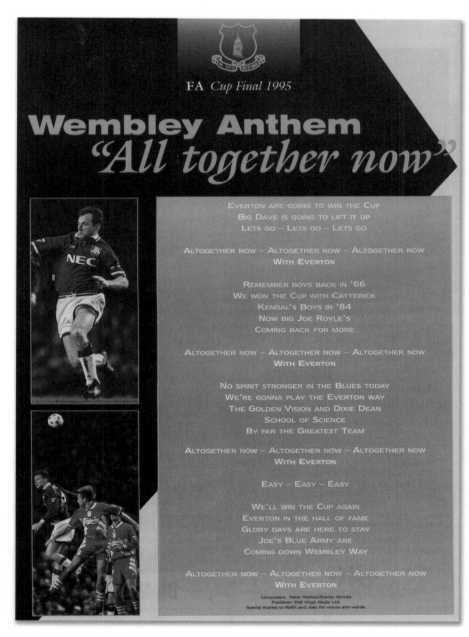

week, although it took five days once!

"This time it will take me about 10 days. I usually meet a lot of people on the way, but I never get the chance to stop and talk to them. This time I will."

Bill plans to take in Everton's match at Coventry on the way.

"After that I'll have a week to get to Wembley and it's only about a hundred miles from there so that will be no problem."

Singing for Wembley: The words to the famous anthem (above) and some Blues fashion-wear fans might have been wearing in 1995 (right)

Cup fever: The Liverpool Echo's FA Cup souvenir special hit the shops

Blue noses conk out

The Liverpool Echo reported: 'Here is the nose news. Sorry folks, they've all gone.

'The good news is there are up to 30,000 of you Blue Noses out there.

'Our final batch of 5,000 colourful conks arrived this morning after being rushed up from the over-worked suppliers in the Midlands.

'They were snapped up at our Old Hall Street offices by True Blues early today.

'None have been available at Everton's Goodison Park Shop after they ran out yesterday.'

Derby foe backs Blues to win

Old foe Ian Rush was tipping the Blues for cup success on the eve of the final.

'Everton will win the FA Cup,' he told the Liverpool Echo. 'United don't seem to like playing Everton and now they've lost the League I reckon it will be even harder to win tomorrow.'

It's in the stars

Everton will repeat their Wembley heroics of 1966 and win 3-2 in a classic FA Cup final.

That was the prediction of National Lottery fortune teller Mystic Meg in the Liverpool Echo.

It was reported: 'Meg's forecast is worth taking seriously. After all, she said Everton would win the cup even before the third-round matches were played back in January.

She also predicts: 'The Blues' scorers will be Paul Rideout, Daniel Amokachi and David Unsworth (pen); Ryan Giggs will score at least one of United's goals; Neville Southall will save a penalty; a female streaker may run onto the pitch.'

Meg explained how she tipped the Blues, saying: "I cast my Rune Stones. This is an ancient alphabet that also has magical powers of prediction. It spelt out a name that looked very like Everton."

Meg's top line showed the letters of the Rune Stones alphabet. The second line revealed how the letters she cast corresponded to the normal alphabet. They spelt the name 'EFERTON'.

The third lines showed how Meg's Rune Stones fell after Everton beat Tottenham in the semi-final.

Mystic Meg said: "This time they give the letters J. R. So it looks like Joe Royle will be celebrating."

Back in January, Meg said that Everton would beat Newcastle at Wembley, a prediction which collapsed when they beat the Geordies 1-0 in the quarter-finals.

But Meg now said: "I saw that Newcastle would be Everton's biggest challenge, so I thought this meant that they would meet in the final. The oracles do need interpreting. And, of course, I don't always do this correctly."

She added: "Neville Southall will save a penalty very late in the final, possibly in extra time. He will be busy and brilliant!"

Two noses are better than one: Duncan Ferguson meets Alder Hey patient Peter Robinson, 14, from Litherland

IT'S IN THE STARS

Ticket cheats exposed

The Liverpool Echo and Everton FC teamed up to expose a London-based agency who had advertised in a national newspaper the chance to obtain tickets for major sporting events. Echo reporter Barry Turnbull, posing as a desperate Merseyside fan, called the company's offices and was offered tickets priced between £300 and £400.

An order was placed for three tickets using the credit card of Everton director Richard Hughes for the £30 face value tickets for the Manchester United section. Everton commercial director Cliff Finch said: "We wanted to get hold of tickets being sold illegally so we could find the source. I am pleased that they have not come from Everton Football Club."

The FA said its undercover team had been unable to obtain a single black market ticket. Under new laws touts could be fined up to £5,000.

1995

ANDY, EVERTON & THE STAFF OF BUZZ NIGHTCLUB WISH JOE ROYLE & THE EVERTON TEAM ALL THE VERY BEST AT WEMBLEY. COME ON YOU BLUES

Lucky stars: Mystic Meg predicts 'Eferton' glory and best wishes from the Buzz

Glass act: An advert from
the final match prgramme

Last orders

A drinking contest between
rival Cup Final fans at a
London pub was scrapped
after protests from police.

Everton and Manchester
United supporters arriving
at Euston Station on
Saturday had been
encouraged to rush to the
Head of Steam bar.

The winners would have
been the fans who drained
their own barrels fastest.

The pub had drafted in
barrels of Cain's beer and
ale from the Oak brewery
in Manchester. Cain's said
beer would not have been
supplied if it was known a
drinking contest was
planned.

Earlier Tony Brookes,
boss of the Newcastle-
based Head of Steam
chain, said he hoped the
competition would be
conducted in a friendly
atmosphere.

Winslow boys in blue:
Evertonians, right, from the
famous pub on Goodison
Road about to set out on the
road to Wembley

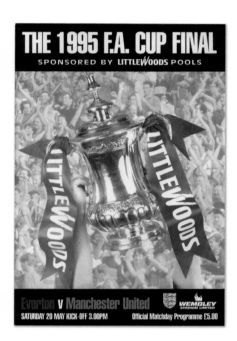

Ebbrell agony

Going into their first final for six years as underdogs, the Blues had only confirmed their Premiership status a couple of weeks before – having began the season with the worst League start in the club's history. However, they had already beaten United in the League earlier in the season and were gunning

for revenge 10 years after the Red Devils denied them a unique treble. Indeed, favourites United had suffered the setback of seeing their Premiership crown being won by Blackburn Rovers the previous Sunday.

Joe Royle was left with a selection poser beforehand, and decided to leave John Ebbrell out of the final 14, the former England U21 midfielder having missed the semi-final. Duncan Ferguson was fit enough only for the bench having recently undergone a hernia operation, while for Alex Ferguson's men Ryan Giggs, who had been out for a month with a hamstring problem, was a sub while Eric Cantona (suspended), Andrei Kanchelskis (injured) and Andy Cole (cup-tied) were unavailable.

Royle line-up: The players and boss Joe Royle prepare to meet Prince Charles on the Wembley pitch (see below, left). Above: The match programme and a ticket

Bookies back a United win

Manchester United to win outright: 4/7
Everton to win outright: 5/4
Everton to win 1-0: 8/1
Paul Rideout to score first goal: 7/1

Omens . . .

Everton had beaten The Rams, The Robins, The Canaries, The Magpies and The Peacocks on their way to the final.

1995

'Big Nev saves the day'

It was 10 years since they last faced United in a final but thankfully the result was not the same – thanks to Paul Rideout and Big Nev

In a tough-tackling affair, Lee Sharpe's header over the bar was the most either side could muster in terms of chances early on, before Anders Limpar's low shot was kept out by Peter Schmeichel at his near post. On the half-hour though, Everton struck.

Paul Ince saw an effort blocked on the edge of the Everton penalty area before Limpar picked up the loose ball. Breaking away the Blues suddenly had United out-numbered four to two in defence. Limpar switched the ball right to Matt Jackson, who cut inside and played in Graham Stuart. Stuart's side-footed effort bounced back off the crossbar but Paul Rideout reacted quickest to head home past the exposed Schmeichel and skipper Steve Bruce covering on the goalline to claim his 16th goal of the season.

From the goal to the half-time interval Everton were the more likely to score again, with Limpar causing problems and Bruce struggling with a thigh injury in the heart of the United defence. Stuart was denied by Schmeichel before the break when Bruce was taken off and Giggs came on, the reshuffle seeing Roy Keane go to right-back and Gary Neville to centre-half.

Duncan Ferguson came on for the hobbling Rideout five minutes after the break and caused problems for Gary Pallister, but it was United who piled on the pressure.

Neville Southall, the only Everton survivor from 1984, showed his quality to pull off a number of vital saves.

Daniel Amokachi was brought on for the injured Anders Limpar and on 72 minutes Paul Scholes was introduced as a last throw of the dice for United and was denied by Southall's double save 13 minutes from time after good work from Giggs.

Schmeichel almost caused chaos after leaving goal for a United corner in the last minute and after Amokachi failed to capitalise at the other end with the Danish keeper out of goal, referee Gerald Ashby blew his whistle to realise the dream of thousands of fans.

EVERTON: Southall, Jackson, Ablett, Unsworth, Watson, Limpar (Amokachi 69), Horne, Parkinson, Stuart, Rideout (Ferguson 51), Hinchcliffe. Sub not used: Kearton.

MANCHESTER UNITED: Schmeichel, G. Neville, Irwin, Bruce (Giggs 46), Pallister, Butt, Keane, Ince, McClair, Hughes, Sharpe (Scholes 72). Sub not used: Walsh.

GOALSCORER: EVERTON Rideout (25).
ATTENDANCE: 79,592.

1995

The cup that cheers:
Paul Rideout wheels away
in celebration after his
all-important goal

'It was for the fans'

Feels nicer because I'm older

"I'm happy with the way the season has turned out but I'm not happy with the way things were. We were a disgrace for part of the season. We gave our fans a torrid time and staying in the Premiership was the main achievement.

"But we had to do something like this for all those people who went to places like Wimbledon and Crystal Palace on cold wet nights. They deserve this – it's for them.

"This one feels nicer because I'm older and can appreciate it more. The next trophy I win could be the Auto Windscreens Shield."

Everton hero, goalkeeper Neville Southall

Fans won us the FA Cup

"Winning the cup was a tremendous feeling – but I'm left wondering if this was my last game for Everton. Being realistic, I have got to think of my long-term future.

"My contract is up this summer, and I don't want to leave – I am desperate to stay. I love the club and would sign for 10 years if I could. I just want to play.

"United didn't really give us too much trouble down their left.

"That was where they were trying to get through. I had a couple of words with Anders (Limpar) early in the game and he said it had woken him up and done him good."

"The fans have done the same all season. It is a simple fact.

"They kept their club up and now they have won them the FA Cup."

Everton defender Matt Jackson

Thinking about Europe now

"They are a great bunch of lads. I don't think we will be anyone's favourites for relegation next season. And we can start thinking about Europe now. The players deserve it."

Everton manager Joe Royle

1995

A Royle celebration

The celebration banquet after the 1995 final was a Royle affair - but there was one man who shunned the bright lights for the simple comforts of home life . . .

Loadsa money

A Liverpool Echo article claimed how three winning games into his tenure, Joe Royle had told the Blues board to: "Put your money on the FA Cup."

Indeed, a 'punting pal' of Royle's had taken the advice of the Everton boss and put £100 on the Blues to win the FA Cup at 33-1.

Crufts class!

Speaking on the famous 'Dogs of War' tag given to Everton, Joe Royle laughed after the final: "We are Crufts now!"

Nev heads for home

Neville Southall left his team-mates to return home to his family straight after the final at Wembley, reportedly walking his dog on Llandudno beach while the FA Cup final banquet was in full swing.

The 36-year-old did not concede a goal in open play during Everton's run, with the clean sheet in the final coming on Southall's 650th appearance.

Big Nev was typically downbeat after the team's success, telling Press: "We're just a pub team!"

Trouble 'n' strife

Michael McGovern missed out on a trip to Wembley for his own match of the day with bride Julie. The couple scored an own goal when, back in August, they set the date for Cup Final day. But Paul Rideout's goal delivered the perfect wedding present.

Sinatra Blues

"I'm delighted we've got this cup because I've followed Kevin Ratcliffe as captain and that's like following Frank Sinatra," joked skipper Dave Watson.

Joe's nerves

Boss Royle paid tribute to the team spirit that brought the Cup home.

He said: "I was slightly nervous in the last five minutes. Beating relegation was the battle when I arrived, but to win the Cup as well is the icing on the cake and we can start thinking about Europe. I've got great lads at the club, and they deserve this."

He also had a special word for the man who chose to snub the official celebration dinner.

Royle said: "That's Neville for you –

nicely awkward. He's not shy, but he is unassuming and he's already on his way back to Llandudno. He didn't want to know about the banquet. We asked him to stay and he said 'Why?' He's his own man, and I just let him get on with it.

"From the first game he's been magnificent and I can honestly say he's not cost us a goal since I've been at the club.

"Nothing goes past him without some kind of comment. He has his own abrasive brand of humour but the rest just laugh and get on with it."

Golden feeling

Daniel Amokachi was delighted at making history. "I got on for about 15 minutes and I've got a gold medal in my pocket, which is cool," he said.

"I was disappointed because the big man wasn't playing and I thought I would be. The manager explained to me that he wanted the same side as the semi-final and so we had to stick together. But I'm the first Nigerian to play in a Cup final. I got some gold in my pocket and it feels great."

Fans 'a credit'

Just nine Everton supporters were arrested – five for being drunk and disorderly, three for being in possession of drugs and one for a breach of the peace.

Of Manchester United fans, 11 were arrested (seven for being drunk and disorderly, one for possession of drugs, one for theft, one for street trading and one for making an unlawful ticket sale).

A spokesman for Merseyside Police's football unit said: "The behaviour was exceptional.

"There were a few isolated incidents but none of the trouble was caused by Everton supporters. They were a credit to the city."

Fergie's verdict

Rival manager Alex Ferguson thought his team deserved better than a 1-0 defeat but had only words of praise for Neville Southall.

He said: "Sometimes you don't get what you deserve, and I thought we deserved better than we got. We defended absolutely terribly for the goal. We had seven men in front of the ball and I can't believe it. That kind of defending in a Cup final is crazy.

"Neville Southall had one of those games where it needed something special to beat him – and we didn't produce it.

"He had a marvellous match. I think he won Everton the Cup. I don't think we deserved to lose."

A thought for Ebbrell

Royle spared a thought for the men who didn't make his Cup final line-up.

He told the Echo: "The hardest part for me was telling John Ebbrell he wasn't going to be playing.

"It was hard with Vinny Samways and Stuart Barlow, but they hadn't played as often as John. I didn't know how to face him and I still don't know how to face him now, because he wouldn't have let us down."

Royle also singled out Anders Limpar for his contribution.

He said: "He is a genius. There was never going to be anybody on that pitch with more ability than him. You can't buy his ability. I've never seen anyone like him."

They gave us space

"Joe Royle is something extra. He dragged me back up after a sad start to the season for me and let me perform," said an ecstatic Anders Limpar.

"He has been brilliant to me. In the first half we all played well. They gave me a lot of space. Denis Irwin backed off and backed off which is great for a winger. I had five minutes when everything clicked, but genius? Steady on! When everything comes off I can have a good game, but I have to be more consistent. I thought we played well until we scored but then nerves started to come in. But it was still a brilliant day."

This is just the start . . .

"People might laugh but I fully intend to be playing for Wales and in the Premier League at 45," said who else but . . . Neville Southall.

King for a day

The FA Cup made a surprise appearance at a restaurant on its way back to Merseyside from London.

Blues defender Matt Jackson told The Evertonian magazine: "We were all split up a bit for the official banquet on the Saturday evening. I remember the alcohol taking hold fairly early.

"The next day was better, when we travelled back on the bus and I think we took the FA Cup into Burger King at one of the service stations on the way back.

"That was a little bit of a strange one for the people behind the counter!"

Stu beauty: David Unsworth and Stuart Barlow celebrate

Celebrate good times: Neville and 'Waggy' salute the fans and (below) Barry Horne with the trophy after swapping shirts

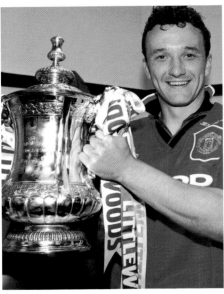

Rideout living the dream

For Paul Rideout, scoring the winning goal in a Cup final had given him a massive boost after what had occasionally been a frustrating time at Everton due to injury.

Speaking to the Liverpool Echo afterwards he admitted: "We were lucky at times.

"They had one or two chances but Neville came to the rescue. He was tremendous, but he's going about like it's any other day.

"To him it is just another day and I am a bit sad he won't be here (at the celebration banquet) tonight.

"Neville Southall has been like a father figure to me. He has always taken it on himself to look after me.

"He gave me one or two nice write-ups in his (Liverpool Echo) column at the right time which lifted me, and it's a bit sad he won't be here.

"To get the winner in a Cup Final against a side like United is an unbelievable feeling.

"It's what dreams are made of. The ball seemed to take a lifetime coming down and then I just headed it.

"It hasn't really sunk in yet. Graham Stuart was tremendous and made so many good runs, but we were wound up before the match today."

Sealed with a kiss: Paul Rideout shares the winning moment with strike partner Graham Stuart

Bluenose day: One of the most famous pictures from the 1995 triumph, left, as Duncan Ferguson dons a blue nose to lift the trophy

A Royle affair

Not everything went according to plan for the Royle family on Cup final day.

There was a brief moment of humour when Prince Charles tried to give the FA Cup to the losing captain, Steve Bruce of Manchester United, instead of Everton's Dave Watson.

Former FA chief executive Graham Kelly relayed the story in his book Sweet FA: "Bruce led his team up first as the losers and the Prince of Wales immediately reached out for the trophy to give to the losing captain, despite the blue and white ribbons and the instructions on the procedure given to him beforehand," Kelly writes.

"For a moment we wrestled with the famous trophy - as I held firmly on to the top of the Cup to stop him giving it to Bruce - before he realised what I was about."

The tale continues: "Last up the stairs was Everton manager Joe Royle and when the Prince congratulated him, Joe could not resist telling him that he was a member of his family but the Prince, not having the vaguest clue who he was, totally ignored the comment Joe passed.

"I could not help but remark that it was another one which had been totally wasted."

1995

189 EFC

A blue religion

More than 300,000 fans welcomed home Joe Royle's conquering Everton team in one of the largest and most joyous turnouts the city has seen in recent years.

The open-topped bus – bearing the symbolic number 10 (1-0) – carried the Everton players, directors and families through the city from Mather Avenue in the south of Liverpool at 3pm. It stopped everything in its tracks on the 90-minute journey.

At Liverpool University's playing fields, cricket was delayed as both sides joined in the celebrations.

Nuns wearing blue scarves clapped and cheered outside St Charles Youth

and Community Centre in Lark Lane.

Thousands were gathered outside Goodison Park and even Liverpool fans celebrated – one banner read: 'A Red for life – but a Blue for today.'

Manager Joe Royle said: "It's tremendous to see so many happy faces.

"The fans have been brilliant all

season and we can only say thanks a million to them."

Daniel Amokachi added: "Football's like a religion here and I can understand why." And goalscoring hero Paul Rideout said: "The fans have been great all season, supporting us when things weren't going well, and today caps it all."

Winning streak

A small article in the Liverpool Echo read: 'Serial streaker Mark Roberts struck again in Scotland Road.

'Wearing just a blue and white G-string he bared almost all in front of the Everton team bus.'

Boys in blue: Even the police were encouraged to take part in the celebrations! Below: The team bus gets a salute from young cadets. Far left: The empty frame of the Everton Megastore which was in the process of being built provided a great viewpoint for some fans

Champagne memories: It was a proud day for Evertonians young and old, at work and play as they took time out to salute their heroes

City united: Even
some Liverpudlians
turned out for the
victory parade.
One 'dog of war'
also enjoyed
the occasion,
decked
out in Everton
colours, left

Rhino the Lion: David Unsworth won an England call-up after the 1995 final

Generation game: The many different members of the Everton family were out in force... even if some younger members found the whole occasion a little tiring!

Unsy caps it off

David Unsworth's FA Cup final display earned the England U21 defender a senior call-up for June's Umbro Cup which saw England take on Japan, Sweden and Brazil.

With Unsworth amongst the Everton squad having departed on a mini-break to Majorca, boss Royle said: "I can see him going all the way with England. Terry Venables already knows all about him.

"He is playing in a position where you have to be mature and although he is only 21, he is mature at a young age.

"Mark Hughes is a physical player but David handled all that.

"He is a strong lad himself - a very powerful boy. His pace is also a big asset. And he can play."

With Everton having kept seven clean sheets in their final eight games, Royle also praised fellow defenders Matt Jackson, skipper Dave Watson and Gary Ablett, who became the first player to appear in - and win - an FA Cup final for both Liverpool and Everton.

Royle added: "Some players struggle to make the switch and to convince fans. David Burrows never quite did it. There were one or two others in the past. David Johnson found it hard. But Gary is winning them over."

1995

No.98

52 seconds . . . and gone!

The third-round visit of First Division Swindon Town in 1997 - managed by Steve McMahon - was seen as a 'potential FA Cup banana skin,' particularly with the Blues ravaged by injury and suspension problems.

Swindon's Mark Robinson said: "The danger is Duncan Ferguson. If we keep them at bay for 45 minutes anything can happen."

Joe Royle was clear in his plan.

He said: "We need a good start and we need to get the crowd on our side."

Swindon Town defender Ian Culverhouse claimed the unwanted record of being the quickest sending off in FA Cup history.

The former Norwich man was dismissed after only 52 seconds for handling the ball on the goal-line from an Andrei Kanchelskis shot.

The Ukrainian scored from the resulting penalty.

Everton eventually cruised through 3-0 (Nick Barmby and Ferguson netting the others) with Paul Rideout, who started his career with the Robins, dominating in an unfamiliar midfield role.

In becoming the then youngest Everton player to appear at Goodison, 17-year-old Richard Dunne enjoyed a successful debut.

The Echo's David Prentice said: "He's the biggest 17-year-old since the Honey Monster sired a son."

Swindon finished with nine men with Gary Elkins dismissed for a second bookable offence.

Fighting back: Paul Gascoigne salutes the crowd after Everton's 1-0 victory over Stoke City in the FA Cup third round of 2002 - a win which helped to ease the mounting pressure on manager Walter Smith

No.99

Gazza's final fling

In January 2002, after seeing off Stoke City, Everton welcomed Third Division opposition to Goodison in the form of Leyton Orient. Despite their lowly ranking, Everton had struggled in these fixtures in recent years. But not in this fourth-round tie as, arguably for the last time in this country, 34-year-old Paul Gascoigne reminded everyone of his class.

His slalom runs through midfield and inch-perfect passes were apparent as he set up three of the goals, the highlight being his run and pass to Kevin Campbell for the fourth goal.

Blues boss Walter Smith said: "We had a touch of vintage Gascoigne out there. A little bit of the old sharpness

The end is nigh: Walter Smith and his coaching staff preside over the debacle at The Riverside in March 2002 above, while Gascoigne salutes the home faithful, left, after his star turn against Orient

Walter's exit

The final game of Walter Smith's reign was a spineless 3-0 quarter-final defeat at Middlesbrough in March 2002, televised live to the nation.

Everton were again struggling in the Premiership but the club's FA Cup run did provide the fans with hope - only for three quick-fire Boro goals in seven minutes before half-time to signal the death knell for Smith and his assistant Archie Knox.

Noel Whelan took advantage of a mix-up between Alessandro Pistone and Steve Simonsen for the opener on 35, before Szilard Nemeth and Paul Ince added the others to put Boro into the last four for only the second time in their history and ensure a third quarter-final defeat in four years for Everton.

Paul Gascoigne made his last appearance in the FA Cup. It was also his last appearance for Everton.

A week later . . . enter David Moyes!

and strength may be missing, but he's still capable of doing things that very few footballers can achieve."

Dave McGhee's spectacular diving header into his own net after 12 minutes was not his first in the competition, having netted in almost identical fashion in the previous round at Portsmouth. Duncan Ferguson and Campbell (who spent some time on loan with the O's while at Arsenal) hit much-needed goals – Ferguson scoring from open play for the first time since April 2001 while it was Campbell's first goals since September.

Boyhood Everton fan and Leyton Orient midfielder Andy Harris said: "I saw the clock had run up and even though he'd (Gazza) said before the game he'd give me the shirt, I knew it was the one everyone wanted. Maybe I should have got a bit closer to him during the game! But I don't think anyone could get near him."

Date	Round	Venue	Opponents	Score	Scorers	Attendance
1887-88						
15th Oct	1	A	Bolton Wanderers	0-1		5,000
29th Oct	1 Replay	H	Bolton Wanderers	2-2	Farmer, Watson	7,000
12th Nov	1 Replay 2	A	Bolton Wanderers	1-1	Farmer	7,000
19th Nov	1 Replay 3	H	Bolton Wanderers	2-1	Goudie, Watson	8,000
1889-90						
18th Jan	1	H	Derby County	11-2	Brady 3, Geary 3, Milward 3, Doyle, Kirkwood	10,000
3rd Feb	2	A	Stoke City	2-4	Geary, Milward	7,000
1890-91						
17th Jan	1	A	Sunderland	0-1		21,000
1891-92						
16th Jan	1	H	Burnley	2-4	Chadwick, Robertson	3,000
1892-93						
21st Jan	1	H	West Bromwich Albion	4-1	Maxwell, Latta, Geary 2	23,867
4th Feb	2	H	Nottingham Forest	4-2	E. Chadwick, Milward 2, Geary	25,000
18th Feb	3	H	Sheffield Wednesday	3-0	E. Chadwick, Geary, Kelso (pen)	30,000
4th Mar	SF	N	Preston North End	2-2	E. Chadwick, Gordon	30,000
16th Mar	SF Replay	N	Preston North End	0-0		15,000
20th Mar	SF Replay 2	N	Preston North End	2-1	Maxwell, Gordon	20,000
25th Mar	F	N	Wolverhampton Wanderers	0-1		45,067
1893-94						
27th Jan	1	A	Stoke City	0-1		14,000
1894-95						
2nd Feb	1	A	Southport	3-0	Bell 3	7,000
16th Feb	2	H	Blackburn Rovers	1-1	Chadwick	20,000
20th Feb	2 Replay	A	Blackburn Rovers	3-2	Chadwick 2, Hartley	20,000
2nd March	3	A	Sheffield Wednesday	0-2		9,000
1895-96						
1st Feb	1	A	Nottingham Forest	2-0	Chadwick, Milward	15,000
15th Feb	2	H	Sheffield United	3-0	Milward (pen), Bell, Cameron	20,000
29th Feb	3	A	Sheffield Wednesday	0-4		12,000
1896-97						
30th Jan	1	H	Burton Wanderers	5-2	Holt, Bell, Milward, Chadwick, Archer o.g.	5,000
13th Feb	2	H	Bury	3-0	Milward, Taylor 2	14,171
27th Feb	3	H	Blackburn Rovers	2-0	Hartley 2	16,000
20th Mar	SF	N	Derby County	3-2	Hartley, Milward, Chadwick	25,000
10th Apr	F	N	Aston Villa	2-3	Bell, Boyle	65,891
1897-98						
29th Jan	1	H	Blackburn Rovers	1-0	Williams	12,000
12th Feb	2	A	Stoke City	0-0		25,000
17th Feb	2 Replay	H	Stoke City	5-1	L Bell 2, Taylor, Chadwick, Cameron	10,000
26th Feb	3	A	Burnley	3-1	Taylor 2, L Bell	20,000
19th Mar	SF	N	Derby County	1-3	Chadwick	30,000
1898-99						
28th Jan	1	H	Jarrow	3-1	Taylor, Chadwick, Proudfoot	3,000
11th Feb	2	H	Nottingham Forest	0-1		23,000
1899-00						
27th Jan	1	A	Southampton	0-3		10,000

	1	2	3	4	5	6	7	8	9	10	11
1887-88											
	Joliffe	Dick	Dobson	Higgins	Gibson	Murray	Cassidy	Farmer	Goudie	Watson	Izat
	Joliffe	Dick	Dobson	Higgins	Gibson	Murray	Cassidy	Farmer	Goudie	Watson	Izat
	Smalley	Dick	Dobson	Higgins	Gibson	Weir	Izat	Farmer	Goudie	Watson	Fleming
	Smalley	Dick	Dobson	Higgins	Gibson	Weir	Izat	Farmer	Goudie	Watson	Briscoe
1889-90											
	Smalley	Hannah	Doyle	Kirkwood	Holt	Parry	Latta	Brady	Geary	Chadwick	Milward
	Smalley	Hannah	Doyle	Kirkwood	Holt	Parry	Latta	Brady	Geary	Chadwick	Milward
1890-91											
	Angus	McLean	Doyle	Kirkwood	Holt	Parry	Latta	Geary	Robertson	Chadwick	Milward
1891-92											
	Williams	Howarth	Earp	Kelso	Holt	Robertson	Latta	Wylie	Gordon	Chadwick	Milward
1892-93											
	Williams	Kelso	Howarth	Boyle	Holt	Stewart	Latta	Maxwell	Geary	Chadwick	Milward
	Williams	Kelso	Howarth	Boyle	Holt	Stewart	Latta	Maxwell	Geary	Chadwick	Milward
	Williams	Kelso	Howarth	Boyle	Holt	Stewart	Latta	Maxwell	Geary	Chadwick	Milward
	Williams	Kelso	Howarth	Boyle	Holt	Stewart	Latta	Gordon	Maxwell	Chadwick	Milward
	Williams	Kelso	Howarth	Boyle	Holt	Stewart	Latta	Gordon	Maxwell	Chadwick	Milward
	Williams	Kelso	Howarth	Boyle	Holt	Stewart	Latta	Gordon	Maxwell	Chadwick	Milward
	Williams	Kelso	Howarth	Boyle	Holt	Stewart	Latta	Gordon	Maxwell	Chadwick	Milward
1893-94											
	Williams	Howarth	Parry	Kelso	Holt	Stewart	Latta	Bell	Southworth	Hartley	Milward
1894-95											
	Williams	Kelso	Parry	Boyle	Holt	Stewart	Reay	McInnes	Hartley	Chadwick	Bell
	Williams	Kelso	Parry	Boyle	Holt	Stewart	Milward	McInnes	Hartley	Chadwick	Bell
	Williams	Kelso	Parry	Boyle	Holt	Stewart	Geary	McInnes	Hartley	Chadwick	Milward
	Cain	Kelso	Parry	Boyle	Storrier	Elliott	Milward	McInnes	Hartley	Chadwick	Bell
1895-96											
	Hillman	Adams	Arridge	Boyle	Holt	Stewart	Bell	Hartley	Cameron	Chadwick	Milward
	Hillman	Adams	Arridge	Boyle	Holt	Stewart	Bell	McInnes	Cameron	Chadwick	Milward
	Hillman	Adams	Kelso	Goldie	Boyle	Stewart	Bell	Cameron	Storrier	Chadwick	Milward
1896-97											
	Menham	Storrier	Arridge	Boyle	Holt	Robertson	Taylor	Bell	Hartley	Chadwick	Milward
	Menham	Meehan	Arridge	Boyle	Holt	Stewart	Taylor	Bell	Hartley	Chadwick	Milward
	Menham	Meehan	Arridge	Boyle	Holt	Stewart	Taylor	Bell	Hartley	Chadwick	Milward
	Menham	Meehan	Storrier	Boyle	Holt	Stewart	Taylor	Bell	Hartley	Chadwick	Milward
	Menham	Meehan	Storrier	Boyle	Holt	Stewart	Taylor	Bell	Hartley	Chadwick	Milward
1897-98											
	Muir	Balmer	Storrier	Taylor	Holt	Robertson	Williams	Cameron	Bell L	Chadwick	Bell J
	Muir	Balmer	Storrier	Stewart	Holt	Robertson	Taylor	Cameron	Bell L	Chadwick	Bell J
	Muir	Balmer	Storrier	Stewart	Holt	Robertson	Taylor	Cameron	Bell L	Chadwick	Bell J
	Muir	Balmer	Storrier	Stewart	Holt	Robertson	Taylor	Divers	Bell L	Chadwick	Bell J
	Muir	Balmer	Storrier	Stewart	Holt	Robertson	Taylor	Divers	Bell L	Chadwick	Bell J
1898-99											
	Muir	Balmer	Molyneux	Wolstenholme	Boyle	Taylor	Bell	Proudfoot	Crompton	Chadwick	Kirwan
	Muir	Balmer	Molyneux	Wolstenholme	Boyle	Taylor	Kirwan	Proudfoot	Bell	Chadwick	Gee
1899-00											
	Muir	Eccles	Balmer	Wolstenholme	Blythe	Abbott	Sharp	Taylor	Proudfoot	Settle	Gray

Date	Round	Venue	Opponents	Score	Scorers	Attendance
1900-01						
9th Feb	1	A	Southampton	3-1	Chadwick, Settle, Taylor	12,000
23rd Feb	2	A	Sheffield United	0-2		24,659
1901-02						
25th Jan	1	A	Liverpool	2-2	Young, Sharp	25,000
30th Jan	1 Replay	H	Liverpool	0-2		20,000
1902-03						
7th Feb	1	H	Portsmouth	5-0	Sharp, Brearley, Abbott, Bell 2	32,000
21st Feb	2	H	Manchester United	3-1	Abbott, Taylor, Booth (pen)	15,000
7th Mar	3	A	Millwall	0-1		14,000
1903-04						
6th Feb	1	H	Tottenham Hotspur	1-2	Taylor	25,000
1904-05						
2nd Feb	1	A	Liverpool	1-1	Makepeace (pen)	28,000
8th Feb	1 Replay	H	Liverpool	2-1	McDermott, Hardman	40,000
18th Feb	2	A	Stoke City	4-0	McDermott 2, Makepeace (pen), Settle	25,700
4th Mar	3	H	Southampton	4-0	McDermott, Settle 3	30,000
25th Mar	SF	N	Aston Villa	1-1	Sharp	35,000
29th Mar	SF Replay	N	Aston Villa	1-2	Sharp	25,000
1905-06						
13th Jan	1	H	West Bromwich Albion	3-1	Hardman, Sharp, Makepeace	18,023
3rd Feb	2	H	Chesterfield	3-0	Settle, Young, Taylor	12,000
24th Feb	3	H	Bradford City	1-0	Makepeace	18,000
10th Mar	4	H	Sheffield Wednesday	4-3	Sharp, Taylor, Bolton, Booth	30,000
31st Mar	SF	N	Liverpool	2-0	Abbott, Hardman	37,000
21st Apr	F	N	Newcastle United	1-0	Young	75,609
1906-07						
12th Jan	1	H	Sheffield United	1-0	Johnson o.g.	35,000
2nd Feb	2	A	West Ham United	2-1	Settle, Sharp	14,000
23rd Feb	3	H	Bolton Wanderers	0-0		52,455
27th Feb	3 Replay	A	Bolton Wanderers	3-0	Taylor, Abbott, Settle	54,470
9th Mar	4	A	Crystal Palace	1-1	Taylor	35,000
13th Mar	4 Replay	H	Crystal Palace	4-0	Hardman, Settle 2, Young	34,340
25th Mar	SF	N	West Bromwich Albion	2-1	Wilson, Sharp	32,381
20th Apr	F	N	Sheffield Wednesday	1-2	Sharp	84,584
1907-08						
11th Jan	1	H	Tottenham Hotspur	1-0	Young	21,000
1st Feb	2	A	Oldham Athletic	0-0		25,690
5th Feb	2 Replay	H	Oldham Athletic	6-1	Young, Abbott, Bolton 4	25,800
22nd Feb	3	A	Bolton Wanderers	3-3	Bolton, Settle 2	30,000
26th Feb	3 Replay	H	Bolton Wanderers	3-1	Settle, Young 2	32,000
7th Mar	4	H	Southampton	0-0		40,000
11th Mar	4 Replay	A	Southampton	2-3	Young, Bolton	21,690
1908-09						
16th Jan	1	H	Barnsley	3-1	Sharp, Coleman, White	15,000
6thFeb	2	A	Manchester United	0-1		35,217
1909-10						
15th Jan	1	A	Middlesbrough	1-1	White	25,000
19th Jan	1 Replay	H	Middlesbrough	5-3	Freeman, Taylor, Young, Makepeace, White	20,000
5th Feb	2	H	Arsenal	5-0	Sharp 2 (1 pen), Barlow, Young, Freeman	30,000
9th Feb	3	H	Sunderland	2-0	Makepeace, Young	45,000
5th Mar	4	A	Coventry City	2-0	Freeman 2	19,095

	1	2	3	4	5	6	7	8	9	10	11
1900-01											
	Muir	Balmer	Eccles	Wolstenholme	Booth	Abbott	Sharp	Taylor	Proudfoot	Settle	Turner
	Muir	Balmer	Eccles	Wolstenholme	Booth	Abbott	Sharp	Taylor	Proudfoot	Settle	Turner
1901-02											
	Kitchen	Balmer	Eccles	Wolstenholme	Booth	Abbott	Sharp J	Taylor	Young	Bowman	Bell
	Kitchen	Balmer	Sharp B	Wolstenholme	Booth	Abbott	Sharp J	Taylor	Young	Bowman	Bell
1902-03											
	Whitley	Henderson	Balmer	Wolstenholme	Booth	Abbott	Sharp	Taylor	Brearley	Settle	Bell
	Whitley	Balmer	Crelley	Wolstenholme	Booth	Abbott	Rankin	Taylor	Brearley	Makepeace	Bell
	Whitley	Henderson	Balmer	Clark	Booth	Abbott	Sharp	Settle	Taylor	Young	Bell
1903-04											
	Kitchen	Balmer	Crelley	Wolstenholme	Booth	Abbott	Sharp	Taylor	Settle	McDermott	Corrin
1904-05											
	Roose	Balmer R	Crelley	Makepeace	Taylor	Abbott	Sharp	McDermott	Young	Settle	Hardman
	Roose	Balmer R	Crelley	Makepeace	Taylor	Abbott	Sharp	McDermott	Young	Settle	Hardman
	Roose	Balmer R	Crelley	Makepeace	Taylor	Abbott	Sharp	McDermott	Young	Settle	Hardman
	Roose	Balmer W	Crelley	Makepeace	Taylor	Abbott	Sharp	McDermott	Young	Settle	Hardman
	Roose	Balmer W	Crelley	Makepeace	Taylor	Abbott	Sharp	McDermitt	Young	Settle	Hardman
	Roose	Balmer W	Crelley	Makepeace	Taylor	Abbott	Sharp	McDermott	Young	Settle	Hardman
1905-06											
	Scott	Hill	Balmer W	Makepeace	Booth	Abbott	Sharp	Taylor	Young	Settle	Hardman
	Scott	Hill	Balmer W	Makepeace	Taylor	Abbott	Sharp	Cook	Young	Settle	Hardman
	Scott	Balmer W	Crelley	Makepeace	Taylor	Abbott	Sharp	Bolton	Oliver	Cook	Hardman
	Scott	Balmer R	Balmer W	Booth	Taylor	Makepeace	Sharp	Bolton	Young	Settle	Hardman
	Scott	Balmer R	Crelley	Makepeace	Taylor	Abbott	Sharp	Bolton	Young	Settle	Hardman
	Scott	Balmer W	Crelley	Makepeace	Taylor	Abbott	Sharp	Bolton	Young	Settle	Hardman
1906-07											
	Scott	Balmer W	Balmer R	Makepeace	Taylor	Chadwick	Donnachie	Bolton	Young	Settle	Wilson
	Scott	Balmer W	Balmer R	Makepeace	Taylor	Abbott	Sharp	Settle	Young	Wilson	Hardman
	Scott	Balmer W	Balmer R	Makepeace	Taylor	Abbott	Sharp	Settle	Young	Rouse	Hardman
	Scott	Balmer W	Balmer R	Makepeace	Taylor	Abbott	Sharp	Settle	Young	Wilson	Hardman
	Scott	Balmer W	Balmer R	Makepeace	Taylor	Abbott	Donnachie	Settle	Young	Wilson	Hardman
	Scott	Balmer W	Balmer R	Makepeace	Taylor	Abbott	Sharp	Settle	Young	Wilson	Hardman
	Scott	Balmer W	Balmer R	Makepeace	Taylor	Abbott	Sharp	Settle	Young	Wilson	Hardman
	Scott	Balmer W	Balmer R	Makepeace	Taylor	Abbott	Sharp	Bolton	Young	Settle	Hardman
1907-08											
	Scott	Stevenson	Balmer R	Makepeace	Taylor	Abbott	Sharp	Bolton	Young	Settle	Hardman
	Scott	Balmer W	Balmer R	Makepeace	Taylor	Abbott	Sharp	Graham	Harris	Settle	Hardman
	Scott	Balmer W	Balmer R	Makepeace	Taylor	Abbott	Sharp	Bolton	Young	Settle	Hardman
	Scott	Balmer W	Balmer R	Makepeace	Taylor	Abbott	Sharp	Bolton	Young	Settle	Hardman
	Scott	Balmer W	Balmer R	Makepeace	Taylor	Abbott	Sharp	Bolton	Young	Settle	Hardman
	Scott	Balmer W	Balmer R	Makepeace	Taylor	Abbott	Sharp	Bolton	Young	Settle	Hardman
	Scott	Balmer W	Balmer R	Makepeace	Taylor	Abbott	Sharp	Bolton	Young	Settle	Hardman
1908-09											
	Scott	Balmer R	Maconnachie	Harris	Clifford	Makepeace	Sharp	Coleman	Freeman	White	Barlow
	Scott	Balmer R	Maconnachie	Harris	Taylor	Makepeace	Sharp	Coleman	Young	White	Dawson
1909-10											
	Scott	Clifford	Maconnachie	Harris	Taylor	Makepeace	Sharp	White	Freeman	Young	Barlow
	Scott	Clifford	Maconnachie	Harris	Taylor	Makepeace	Sharp	White	Freeman	Young	Barlow
	Scott	Clifford	Maconnachie	Harris	Taylor	Makepeace	Sharp	White	Freeman	Young	Barlow
	Scott	Clifford	Maconnachie	Harris	Taylor	Makepeace	Sharp	White	Freeman	Young	Barlow
	Scott	Clifford	Maconnachie	Harris	Taylor	Makepeace	Sharp	White	Freeman	Young	Barlow

Date	Round	Venue	Opponents	Score	Scorers	Attendance
1909-10 (Cont)						
26th Mar	SF	N	Barnsley	0-0		35,000
31st Mar	SF Replay	N	Barnsley	0-3		55,000
1910-11						
14th Jan	1	A	Crystal Palace	4-0	A Young, Magnier, Gourlay, R Young	35,000
4th Feb	2	H	Liverpool	2-1	A Young 2	50,000
25th Feb	3	A	Derby County	0-5		22,892
1911-12						
13th Jan	1	A	Leyton Orient	2-1	Beare, Browell	11,000
3rd Feb	2	H	Bury	1-1	Maconnachie	32,000
8th Feb	2 Replay	A	Bury	6-0	Browell 4, Jefferis, Davidson	25,000
			(Played at Goodison Park)			
24th Feb	3	A	Oldham Athletic	2-0	Browell 2	35,473
9th Mar	4	A	Swindon Town	1-2	Makepeace	13,989
1912-13						
15th Jan	1	H	Stockport County	5-1	Wareing, T Browell 3, Bradshaw	10,000
1st Feb	2	A	Brighton & Hove Alb.	0-0		11,000
5th Feb	2 Replay	H	Brighton & Hove Alb.	1-0	Jefferis	30,000
22nd Feb	3	A	Bristol Rovers	4-0	Jefferis, Fleetwood, Harris, T Browell	15,719
8th Mar	4	H	Oldham Athletic	0-1		43,000
1913-14						
10th Jan	1	A	Glossop North End	1-2	Bradshaw	5,000
1914-15						
9th Jan	1	H	Barnsley	3-0	Galt 2, Parker	18,000
30th Jan	2	H	Bristol City	4-0	Clennell, Kirsopp, Parker, Wareing	24,000
20th Feb	3	A	Queens Park Rangers	2-1	Clennell, Broster o.g.	33,000
6th Mar	4	A	Bradford City	2-0	Chedgzoy, Clennell	26,100
27th Mar	SF	N	Chelsea	0-2		22,000
1919-20						
10th Jan	1	A	Birmingham City	0-2		44,000
1920-21						
8th Jan	1	H	Stockport County	1-0	Brewster	25,000
29 Jan	2	H	Sheffield Wednesday	1-1	Parker	44,000
3rd Feb	2 Replay	A	Sheffield Wednesday	1-0	Crossley	62,407
19th Feb	3	H	Newcastle United	3-0	Crossley 2, Davies	54,205
5th Mar	4	H	Wolverhampton Wanderers	0-1		53,246
1921-22						
7th Jan	1	H	Crystal Palace	0-6		41,000
1922-23						
13th Jan	1	H	Bradford Park Avenue	1-1	Chedgzoy	18,000
17th Jan	1 Replay	A	Bradford Park Avenue	0-1		15,000
1923-24						
12th Jan	1	H	Preston North End	3-1	Chadwick, Chedgzoy, Cock	33,000
2nd Feb	2	A	Brighton & Hove Albion	2-5	Chadwick, Cock	27,450
1924-25						
10th Jan	1	H	Burnley	2-1	Chadwick 2	28,315

	1	2	3	4	5	6	7	8	9	10	11
1909-10 (Cont)											
	Scott	Clifford	Maconnachie	Harris	Taylor	Makepeace	Sharp	White	Freeman	Young	Barlow
	Scott	Clifford	Maconnachie	Harris	Taylor	Makepeace	Sharp	White	Freeman	Young	Barlow
1910-11											
	Scott	Stevenson	Balmer R	Harris	Young R	Makepeace	Berry	Gourlay	Magner	Young A	Beare
	Scott	Stevenson	Maconnachie	Harris	Young R	Makepeace	Lacey	Gourlay	Magner	Young A	Beare
	Scott	Stevenson	Maconnachie	Harris	Young R	Makepeace	Berry	Lacey	Magner	Young A	Beare
1911-12											
	Scott	Stevenson	Maconnachie	Harris	Fleetwood	Makepeace	Beare	Jefferis	Browell	Bradshaw	Davidson
	Scott	Stevenson	Maconnachie	Harris	Fleetwood	Makepeace	Beare	Jefferis	Browell	Bradshaw	Davidson
	Scott	Stevenson	Maconnachie	Harris	Fleetwood	Makepeace	Beare	Jefferis	Browell	Gourlay	Davidson
	Scott	Stevenson	Maconnachie	Harris	Fleetwood	Makepeace	Beare	Jefferis	Browell	Bradshaw	Lacey
	Scott	Stevenson	Maconnachie	Harris	Fleetwood	Makepeace	Beare	Jefferis	Browell	Bradshaw	Davidson
1912-13											
	Caldwell	Stevenson	Maconnachie	Harris	Wareing	Grenyer	Beare	Jefferis	Browell	Bradshaw	Davidson
	Caldwell	Stevenson	Maconnachie	Harris	Wareing	Grenyer	Beare	Jefferis	Browell	Bradshaw	Davidson
	Caldwell	Stevenson	Maconnachie	Harris	Wareing	Makepeace	Beare	Jefferis	Browell	Gourlay	Davidson
	Caldwell	Stevenson	Maconnachie	Harris	Wareing	Grenyer	Houston	Jefferis	Fleetwood	Browell	Beare
	Caldwell	Stevenson	Maconnachie	Fleetwood	Harris	Grenyer	Houston	Jefferis	Browell	Bradshaw	Beare
1913-14											
	Fern	Thompson	Maconnachie	Harris	Fleetwood	Makepeace	Beare	Jefferis	Parker	Bradshaw	Harrison
1914-15											
	Fern	Thompson	Maconnachie	Fleetwood	Galt	Makepeace	Chedgzoy	Kirsopp	Parker	Clennell	Harrison
	Fern	Thompson	Simpson	Fleetwood	Wareing	Makepeace	Chedgzoy	Kirsopp	Parker	Clennell	Palmer
	Fern	Thompson	Maconnachie	Fleetwood	Galt	Makepeace	Chedgzoy	Kirsopp	Parker	Clennell	Harrison
	Fern	Thompson	Maconnachie	Fleetwood	Galt	Makepeace	Chedgzoy	Kirsopp	Parker	Clennell	Harrison
	Mitchell	Thompson	Simpson	Fleetwood	Galt	Makepeace	Chedgzoy	Kirsopp	Parker	Clennell	Harrison
1919-20											
	Fern	Page	Weller	Brown	Fleetwood	Grenyer	Chedgzoy	Jefferis	Gault	Clennell	Harrison
1920-21											
	Fern	Downs	McDonald	Weller	Brewster	Peacock	Chedgzoy	Fazackerley	Parker	Crossley	Harrison
	Fern	Downs	McDonald	Peacock	Fleetwood	Grenyer	Chedgzoy	Fazackerley	Parker	Crossley	Harrison
	Fern	Downs	McDonald	Fleetwood	Brewster	Weller	Chedgzoy	Fazackerley	Blair	Crossley	Harrison
	Fern	Downs	McDonald	Fleetwood	Brewster	Weller	Chedgzoy	Fazackerley	Davies	Crossley	Harrison
	Fern	Downs	McDonald	Fleetwood	Brewster	Weller	Chedgzoy	Fazackerley	Davies	Crossley	Harrison
1921-22											
	Fern	McDonald	Livingstone	Brown	Fleetwood	Peacock	Chedgzoy	Fazackerley	Irvine	Wall	Harrison
1922-23											
	Harland	Raitt	Livingstone	Brown	Fleetwood	Hart	Chedgzoy	Peacock	Chadwick	Williams	Harrison
	Harland	Raitt	Livingstone	Brown	Fleetwood	Hart	Chedgzoy	Peacock	Irvine	Williams	Reid
1923-24											
	Harland	McDonald	Livingstone	Brown	McBain	Hart	Chedgzoy	Irvine	Cock	Chadwick	Troup
	Harland	McDonald	Livingstone	Brown	McBain	Peacock	Chedgzoy	Irvine	Cock	Chadwick	Troup
1924-25											
	Harland	Raitt	McDonald	Brown	McBain	Virr	Parry	Peacock	Broad	Chadwick	Weaver

Date	Round	Venue	Opponents	Score	Scorers	Attendance
1924-25 (Cont)						
31st Jan	2	A	Sunderland	0-0		35,000
4th Feb	2 Replay	H	Sunderland	2-1	Irvine, Chadwick	40,000
21st Feb	3	A	Sheffield United	0-1		51,745
1925-26						
9th Jan	1	H	Fulham	1-1	Dean	46,000
14th Jan	1 Replay	A	Fulham	0-1		20,116
1926-27						
8th Jan	1	H	Poole Town	3-1	Dean, Troup, Irvine	34,250
29th Jan	2	A	Hull City	1-1	Virr	22,000
2nd Feb	2 Replay 1	H	Hull City	2-2	Troup, Dean	45,000
7th Feb	2 Replay 2	N	Hull City	2-3	Dean, Dominy	6,800
1927-28						
14th Jan	1	A	Preston North End	3-0	Ward o.g., Dean, Irvine	39,215
28th Jan	2	A	Arsenal	3-4	Troup, Dean 2	44,328
1928-29						
12th Jan	1	A	Chelsea	0-2		61,316
1929-30						
11th Jan	1	A	Carlisle United	4-2	Critchley 2, Dean 2 (1 pen)	20,000
25th Jan	2	A	Blackburn Rovers	1-4	Martin	53,000
1930-31						
10th Jan	1	A	Plymouth Argyle	2-0	Stein, Dunn	33,000
24th Jan	2	A	Crystal Palace	6-0	Dean 4, Johnson, Wilde o.g.	38,000
14th Feb	3	H	Grimsby Town	5-3	Stein 2, Johnson 2 (1 pen), Dean	65,534
28th Feb	4	H	Southport	9-1	Dean 4, Dunn 2, Critchley 2, Johnson	45,647
14th Mar	SF	N	West Bromwich Albion	0-1		69,241
1931-32						
19th Jan	1	H	Liverpool	1-2	Dean	57,090
1932-33						
14th Jan	1	A	Leicester City	3-2	Dean, Dunn, Stein	-
28th Jan	2	H	Bury	3-1	Johnson 2, Dean	45,478
18th Feb	3	H	Leeds United	2-0	Dean, Stein	58,073
3rd Mar	4	H	Luton Town	6-0	Johnson 2, Stein 2, Dean, Dunn	55,431
18th Mar	SF	N	West Ham United	2-1	Dunn, Critchley	37,936
29th Apr	F	N	Manchester City	3-0	Stein, Dean, Dunn	92,900
1933-34						
13th Jan	1	A	Tottenham Hotspur	0-3		45,637
1934-35						
12th Jan	1	H	Grimsby Town	6-3	Geldard 3, Stevenson 2, Cunliffe	44,850
26th Jan	2	A	Sunderland	1-1	Cunliffe	45,000
30th Jan	2 Replay	H	Sunderland	6-4 aet	Coulter 3, Stevenson, Geldard 2	60,000
16th Feb	3	H	Derby County	3-1	Dean, Coulter 2	62,230
2nd Mar	4	H	Bolton Wanderers	1-2	Coulter	67,696
1935-36						
11th Jan	1	H	Preston North End	1-3	Geldard	35,000

	1	2	3	4	5	6	7	8	9	10	11
1924-25 (Cont)											
	Harland	Raitt	McDonald	Brown	McBain	Reid	Chedgzoy	Irvine	Broad	Chadwick	Weaver
	Kendall	Raitt	McDonald	Brown	McBain	Reid	Chedgzoy	Irvine	Cock	Chadwick	Weaver
	Kendall	Raitt	McDonald	McBain	Bain	Reid	Chedgzoy	Irvine	Broad	Chadwick	Weaver
1925-26											
	Hardy	Raitt	McDonald	Peacock	Bain	Virr	Chedgzoy	Irvine	Dean	O'Donnell	Troup
	Hardy	Raitt	McDonald	Peacock	Bain	Virr	Chedgzoy	Irvine	Dean	O'Donnell	Troup
1926-27											
	Hardy	Raitt	O'Donnell	Rooney	Bain	Virr	Parker	Irvine	Dean	Dominy	Troup
	Hardy	McDonald	Kerr	Peacock	Hart	Virr	Moffat	Irvine	Dean	Dominy	Troup
	Hardy	McDonald	Kerr	Rooney	Hart	Virr	Irvine	Bain	Dean	Dominy	Troup
	Davies	O'Donnell	Kerr	Rooney	Hart	Virr	Millington	Irvine	Dean	Dominy	Troup
1927-28											
	Taylor	Cresswell	O'Donnell	Kelly	Hart	Rooney	Critchley	Irvine	Dean	Weldon	Troup
	Taylor	Cresswell	O'Donnell	Kelly	Hart	Virr	Critchley	Irvine	Dean	Weldon	Troup
1928-29											
	Davies	Cresswell	O'Donnell	Griffiths	Hart	Virr	Ritchie	Dunn	Dean	Weldon	Stein
1929-30											
	Davies	Williams	O'Donnell	Robson	Griffiths	Hart	Critchley	Dunn	Dean	Rigby	Stein
	Sagar	Williams	O'Donnell	Robson	Hart	McPherson	Critchley	Martin	Dean	Rigby	Stein
1930-31											
	Coggins	Williams	Cresswell	McClure	Gee	Thomson	Critchley	Dunn	Dean	Johnson	Stein
	Coggins	Williams	Cresswell	McClure	Gee	Thomson	Critchley	Dunn	Dean	Johnson	Stein
	Coggins	Williams	Cresswell	McClure	Gee	Thomson	Critchley	Dunn	Dean	Johnson	Stein
	Coggins	Williams	Cresswell	McClure	Gee	Thomson	Critchley	Dunn	Dean	Johnson	Stein
	Coggins	Williams	Cresswell	McClure	Gee	Thomson	Wilkinson	Dunn	Dean	Johnson	Stein
1931-32											
	Sagar	Williams	Bocking	Clark	Gee	Thomson	Critchley	White	Dean	Johnson	Stein
1932-33											
	Sagar	Cook	Cresswell	Britton	White	Thomson	Geldard	Dunn	Dean	Johnson	Stein
	Sagar	Cook	Cresswell	Britton	White	Thomson	Geldard	Dunn	Dean	Johnson	Stein
	Sagar	Cook	Cresswell	Britton	White	Thomson	Geldard	Dunn	Dean	Johnson	Stein
	Sagar	Cook	Cresswell	Britton	White	Thomson	Critchley	Dunn	Dean	Johnson	Stein
	Sagar	Cook	Cresswell	Britton	White	Thomson	Critchley	Dunn	Dean	Johnson	Stein
	Sagar	Cook	Cresswell	Britton	White	Thomson	Geldard	Dunn	Dean	Johnson	Stein
1933-34											
	Sagar	Cresswell	Cook	Britton	White	Thomson	Critchley	Dunn	Cunliffe	Johnson	Stein
1934-35											
	Sagar	Cresswell	Cook	Britton	Gee	Thomson	Geldard	Cunliffe	Dean	Stevenson	Coulter
	Sagar	Cook	Jones	Britton	Gee	Thomson	Geldard	Cunliffe	Dean	Stevenson	Coulter
	Sagar	Cook	Jones	Britton	Gee	Thomson	Geldard	Cunliffe	Dean	Stevenson	Coulter
	Sagar	Jackson	Cook	Britton	Gee	Thomson	Geldard	Cunliffe	Dean	Stevenson	Coulter
	Bradshaw	Cook	Jones	Britton	Gee	Thomson	Geldard	Cunliffe	Dean	Stevenson	Coulter
1935-36											
	King	Cook	Jones	Britton	White	Mercer	Geldard	Bentham	Cunliffe	Miller	Gillick

Date	Round	Venue	Opponents	Score	Scorers	Attendance
1936-37						
16th Jan	1	H	Bournemouth	5-0	Gillick 2, Cunliffe, Stevenson 2	35,468
30th Jan	2	H	Sheffield Wednesday	3-0	Britton (pen), Dean, Coulter	35,807
20th Feb	3	H	Tottenham Hotspur	1-1	Coulter	57,149
22nd Feb	3 Replay	A	Tottenham Hotspur	3-4	Lawton, Dean 2	46,972
1937-38						
8th Jan	1	A	Chelsea	1-0	Stevenson	41,946
22nd Jan	2	H	Sunderland	0-1		68,158
1938-39						
7th Jan	1	A	Derby County	1-0	Boyes	22,237
21st Jan	2	H	Doncaster Rovers	8-0	Boyes 2, Lawton 4, Stevenson, Gillick	41,115
11th Feb	3	A	Birmingham City	2-2	Boyes, Stevenson	67,341
15th Feb	3 Replay	H	Birmingham City	2-1	Gillick, Cook (pen)	64,796
4th Mar	4	A	Wolverhampton W.	0-2		59,545
1945-46						
5th Jan	3 1st Leg	A	Preston North End	1-2	Catterick	25,000
9th Jan	3 2nd Leg	H	Preston North End	2-2 aet	Mercer (pen), Elliott	25,000
1946-47						
11th Jan	3	H	Southend United	4-2	Jones, McIlhatton, Wainwright, Fielding	50,124
25th Jan	4	A	Sheffield Wednesday	1-2	Wainwright	62,250
1947-48						
10th Jan	3	A	Grimsby Town	4-1	Wainwright 2, Farrell, Dodds	19,000
24th Jan	4	A	Wolverhampton W.	1-1	Catterick	45,085
31st Jan	4 Replay	H	Wolverhampton W.	3-2	Fielding 2, Grant	72,569
7th Feb	5	A	Fulham	1-1	Eglington	37,500
14th Feb	5 Replay	H	Fulham	0-1		71,587
1948-49						
8th Jan	3	H	Manchester City	1-0	Higgins	63,459
29th Jan	4	A	Chelsea	0-2		56,671
1949-50						
7th Jan	3	A	Queens Park Rangers	2-0	Buckle, Catterick	22,433
28th Jan	4	A	West Ham United	2-1	Catterick 2	26,800
11th Feb	5	H	Tottenham Hotspur	1-0	Wainwright (pen)	72,921
4th Mar	6	A	Derby County	2-1	Wainwright, Buckle	32,128
25th Mar	SF	N	Liverpool	0-2		72,000
1950-51						
6th Jan	3	A	Hull City	0-2		36,465
1951-52						
12th Jan	3	A	Leyton Orient	0-0		21,240
16th Jan	3 Replay	H	Leyton Orient	1-3	Parker	39,750
1952-53						
10th Jan	3	H	Ipswich Town	3-2	Fielding, Hickson 2	42,252
31st Jan	4	H	Nottingham Forest	4-1	Clinton, Parker 2, Eglington	48,904
14th Feb	5	H	Manchester United	2-1	Eglington, Hickson	77,920
28th Feb	6	A	Aston Villa	1-0	Hickson	60,658
21st Mar	SF	N	Bolton Wanderers	3-4	Parker 2, Farrell	75,000
1953-54						
9th Jan	3	H	Notts County	2-1	Eglington, Hickson	49,737

	1	2	3	4	5	6	7	8	9	10	11
1936-37											
	Sagar	Cook	Jones	Britton	Gee	Mercer	Gillick	Cunliffe	Dean	Stevenson	Coulter
	Sagar	Cook	Jones	Britton	Gee	Mercer	Gillick	Cunliffe	Dean	Stevenson	Coulter
	Sagar	Cook	Jones	Britton	Gee	Mercer	Gillick	Cunliffe	Dean	Stevenson	Coulter
	Sagar	Cook	Jones	Britton	Gee	Mercer	Geldard	Cunliffe	Dean	Lawton	Gillick
1937-38											
	Morton	Cook	Jones J	Britton	Jones TG	Mercer	Geldard	Cunliffe	Lawton	Stevenson	Gillick
	Morton	Cook	Jones J	Britton	Jones TG	Mercer	Gillick	Cunliffe	Lawton	Stevenson	Trentham
1938-39											
	Sagar	Cook	Greenhalgh	Mercer	Jones	Thomson	Gillick	Bentham	Lawton	Stevenson	Boyes
	Sagar	Cook	Greenhalgh	Mercer	Jones	Thomson	Gillick	Bentham	Lawton	Stevenson	Boyes
	Sagar	Cook	Greenhalgh	Mercer	Jones	Thomson	Gillick	Bentham	Lawton	Stevenson	Boyes
	Sagar	Cook	Greenhalgh	Mercer	Jones	Thomson	Gillick	Bentham	Lawton	Stevenson	Boyes
	Sagar	Cook	Greenhalgh	Mercer	Jones	Watson	Gillick	Bentham	Lawton	Stevenson	Boyes
1945-46											
	Burnett	Jackson	Greenhalgh	Bentham	Humphreys	Mercer	Rawlings	Elliott	Catterick	Fielding	Boyes
	Burnett	Jackson	Greenhalgh	Bentham	Humphreys	Mercer	Rawlings	Elliott	Catterick	Fielding	Boyes
1946-47											
	Sagar	Saunders	Greenhalgh	Bentham	Jones	Farrell	McIlhatton	Wainwright	Dodds	Fielding	Eglington
	Sagar	Jackson	Greenhalgh	Bentham	Humphreys	Farrell	McIlhatton	Wainwright	Dodds	Fielding	Eglington
1947-48											
	Sagar	Saunders	Watson	Bentham	Humphreys	Farrell	Grant	Wainwright	Dodds	Fielding	Eglington
	Sagar	Saunders	Dugdale	Bentham	Humphreys	Watson	Grant	Wainwright	Catterick	Fielding	Eglington
	Sagar	Saunders	Dugdale	Bentham	Humphreys	Watson	Grant	Wainwright	Catterick	Fielding	Eglington
	Sagar	Saunders	Dugdale	Bentham	Humphreys	Farrell	Grant	Wainwright	Catterick	Fielding	Eglington
	Sagar	Saunders	Dugdale	Farrell	Humphreys	Watson	Grant	Bentham	Catterick	Fielding	Eglington
1948-49											
	Sagar	Hedley	Dugdale	Lindley	Jones	Farrell	Grant	Stevenson	Higgins	Fielding	Eglington
	Sagar	Saunders	Hedley	Farrell	Jones	Lello	McIlhatton	Wainwright	Catterick	Fielding	Eglington
1949-50											
	Burnett	Moore	Hedley	Grant	Falder	Lello	Buckle	Wainwright	Catterick	Farrell	Eglington
	Burnett	Moore	Hedley	Grant	Falder	Lello	Buckle	Wainwright	Catterick	Farrell	Eglington
	Burnett	Moore	Hedley	Grant	Falder	Farrell	Buckle	Wainwright	Catterick	Fielding	Eglington
	Burnett	Moore	Hedley	Grant	Falder	Farrell	Buckle	Wainwright	Catterick	Fielding	Eglington
	Burnett	Moore	Hedley	Grant	Falder	Farrell	Buckle	Wainwright	Catterick	Fielding	Eglington
1950-51											
	Sagar	Moore	Rankin	Grant	Jones	Farrell	Fielding	Hold	McIntosh	Potts	Eglington
1951-52											
	Leyland	Clinton	Lindsay	Donovan	Lindley	Farrell	McNamara	Fielding	Hickson	Parker	Eglington
	Leyland	Clinton	Lindsay	Donovan	Lindley	Farrell	Buckle	Fielding	Hickson	Parker	Eglington
1952-53											
	O'Neill	Clinton	Lindsay	Farrell	Jones	Lello	Fielding	Potts	Hickson	Cummins	Eglington
	O'Neill	Clinton	Lindsay	Farrell	Jones	Lello	Buckle	Cummins	Hickson	Parker	Eglington
	O'Neill	Clinton	Lindsay	Farrell	Jones	Lello	Buckle	Cummins	Hickson	Parker	Eglington
	O'Neill	Clinton	Lindsay	Farrell	Jones	Lello	Buckle	Cummins	Hickson	Parker	Eglington
	O'Neill	Clinton	Lindsay	Farrell	Jones	Lello	Buckle	Cummins	Hickson	Parker	Eglington
1953-54											
	O'Neill	Donovan	Lindsay	Farrell	Jones	Lello	Wainwright	Fielding	Hickson	Parker	Eglington

Date	Round	Venue	Opponents	Score	Scorers	Attendance
1953-54 (cont)						
30th Jan	4	H	Swansea City	3-0	Parker 2, Hickson	61,619
20th Feb	5	A	Sheffield Wednesday	1-3	Hickson	65,000
1954-55						
8th Jan	3	H	Southend United	3-1	Potts, Fielding, Hickson	53,043
29th Jan	4	H	Liverpool	0-4		72,000
1955-56						
7th Jan	3	H	Bristol City	3-1	Eglington, Wainwright, J. Harris	46,493
28th Jan	4	A	Port Vale	3-2	Eglington, B. Harris, Wainwright	44,278
18th Feb	5	H	Chelsea	1-0	Farrell	61,572
3rd Mar	6	A	Manchester City	1-2	J. Harris	76,129
1956-57						
5th Jan	3	H	Blackburn Rovers	1-0	J. Harris (pen)	56,293
26th Jan	4	H	West Ham United	2-1	Gauld, Farrell	55,245
16th Feb	5	A	Manchester United	0-1		61,803
1957-58						
4th Jan	3	A	Sunderland	2-2	Hickson 2	34,602
8th Jan	3 Replay	H	Sunderland	3-1	Keeley 2, Hickson	56,952
29th Jan	4	H	Blackburn Rovers	1-2	J. Harris	75,818
1958-59						
10th Jan	3	H	Sunderland	4-0	Hickson 2, J. Harris, Thomas	57,788
24th Jan	4	A	Charlton Athletic	2-2	Thomas, Collins	44,094
28th Jan	4 Replay	H	Charlton Athletic	4-1	Hickson 2, Collins 2	74,782
14th Feb	5	H	Aston Villa	1-4	Hickson	60,225
1959-60						
9th Jan	3	A	Bradford City	0-3		23,550
1960-61						
7th Jan	3	H	Sheffield United	0-1		48,593
1961-62						
6th Jan	3	H	King's Lynn	4-0	Collins, Vernon (pen), Bingham, Fell	44,916
27th Jan	4	H	Manchester City	2-0	Vernon, Lill	56,980
17th Feb	5	A	Burnley	1-3	Collins	50,514
1962-63						
15th Jan	3	A	Barnsley	3-0	B. Harris, Stevens, Vernon	30,011
29th Jan	4	A	Swindon Town	5-1	Vernon 2, Gabriel, Bingham, Morrissey	26,239
16th Mar	5	A	West Ham United	0-1		31,770
1963-64						
4th Jan	3	A	Hull City	1-1	Scott	36,478
7th Jan	3 Replay	H	Hull City	2-1	Scott, B. Harris	56,613
25th Jan	4	A	Leeds United	1-1	Vernon (pen)	48,826
28th Jan	4 Replay	H	Leeds United	2-0	Vernon, Gabriel	66,167
15th Feb	5	A	Sunderland	1-3	B. Harris	62,817
1964-65						
9th Jan	3	H	Sheffield Wednesday	2-2	Burgin o.g., Pickering	44,732
13th Jan	3 Replay	A	Sheffield Wednesday	3-0	Pickering, Harvey, Temple	50,080
30th Jan	4	A	Leeds United	1-1	Pickering (pen)	50,051
2nd Feb	4 Replay	H	Leeds United	1-2	Pickering	65,940

	1	2	3	4	5	6	7	8	9	10	11
1953-54 (cont)											
	O'Neill	Moore	Lindsay	Farrell	Jones	Lello	Wainwright	Fielding	Hickson	Parker	Eglington
	O'Neill	Donovan	Lindsay	Farrell	Jones	Lello	Wainwright	Fielding	Hickson	Parker	Eglington
1954-55											
	O'Neill	Moore	Rankin	Farrell	Jones	Lello	Wainwright	Fielding	Hickson	Potts	Eglington
	O'Neill	Moore	Rankin	Farrell	Jones	Lello	Wainwright	Fielding	Hickson	Potts	Eglington
1955-56											
	O'Neill	Moore	Tansey	Farrell	Jones	Lello	Harris B	Wainwright	Harris J	Fielding	Eglington
	Leyland	Moore	Tansey	Farrell	Jones	Lello	Harris B	Wainwright	Harris J	Fielding	Eglington
	Leyland	Moore	Tansey	Farrell	Jones	Lello	Harris B	Wainwright	Harris J	Fielding	Eglington
	O'Neill	Moore	Tansey	Farrell	Jones	Lello	Harris B	Wainwright	Harris J	Fielding	Eglington
1956-57											
	Dunlop	Sutherland	Tansey	Birch	Donovan	Rea	McNamara	Gauld	Harris J	Fielding	Eglington
	Dunlop	Sutherland	Tansey	Farrell	Donovan	Rea	Mayers	Gauld	Kirby	Fielding	Eglington
	Dunlop	Donovan	Tansey	Farrell	Jones	Rea	Payne	Gauld	Harris J	Fielding	Eglington
1957-58											
	Dunlop	Sanders	Tansey	Rea	Jones	Meagan	Harris J	Thomas	Hickson	Keeley	Harris B
	Dunlop	Sanders	Tansey	Rea	Jones	Meagan	Harris J	Thomas	Hickson	Keeley	Harris B
	Dunlop	Sanders	Donovan	Birch	Jones	Meagan	Harris J	Thomas	Temple	Keeley	Harris B
1958-59											
	Dunlop	Sanders	Bramwell	Parker	Jones	Harris B	Harris J	Thomas	Hickson	Collins	Williams
	Dunlop	Sanders	Bramwell	Parker	Jones	Harris B	Harris J	Thomas	Hickson	Collins	Williams
	Dunlop	Sanders	Bramwell	Parker	Jones	Harris B	Harris J	Thomas	Hickson	Collins	O'Hara
	Dunlop	Sanders	Bramwell	Parker	Jones	Harris B	Harris J	Thomas	Hickson	Collins	O'Hara
1959-60											
	Dunlop	Parker	Jones	King	Labone	Harris B	Harris J	Wignall	Shackleton	Collins	Laverick
1960-61											
	Dunlop	Parker	Jones	Gabriel	Labone	Harris	Bingham	Collins	Wignall	Vernon	Tyrer
1961-62											
	Dunlop	Parker	Thomson	Gabriel	Labone	Harris	Bingham	Collins	Young	Vernon	Fell
	Dunlop	Parker	Green	Gabriel	Labone	Harris	Bingham	Collins	Young	Vernon	Lill
	Dunlop	Parker	Green	Gabriel	Labone	Harris	Bingham	Collins	Young	Vernon	Lill
1962-63											
	West	Parker	Meagan	Gabriel	Labone	Harris	Bingham	Stevens	Young	Vernon	Morrissey
	West	Parker	Meagan	Gabriel	Labone	Kay	Bingham	Stevens	Young	Vernon	Morrissey
	West	Parker	Meagan	Gabriel	Labone	Kay	Bingham	Stevens	Young	Vernon	Morrissey
1963-64											
	Rankin	Brown	Meagan	Gabriel	Heslop	Harris	Scott	Stevens	Young	Vernon	Temple
	Rankin	Brown	Meagan	Gabriel	Labone	Harris	Scott	Stevens	Young	Vernon	Temple
	West	Brown	Harris	Gabriel	Labone	Kay	Scott	Stevens	Young	Vernon	Temple
	West	Brown	Meagan	Harris	Labone	Kay	Scott	Stevens	Gabriel	Vernon	Temple
	West	Brown	Meagan	Harris	Labone	Kay	Scott	Stevens	Gabriel	Vernon	Temple
1964-65											
	West	Brown	Wilson	Gabriel	Labone	Harvey	Scott	Young	Pickering	Temple	Morrissey
	West	Wright	Wilson	Gabriel	Labone	Harris	Scott	Harvey	Pickering	Temple	Morrissey
	West	Wright	Wilson	Gabriel	Labone	Stevens	Scott	Harvey	Pickering	Temple	Morrissey
	West	Wright	Wilson	Gabriel	Labone	Stevens	Scott	Harvey	Pickering	Temple	Morrissey

Date	Round	Venue	Opponents	Score	Scorers	Attendance
1965-66						
22nd Jan	3	H	Sunderland	3-0	Temple, Pickering, Young	47,893
12th Feb	4	A	Bedford Town	3-0	Temple 2, Pickering	18,407
3rd Mar	5	H	Coventry City	3-0	Young, Temple, Pickering	60,350
26th Mar	6	A	Manchester City	0-0		63,034
29th Mar	6 Replay 1	H	Manchester City	0-0		60,349
5th Apr	6 Replay 2	N	Manchester City	2-0	Temple, Pickering	27,948
23rd Apr	SF	N	Manchester United	1-0	Harvey	60,000
14th May	F	N	Sheffield Wednesday	3-2	Trebilcock 2, Temple	100,000
1966-67						
28th Jan	3	A	Burnley	0-0		42,482
31st Jan	3 Replay	H	Burnley	2-1	Young 2	57,449
18th Feb	4	A	Wolverhampton W.	1-1	Ball (pen)	53,439
21st Feb	4 Replay	H	Wolverhampton W.	3-1	Husband 2, Temple	60,020
11th Mar	5	H	Liverpool	1-0	Ball	64,851
8th Apr	6	A	Nottingham Forest	2-3	Husband 2	47,510
1967-68						
27th Jan	3	A	Southport	1-0	Royle	18,795
17th Feb	4	A	Carlisle United	2-0	Husband, Royle	25,000
9th Mar	5	H	Tranmere Rovers	2-0	Royle, Morrissey	61,982
30th Mar	6	A	Leicester City	3-1	Husband 2, Kendall	43,519
27th Apr	SF	N	Leeds United	1-0	Morrissey (pen)	63,000
18th May	F	N	West Bromwich Albion	0-1 aet		99,665
1968-69						
4th Jan	3	H	Ipswich Town	2-1	Royle, Hurst	49,047
25th Jan	4	H	Coventry City	2-0	Royle, Hurst	53,289
12th Feb	5	H	Bristol Rovers	1-0	Royle	55,294
1st Mar	6	A	Manchester United	1-0	Royle	63,464
22nd Mar	SF	N	Manchester City	0-1		63,025
1969-70						
3rd Jan	3	A	Sheffield United	1-2	Ball (pen)	29,116
1970-71						
2nd Jan	3	H	Blackburn Rovers	2-0	Husband 2	40,471
23rd Jan	4	H	Middlesbrough	3-0	H. Newton, Harvey, Royle	54,875
13th Feb	5	H	Derby County	1-0	Johnson	53,490
6th Mar	6	H	Colchester United	5-0	Kendall 2, Royle, Husband, Ball	53,028
27th Mar	SF	N	Liverpool	1-2	Ball	62,144
1971-72						
15th Jan	3	A	Crystal Palace	2-2	Whittle, Harvey	32,331
18th Jan	3 Replay	H	Crystal Palace	3-2	Scott, Kenyon, Hurst	45,408
5th Feb	4	H	Walsall	2-1	Johnson, Whittle	45,462
26th Feb	5	H	Tottenham Hotspur	0-2		50,511
1972-73						
13th Jan	3	H	Aston Villa	3-2	Belfitt, Buckley, Harper	42,222
3rd Feb	4	H	Millwall	0-2		37,277
1973-74						
5th Jan	3	H	Blackburn Rovers	3-0	Harper, Hurst, Clements	31,940
27th Jan	4	H	West Bromwich Albion	0-0		53,509
30th Jan	4 Replay	A	West Bromwich Albion	0-1		27,556
1974-75						
4th Jan	3	H	Altrincham	1-1	Clements (pen)	34,519

	1	2	3	4	5	6	7	8	9	10	11	Used Sub
1965-66												
	West	Wright	Wilson	Gabriel	Labone	Harris	Scott	Young	Pickering	Harvey	Temple	
	West	Wright	Wilson	Gabriel	Labone	Harris	Scott	Young	Pickering	Harvey	Temple	
	West	Brown	Wilson	Gabriel	Labone	Harris	Scott	Young	Pickering	Harvey	Temple	
	West	Wright	Wilson	Brown	Labone	Harris	Scott	Young	Temple	Harvey	Morrissey	
	West	Wright	Wilson	Brown	Labone	Harris	Scott	Young	Pickering	Harvey	Temple	
	West	Wright	Wilson	Gabriel	Labone	Harris	Scott	Young	Pickering	Harvey	Temple	
	West	Brown	Wilson	Gabriel	Labone	Harris	Scott	Trebilcock	Young	Harvey	Temple	
	West	Wright	Wilson	Gabriel	Labone	Harris	Scott	Trebilcock	Young	Harvey	Temple	
1966-67												
	West	Wright	Wilson	Hurst	Labone	Harvey	Gabriel	Ball	Temple	Husband	Morrissey	Brown
	West	Wright	Wilson	Hurst	Labone	Harvey	Young	Ball	Gabriel	Husband	Morrissey	Brown
	West	Wright	Wilson	Hurst	Labone	Harvey	Young	Ball	Gabriel	Husband	Morrissey	
	West	Wright	Wilson	Hurst	Labone	Harvey	Young	Ball	Temple	Husband	Morrissey	Brown
	West	Wright	Wilson	Hurst	Labone	Harvey	Young	Ball	Temple	Husband	Morrissey	
	Rankin	Wright	Wilson	Hurst	Labone	Harvey	Young	Ball	Brown	Husband	Morrissey	
1967-68												
	West	Wright	Wilson	Kendall	Labone	Harvey	Ball	Young	Royle	Hurst	Husband	Brown
	West	Wright	Wilson	Kendall	Labone	Harvey	Husband	Ball	Royle	Hurst	Morrissey	
	West	Wright	Wilson	Kendall	Labone	Hurst	Husband	Young	Royle	Hunt	Morrissey	Brown
	West	Wright	Wilson	Kendall	Labone	Kenyon	Husband	Ball	Royle	Hurst	Morrissey	Young
	West	Wright	Wilson	Jackson	Labone	Harvey	Husband	Kenyon	Royle	Kendall	Morrissey	Young
	West	Wright	Wilson	Kendall	Labone	Harvey	Husband	Ball	Royle	Hurst	Morrissey	
1968-69												
	West	Wright	Brown	Kendall	Labone	Harvey	Husband	Ball	Royle	Hurst	Morrissey	
	West	Wright	Wilson	Kendall	Labone	Brown	Husband	Ball	Royle	Hurst	Morrissey	
	West	Wright	Wilson	Brown	Labone	Harvey	Husband	Ball	Royle	Hurst	Morrissey	
	West	Wright	Brown	Jackson	Labone	Harvey	Husband	Ball	Royle	Hurst	Morrissey	D'Arcy Kenyon
	West	Wright	Brown	Kendall	Labone	Harvey	Husband	Ball	Royle	Hurst	Morrissey	Jackson
1969-70												
	West	Wright	Newton	Kendall	Labone	Jackson	Whittle	Ball	Royle	Hurst	Morrissey	Brown
1970-71												
	Rankin	Wright	Newton H	Kendall	Labone	Harvey	Husband	Ball	Royle	Hurst	Morrissey	
	Rankin	Wright	Newton H	Kendall	Labone	Harvey	Husband	Ball	Royle	Hurst	Morrissey	
	West	Wright	Newton H	Kendall	Kenyon	Harvey	Husband	Ball	Royle	Hurst	Johnson	
	Rankin	Wright	Newton H	Kendall	Kenyon	Harvey	Husband	Ball	Royle	Hurst	Morrissey	Brown
	Rankin	Wright	Newton K	Kendall	Labone	Harvey	Whittle	Ball	Royle	Hurst	Morrissey	Brown
1971-72												
	West	Scott	McLaughlin	Kendall	Kenyon	Darracott	Johnson	Harvey	Royle	Lyons	Whittle	
	West	Scott	McLaughlin	Kendall	Kenyon	Darracott	Husband	Harvey	Johnson	Lyons	Whittle	Hurst
	West	Wright	McLaughlin	Kendall	Lyons	Newton	Johnson	Harvey	Royle	Hurst	Whittle	
	West	Scott	McLaughlin	Kendall	Kenyon	Newton	Johnson	Whittle	Royle	Lyons	Jones	Hurst
1972-73												
	Lawson	Wright	Styles	Kendall	Kenyon	Hurst	Harper	Bernard	Belfitt	Buckley	Connolly	Lyons
	Lawson	Wright	Styles	Kendall	Kenyon	Hurst	Harper	Bernard	Belfitt	Buckley	Connolly	Jones
1973-74												
	Lawson	Darracott	Styles	Clements	Kenyon	Hurst	Bernard	Buckley	Royle	Lyons	Harper	Jones
	Lawson	Darracott	McLaughlin	Clements	Lyons	Hurst	Bernard	Buckley	Royle	Jones	Harper	Telfer
	Lawson	Darracott	Styles	Kendall	Lyons	Hurst	Bernard	Buckley	Royle	Jones	Telfer	
1974-75												
	Davies	Bernard	McLaughlin	Clements	McNaught	Lyons	Jones	Pearson	Irving	Latchford	Connolly	Telfer

Date	Round	Venue	Opponents	Score	Scorers	Attendance
1974-75 (cont)						
7th Jan	3 Replay	A	Altrincham (Played at Old Trafford)	2-0	Latchford, Lyons	35,530
25th Jan	4	A	Plymouth Argyle	3-1	Pearson, Lyons 2	38,000
15th Feb	5	H	Fulham	1-2	Kenyon	45,233
1975-76						
3rd Jan	3	A	Derby County	1-2	G. Jones	31,647
1976-77						
8th Jan	3	H	Stoke City	2-0	Lyons, McKenzie (pen)	32,981
29th Jan	4	A	Swindon Town	2-2	McKenzie, Latchford	24,347
1st Feb	4 Replay	H	Swindon Town	2-1	Dobson, Jones	38,063
26th Feb	5	A	Cardiff City	2-1	Latchford, McKenzie	35,582
19th Mar	6	H	Derby County	2-0	Latchford, Pearson	42,409
23rd Apr	SF	N	Liverpool	2-2	McKenzie, Rioch	52,637
27th Apr	SF Replay	N	Liverpool	0-3		52,579
1977-78						
7th Jan	3	H	Aston Villa	4-1	King, Ross (pen), McKenzie, Latchford	46,320
28th Jan	4	A	Middlesbrough	2-3	Telfer, Lyons	33,652
1978-79						
10th Jan	3	A	Sunderland	1-2	Dobson	28,602
1979-80						
5th Jan	3	H	Aldershot	4-1	Latchford, Hartford, King, Kidd	23,700
26th Jan	4	H	Wigan Athletic	3-0	McBride, Latchford, Kidd	51,853
16th Feb	5	H	Wrexham	5-2	Megson, Eastoe 2, Ross (pen), Latchford	44,830
8th Mar	6	H	Ipswich Town	2-1	Latchford, Kidd	45,104
12th Apr	SF	N	West Ham United	1-1	Kidd (pen)	47,685
16th Apr	SF Replay	N	West Ham United	1-2 aet	Latchford	40,720
1980-81						
3rd Jan	3	H	Arsenal	2-0	Sansom o.g., Lyons	34,236
24th Jan	4	H	Liverpool	2-1	Eastoe, Varadi	53,804
14th Feb	5	A	Southampton	0-0		24,152
17th Feb	5 Replay	H	Southampton	1-0 aet	O'Keefe	49,192
7th Mar	6	H	Manchester City	2-2	Eastoe, Ross (pen)	52,791
11th Mar	6 Replay	A	Manchester City	1-3	Eastoe	52,532
1981-82						
2nd Jan	3	A	West Ham United	1-2	Eastoe	24,431
1982-83						
8th Jan	3	A	Newport County	1-1	Sheedy	9,527
11th Jan	3 Replay	H	Newport County	2-1	Sharp, King	18,565
30th Jan	4	H	Shrewsbury Town	2-1	Sheedy, Heath	35,188
19th Feb	5	H	Tottenham Hotspur	2-0	King, Sharp	42,995
12th Mar	6	A	Manchester United	0-1		58,198
1983-84						
6th Jan	3	A	Stoke City	2-0	Gray, Irvine	16,462
28th Jan	4	H	Gillingham	0-0		22,380
31st Jan	4 Replay 1	A	Gillingham	0-0		15,339
6th Feb	4 Replay 2	A	Gillingham	3-0	Sheedy 2, Heath	17,817
18th Feb	5	H	Shrewsbury Town	3-0	Irvine, Reid, Griffin o.g.	27,106
10th Mar	6	A	Notts County	2-1	Richardson, Gray	19,534
14th Apr	SF	N	Southampton	1-0 aet	Heath	46,587
19th May	F	N	Watford	2-0	Sharp, Gray	100,000

1	2	3	4	5	6	7	8	9	10	11	Used Sub
1974-75 (cont)											
Davies	Scott	McLaughlin	Clements	McNaught	Lyons	Jones	Dobson	Pearson	Latchford	Telfer	
Davies	Scott	Seargeant	Clements	Kenyon	McNaught	Marshall	Dobson	Pearson	Lyons	Telfer	Bernard
Davies	Bernard	Seargeant	Clements	Kenyon	Hurst	Jones	Dobson	Lyons	Latchford	Pearson	Telfer
1975-76											
Davies	Bernard	Darracott	Hurst	Kenyon	Lyons	Hamilton	Dobson	Latchford	Pearson	Jones	Connolly
1976-77											
Lawson	Robinson	Jones	Lyons	McNaught	Rioch	King	Dobson	Latchford	McKenzie	Goodlass	
Lawson	Darracott	Jones	Lyons	McNaught	Rioch	King	Dobson	Latchford	McKenzie	Goodlass	Hamilton
Lawson	Bernard	Jones	Lyons	McNaught	Rioch	King	Dobson	Latchford	McKenzie	Goodlass	
Lawson	Jones	Pejic	Lyons	McNaught	Rioch	Hamilton	Dobson	Latchford	McKenzie	Goodlass	
Lawson	Darracott	Pejic	Lyons	McNaught	King	Rioch	Kenyon	Latchford	Pearson	Goodlass	Telfer
Lawson	Darracott	Pejic	Lyons	McNaught	Rioch	Buckley	Dobson	Pearson	McKenzie	Goodlass	Hamilton
Lawson	Darracott	Pejic	Lyons	McNaught	Rioch	Buckley	Dobson	Pearson	McKenzie	Goodlass	King
1977-78											
Wood	Darracott	Pejic	Lyons	Higgins	Ross	King	Dobson	Latchford	McKenzie	Thomas	
Wood	Jones	Pejic	Lyons	Kenyon	Ross	King	Dobson	Latchford	Telfer	Pearson	McKenzie
1978-79											
Wood	Todd	Darracott	Lyons	Wright	Ross	King	Dobson	Latchford	Walsh	Thomas	
1979-80											
Hodge	Gidman	Bailey	Wright	Lyons	King	Hartford	Stanley	Latchford	Kidd	McBride	
Hodge	Gidman	Bailey	Wright	Lyons	Stanley	Hartford	Eastoe	Latchford	Kidd	McBride	
Hodge	Gidman	Bailey	Wright	Lyons	Ross	Megson	Eastoe	Latchford	Hartford	McBride	
Wood	Gidman	Bailey	Wright	Lyons	King	Megson	Eastoe	Latchford	Kidd	McBride	
Hodge	Gidman	Bailey	Wright	Lyons	King	Megson	Eastoe	Kidd	Hartford	Ross	Latchford
Hodge	Gidman	Bailey	Wright	Lyons	Ratcliffe	Eastoe	King	Latchford	Hartford	Ross	Varadi
1980-81											
McDonagh	Gidman	Bailey	Wright	Ratcliffe	Ross	McMahon	Eastoe	Varadi	Hartford	McBride	Lyons
Hodge	Ratcliffe	Bailey	Wright	Lyons	Ross	McMahon	Eastoe	Varadi	Hartford	O'Keefe	
McDonagh	Ratcliffe	Bailey	Wright	Lyons	Gidman	Ross	Eastoe	Varadi	Hartford	O'Keefe	
McDonagh	Gidman	Ratcliffe	Wright	Lyons	Ross	McMahon	Eastoe	Varadi	Hartford	O'Keefe	
McDonagh	Gidman	Ratcliffe	Wright	Lyons	Ross	McMahon	Eastoe	Varadi	Hartford	O'Keefe	Stanley
McDonagh	Gidman	Bailey	Wright	Lyons	Ross	McMahon	Eastoe	Varadi	Hartford	McBride	
1981-82											
Southall	Stevens	Ratcliffe	Higgins	Lyons	Kendall	Richardson	Ross	Sharp	Eastoe	Lodge	O'Keefe
1982-83											
Arnold	Stevens	Bailey	Ratcliffe	Higgins	McMahon	Heath	Sharp	King	Reid	Sheedy	
Arnold	Stevens	Bailey	Ratcliffe	Higgins	McMahon	Heath	Sharp	King	Reid	Sheedy	
Arnold	Stevens	Bailey	Ratcliffe	Higgins	McMahon	Heath	Sharp	King	Reid	Sheedy	
Arnold	Stevens	Bailey	Ratcliffe	Higgins	Richardson	Irvine	King	Sharp	Heath	Sheedy	
Arnold	Stevens	Bailey	Ratcliffe	Higgins	Richardson	Irvine	McMahon	Sharp	Heath	Sheedy	
1983-84											
Southall	Stevens	Bailey	Ratcliffe	Mountfield	Reid	Irvine	Heath	Sharp	Gray	Sheedy	
Southall	Stevens	Harper	Ratcliffe	Mountfield	Reid	Irvine	Heath	Sharp	Gray	Sheedy	
Southall	Stevens	Bailey	Ratcliffe	Mountfield	Reid	Irvine	Heath	Sharp	Richardson	Sheedy	Gray
Southall	Stevens	Bailey	Ratcliffe	Mountfield	Reid	Irvine	Heath	Gray	Richardson	Sheedy	
Southall	Stevens	Bailey	Ratcliffe	Mountfield	Reid	Irvine	Heath	Gray	King	Sheedy	Sharp
Southall	Stevens	Bailey	Ratcliffe	Mountfield	Reid	Irvine	Richardson	Sharp	Gray	Sheedy	Harper
Southall	Stevens	Bailey	Ratcliffe	Mountfield	Reid	Curran	Heath	Gray	Steven	Richardson	Sharp
Southall	Stevens	Bailey	Ratcliffe	Mountfield	Reid	Steven	Heath	Sharp	Gray	Richardson	

Date	Round	Venue	Opponents	Score	Scorers	Attendance
1984-85						
5th Jan	3	A	Leeds United	2-0	Sharp (pen), Sheedy	21,211
26th Jan	4	H	Doncaster Rovers	2-0	Steven, Stevens	37,535
16th Feb	5	H	Telford United	3-0	Reid, Sheedy (pen), Steven	47,402
9th Mar	6	H	Ipswich Town	2-2	Sheedy, Mountfield	36,468
13th Mar	6 Replay	A	Ipswich Town	1-0	Sharp (pen)	27,737
13th Apr	SF	N	Luton Town	2-1 aet	Sheedy, Mountfield	45,289
18th May	F	N	Manchester United	0-1		100,000
1985-86						
5th Jan	3	H	Exeter City	1-0	Stevens	22,726
25th Jan	4	H	Blackburn Rovers	3-1	Van den Hauwe, Lineker 2	41,831
4th Mar	5	A	Tottenham Hotspur	2-1	Heath, Lineker	23,338
8th Mar	6	A	Luton Town	2-2	Donaghy o.g., Heath	15,529
12th Mar	6 Replay	H	Luton Town	1-0	Lineker	44,264
5th Apr	SF	N	Sheffield Wednesday	2-1 aet	Harper, Sharp	47,711
10th May	F	N	Liverpool	1-3	Lineker	98,000
1986-87						
10th Jan	3	H	Southampton	2-1	Sharp 2	32,320
31st Jan	4	A	Bradford City	1-0	Snodin	15,519
22nd Feb	5	A	Wimbledon	1-3	Wilkinson	9,924
1987-88						
9th Jan	3	A	Sheffield Wednesday	1-1	Reid	33,304
13th Jan	3 Replay 1	H	Sheffield Wednesday	1-1 aet	Sharp	32,935
25th Jan	3 Replay 2	H	Sheffield Wednesday	1-1 aet	Steven	37,414
27th Jan	3 Replay 3	A	Sheffield Wednesday	5-0	Sharp 3, Heath, Snodin	38,953
30th Jan	4	H	Middlesbrough	1-1	Sharp	36,564
3rd Feb	4 Replay 1	A	Middlesbrough	2-2 aet	Watson, Steven	25,235
9th Feb	4 Replay 2	H	Middlesbrough	2-1	Sharp, Mowbray o.g.	32,222
21st Feb	5	H	Liverpool	0-1		48,270
1988-89						
7th Jan	3	A	West Bromwich Albion	1-1	Sheedy (pen)	31,186
11th Jan	3 Replay	H	West Bromwich Albion	1-0	Sheedy	31,697
28th Jan	4	A	Plymouth Argyle	1-1	Sheedy (pen)	27,566
31st Jan	4 Replay	H	Plymouth Argyle	4-0	Nevin, Sharp 2, Sheedy	28,542
18th Feb	5	A	Barnsley	1-0	Sharp	32,551
19th Mar	6	H	Wimbledon	1-0	McCall	24,562
15th Apr	SF	N	Norwich City	1-0	Nevin	46,553
20th May	F	N	Liverpool	2-3 aet	McCall 2	82,800
1989-90						
6th Jan	3	A	Middlesbrough	0-0		20,075
10th Jan	3 Replay 1	H	Middlesbrough	1-1 aet	Sheedy	24,352
17th Jan	3 Replay 2	H	Middlesbrough	1-0	Whiteside	23,866
28th Jan	4	A	Sheffield Wednesday	2-1	Whiteside 2	31,754
17th Feb	5	A	Oldham Athletic	2-2	Sharp, Cottee	19,320
21st Feb	5 Replay 1	H	Oldham Athletic	1-1 aet	Sheedy (pen)	36,663
10th Mar	5 Replay 2	A	Oldham Athletic	1-2 aet	Cottee	19,346
1990-91						
5th Jan	3	A	Charlton Athletic	2-1	Ebbrell 2	12,234
27th Jan	4	A	Woking (Played at Goodison Park)	1-0	Sheedy	34,724
17th Feb	5	A	Liverpool	0-0		38,323
20th Feb	5 Replay 1	H	Liverpool	4-4 aet	Sharp 2, Cottee 2	37,766
27th Feb	5 Replay 2	H	Liverpool	1-0	Watson	40,201
11th Mar	6	A	West Ham United	1-2	Watson	28,162
1991-92						
4th Jan	3	H	Southend United	1-0	Beardsley	22,606

1	2	3	4	5	6	7	8	9	10	11	Used Subs
1984-85											
Southall	Stevens	V d Hauwe	Ratcliffe	Mountfield	Reid	Steven	Gray	Sharp	Bracewell	Sheedy	Atkins
Southall	Stevens	V d Hauwe	Ratcliffe	Mountfield	Reid	Steven	Gray	Sharp	Bracewell	Sheedy	
Southall	Stevens	V d Hauwe	Ratcliffe	Mountfield	Reid	Steven	Gray	Sharp	Bracewell	Sheedy	Harper
Southall	Stevens	V d Hauwe	Ratcliffe	Mountfield	Reid	Steven	Curran	Gray	Bracewell	Sheedy	
Southall	Stevens	V d Hauwe	Ratcliffe	Mountfield	Reid	Steven	Sharp	Gray	Bracewell	Harper	
Southall	Stevens	V d Hauwe	Ratcliffe	Mountfield	Reid	Steven	Sharp	Gray	Bracewell	Sheedy	
Southall	Stevens	V d Hauwe	Ratcliffe	Mountfield	Reid	Steven	Sharp	Gray	Bracewell	Sheedy	
1985-86											
Southall	Stevens	Pointon	Ratcliffe	V d Hauwe	Heath	Harper	Lineker	Sharp	Richardson	Wilkinson	
Southall	Stevens	Pointon	Ratcliffe	V d Hauwe	Richardson	Steven	Lineker	Sharp	Bracewell	Sheedy	Harper
Southall	Harper	Pointon	Ratcliffe	V d Hauwe	Reid	Steven	Lineker	Sharp	Bracewell	Richardson	Heath
Southall	Stevens	Pointon	Harper	V d Hauwe	Reid	Steven	Lineker	Sharp	Bracewell	Richardson	Heath
Southall	Stevens	Pointon	Harper	V d Hauwe	Reid	Steven	Lineker	Sharp	Bracewell	Sheedy	Heath
Mimms	Stevens	V d Hauwe	Ratcliffe	Mountfield	Reid	Steven	Heath	Sharp	Bracewell	Richardson	Harper
Mimms	Stevens	V d Hauwe	Ratcliffe	Mountfield	Reid	Steven	Lineker	Sharp	Bracewell	Sheedy	Heath
1986-87											
Southall	Stevens	Pointon	Ratcliffe	Watson	Power	Steven	Heath	Sharp	Harper	Sheedy	
Southall	Stevens	V d Hauwe	Ratcliffe	Watson	Reid	Steven	Heath	W'inson	Snodin	Power	
Southall	Stevens	V d Hauwe	Ratcliffe	Watson	Reid	Steven	Heath	W'inson	Snodin	Power	Pointon/Harper
1987-88											
Southall	Stevens	V d Hauwe	Ratcliffe	Watson	Reid	Steven	Clarke	Sharp	Snodin	Wilson	Harper/Heath
Southall	Stevens	Pointon	V d Hauwe	Watson	Reid	Steven	Heath	Sharp	Snodin	Wilson	Clarke
Southall	Stevens	Pointon	V d Hauwe	Watson	Reid	Steven	Heath	Sharp	Snodin	Wilson	Clarke/Harper
Southall	Stevens	Pointon	V d Hauwe	Watson	Reid	Steven	Heath	Sharp	Snodin	Harper	Bra'well/Clarke
Southall	Stevens	Pointon	V d Hauwe	Watson	Reid	Steven	Heath	Sharp	Snodin	Harper	Clarke
Southall	Stevens	Pointon	V d Hauwe	Watson	Reid	Steven	Heath	Sharp	Snodin	Harper	Clarke
Southall	Stevens	Pointon	V d Hauwe	Watson	Reid	Steven	Heath	Sharp	Snodin	Power	Clarke
Southall	Stevens	Pointon	V d Hauwe	Watson	Reid	Steven	Heath	Sharp	Snodin	Power	Bra'well/Harper
1988-89											
Southall	Snodin	Pointon	Ratcliffe	V d Hauwe	Bracewell	Steven	Reid	Nevin	Cottee	Sheedy	Clarke
Southall	Snodin	V d Hauwe	Ratcliffe	Watson	Bracewell	Nevin	Reid	Clarke	Cottee	Sheedy	Pointon
Southall	Snodin	V d Hauwe	Ratcliffe	Watson	Bracewell	Steven	McCall	Sharp	Cottee	Sheedy	
Southall	Snodin	V d Hauwe	Ratcliffe	Watson	Steven	Nevin	McCall	Sharp	Cottee	Sheedy	Wilson/Clarke
Southall	McDonald	Pointon	Ratcliffe	Watson	Snodin	Steven	McCall	Sharp	Cottee	Sheedy	Nevin
Southall	McDonald	Pointon	Ratcliffe	Watson	Bracewell	Steven	McCall	Sharp	Cottee	Sheedy	
Southall	McDonald	V d Hauwe	Ratcliffe	Watson	Bracewell	Nevin	Steven	Sharp	Cottee	Sheedy	
Southall	McDonald	V d Hauwe	Ratcliffe	Watson	Bracewell	Nevin	Steven	Sharp	Cottee	Sheedy	McCall/Wilson
1989-90											
Southall	Snodin	McDonald	Ratcliffe	Watson	Whiteside	Atteveld	McCall	Sharp	Newell	Beagrie	
Southall	Snodin	McDonald	Ratcliffe	Keown	Whiteside	Beagrie	McCall	Sharp	Newell	Sheedy	Cottee/Nevin
Southall	Snodin	McDonald	Ratcliffe	Keown	Whiteside	Nevin	McCall	Sharp	Newell	Sheedy	Cottee/Atteveld
Southall	Snodin	McDonald	Ratcliffe	Watson	Whiteside	Keown	McCall	Sharp	Newell	Sheedy	Nevin
Southall	Snodin	McDonald	Ratcliffe	Watson	Whiteside	Ebbrell	McCall	Sharp	Cottee	Sheedy	
Southall	Snodin	McDonald	Ratcliffe	Watson	Whiteside	Atteveld	McCall	Sharp	Cottee	Sheedy	Nevin/Newelll
Southall	Snodin	McDonald	Ratcliffe	Keown	Ebbrell	Atteveld	McCall	Sharp	Cottee	Sheedy	Newell/Beagrie
1990-91											
Southall	McDonald	Hinchcliffe	Ratcliffe	Watson	Ebbrell	Nevin	McCall	Sharp	Sheedy	Beagrie	Newell
Southall	McDonald	Hinchcliffe	Ratcliffe	Watson	McCall	Nevin	Cottee	Sharp	Sheedy	Ebbrell	Beagrie/Keown
Southall	McDonald	Ebbrell	Ratcliffe	Watson	Keown	Atteveld	McCall	Sharp	Sheedy	Nevin	Cottee
Southall	Atteveld	Hinchcliffe	Ratcliffe	Watson	Keown	Nevin	McDonald	Sharp	Newell	Ebbrell	McCall/Cottee
Southall	McDonald	Hinchcliffe	Ratcliffe	Watson	Keown	Atteveld	McCall	Sharp	Newell	Ebbrell	Nevin
Southall	McDonald	Hinchcliffe	Ratcliffe	Watson	Keown	Nevin	McCall	Sharp	Milligan	Ebbrell	Cottee/Newell
1991-92											
Southall	Jackson	Harper	Ebbrell	Watson	Keown	Warzycha	Beardsley	Johnston	Ward	Beagrie	Cottee/Nevin

Date	Round	Venue	Opponents	Score	Scorers	Attendance
1991-92 (cont)						
26th Jan	4	A	Chelsea	0-1		21,152
1992-93						
2nd Jan	3	A	Wimbledon	0-0		7,818
12th Jan	3 Replay	H	Wimbledon	1-2	Watson	15,293
1993-94						
8th Jan	3	A	Bolton Wanderers	1-1	Rideout	21,702
19th Jan	3 Replay	H	Bolton Wanderers	2-3 aet	Barlow 2	34,642
1994-95						
7th Jan	3	H	Derby County	1-0	Hinchcliffe	29,406
29th Jan	4	A	Bristol City	1-0	Jackson	19,816
18th Feb	5	H	Norwich City	5-0	Limpar, Parkinson, Rideout, Ferguson, Stuart	31,616
12th Mar	6	H	Newcastle United	1-0	Watson	35,203
9th Apr	SF	N	Tottenham Hotspur	4-1	Jackson, Stuart, Amokachi 2	38,226
20th May	F	N	Manchester United	1-0	Rideout	79,592
1995-96						
7th Jan	3	H	Stockport County	2-2	Ablett, Stuart	28,921
17th Jan	3 Replay	A	Stockport County	3-2	Ferguson, Stuart, Ebbrell	11,283
27th Jan	4	H	Port Vale	2-2	Amokachi, Ferguson	33,168
14th Feb	4 Replay	A	Port Vale	1-2	Stuart	19,197
1996-97						
5th Jan	3	H	Swindon Town	3-0	Kanchelskis (pen), Barmby, Ferguson	20,411
25th Jan	4	H	Bradford City	2-3	O'Brien o.g., Speed	30,007
1997-98						
4th Jan	3	H	Newcastle United	0-1		20,885
1998-99						
2nd Jan	3	A	Bristol City	2-0	Bakayoko 2	19,608
23rd Jan	4	H	Ipswich Town	1-0	Barmby	28,854
13th Feb	5	H	Coventry City	2-1	Jeffers, Oster	33,907
7th Mar	6	A	Newcastle United	1-4	Unsworth	36,504
1999-2000						
11th Dec	3	A	Exeter City	0-0		6,045
21st Dec	3 Replay	H	Exeter City	1-0	Barmby	16,869
8th Jan	4	H	Birmingham City	2-0	Unsworth 2 (2 pens)	25,405
29th Jan	5	H	Preston North End	2-0	Unsworth, Moore	37,486
20th Feb	6	H	Aston Villa	1-2	Moore	35,331
2000-01						
6th Jan	3	A	Watford	2-1	Hughes, Watson	15,635
27th Jan	4	H	Tranmere Rovers	0-3		39,207
2001-02						
5th Jan	3	A	Stoke City	1-0	Stubbs	28,218
26th Jan	4	H	Leyton Orient	4-1	McGhee o.g., Ferguson, Campbell	35,851
17th Feb	5	H	Crewe Alexandra	0-0		29,939
26th Feb	5 Replay	A	Crewe Alexandra	2-1	Radzinski, Campbell	10,073
10th Mar	6	A	Middlesbrough	0-3		26,950
2002-03						
4th Jan	3	A	Shrewsbury Town	1-2	Alexandersson	7,800

	1	2	3	4	5	6	7	8	9	10	11	Used Subs
1991-92 (cont)												
	Southall	Jackson	Ablett	Ebbrell	Watson	Keown	Nevin	Beardsley	Cottee	Ward	Beagrie	Warzycha
1992-93												
	Southall	Jackson	Ablett	Snodin	Watson	Keown	Harper	Beardsley	Rideout	Kenny	Ebbrell	Barlow/Horne
	Kearton	Jackson	Ablett	Snodin	Watson	Keown	Radosavijevic	Beardsley	Barlow	Kenny	Ebbrell	Warzycha/Harper
1993-94												
	Southall	Holmes	Ablett	Horne	Jackson	Snodin	Ward	Stuart	Cottee	Rideout	Beagrie	Barlow
	Southall	Jackson	Hinchcliffe	Ebbrell	Snodin	Ablett	Ward	Horne	Cottee	Barlow	Beagrie	Stuart/Warzycha
1994-95												
	Southall	Jackson	Burrows	Ebbrell	Watson	Unsworth	Horne	Parkinson	Ferguson	Rideout	Hinchcliffe	Limpar
	Southall	Jackson	Burrows	Horne	Watson	Unsworth	Limpar	Parkinson	Barlow	Rideout	Hinchcliffe	Stuart
	Southall	Jackson	Hinchcliffe	Ebbrell	Watson	Ablett	Stuart	Parkinson	Ferguson	Rideout	Limpar	Barlow
	Southall	Jackson	Ablett	Ebbrell	Watson	Unsworth	Horne	Parkinson	Ferguson	Barlow	Limpar	Stuart
	Southall	Jackson	Ablett	Parkinson	Watson	Unsworth	Limpar	Horne	Stuart	Rideout	Hinchcliffe	Amokachi
	Southall	Jackson	Ablett	Parkinson	Watson	Unsworth	Limpar	Horne	Stuart	Rideout	Hinchcliffe	Amokachi/Ferguson
1995-96												
	Southall	Jackson	Unsworth	Ebbrell	Watson	Ablett	Kanchelskis	Horne	Stuart	Rideout	Limpar	Hinchcliffe/Grant
	Southall	Ebbrell	Ablett	Parkinson	Watson	Short	Kanchelskis	Horne	Ferguson	Stuart	Limpar	Amokachi
	Southall	Ebbrell	Ablett	Parkinson	Watson	Short	Kanchelskis	Horne	Ferguson	Amokachi	Stuart	Hinchcliffe/Limpar
	Southall	Jackson	Unsworth	Ebbrell	Watson	Short	Kanchelskis	Horne	Amokachi	Stuart	Hinchcliffe	Limpar/Rideout
1996-97												
	Southall	Barrett	Speed	Rideout	Watson	Dunne	Kanc'lskis	Barmby	Ferguson	Branch	Stuart	Grant
	Southall	Barrett	Phelan	Parkinson	Watson	Short	Kanc'lskis	Barmby	Ferguson	Stuart	Speed	Grant
1997-98												
	Myhre	Thomas	Ball	Thomsen	Dunne	Tiler	Farrelly	Barmby	Ferguson	Grant	Cadamarteri	Oster
1998-99												
	Myhre	Dunne	Ball	Bilic	Watson	Unsworth	Cadamarteri	Barmby	Bakayoko	Dacourt	Hutchison	Branch/Oster/Grant
	Myhre	Ward	Ball	Cleland	M'razzi	Unsworth	Grant	Barmby	Ca'marteri	Oster	Hutchison	O'Kane/Branch
	Myhre	Ward	Ball	Grant	Watson	Dunne	Oster	Barmby	Jeffers	Dacourt	Hutchison	O'Kane/Bakayoko/C'rteri
	Myhre	Weir	O'Kane	Materazzi	Watson	Unsworth	Grant	Barmby	Ca'marteri	Jeffers	Hutchison	Bakayoko/Oster
1999-2000												
	Gerrard	Weir	Unsworth	Pembridge	Dunne	Xavier	Collins	Barmby	Campbell	Hutchison	Jeffers	Moore/Ball
	Gerrard	Cleland	Unsworth	Weir	Dunne	Pembridge	Collins	Barmby	Campbell	Hutchison	Jeffers	
	Gerrard	Weir	Unsworth	P'bridge	Dunne	Gough	Collins	Barmby	Campbell	Hutchison	Jeffers	Watson/Gemmill
	Myhre	Weir	Ball	Unsworth	Dunne	Gough	Pembridge	Barmby	Campbell	Hutchison	Jeffers	Cadamarteri/Moore
	Myhre	Weir	Unsworth	P'bridge	Gough	Xavier	Collins	Barmby	Campbell	Hutchison	Moore	Cadamarteri/Jeffers
2000-01												
	Myhre	Watson	Naysmith	Gravesen	Weir	Ball	A'dersson	Pembridge	Ca'marteri	Ferguson	Hughes	Gemmill/Tal/Moore
	Myhre	Xavier	Unsworth	Gravesen	Watson	Ball	Gemmill	Pembridge	Campbell	Ca'marteri	Hughes	Gough/Tal/Moore
2001-02												
	Simonsen	Xavier	Naysmith	Stubbs	Weir	Unsworth	Blomqvist	Gascoigne	Moore	Ferguson	Gemmill	
	Simonsen	Hibbert	Unsworth	Stubbs	Weir	Gemmill	A'dersson	Gascoigne	Campbell	Ferguson	N'smith	Tal/Moore
	Simonsen	Clarke	Naysmith	Stubbs	Weir	Linderoth	A'dersson	Gemmill	Campbell	Ginola	Blomqvist	P'bridge/Gasc'gne/Moore
	Simonsen	Clarke	Naysmith	Stubbs	Weir	Pembridge	A'dersson	Gemmill	Campbell	Radzinski	Ginola	Unsworth/L'roth/G'vsen
	Simonsen	Pistone	Unsworth	Stubbs	Weir	Clarke	Linderoth	Gascoigne	Moore	Radzinski	Gemmill	A'dersson/C'wick/Bl'vist
2002-03												
	Wright	Clarke	Unsworth	Stubbs	Weir	Carsley	Gemmill	Gravesen	Rooney	Radzinski	Naysmith	A'dersson/McLeod/Tie

Date	Round	Venue	Opponents	Score	Scorers	Attendance
2003-04						
3rd Jan	3	H	Norwich City	3-1	Kilbane, Ferguson 2 (2 pens)	29,955
25th Jan	4	H	Fulham	1-1	Jeffers	27,862
4th Feb	4 Replay	A	Fulham	1-2 aet	Jeffers	11,551
2004-05						
8th Jan	3	A	Plymouth Argyle	3-1	Osman, McFadden, Chadwick	20,112
29th Jan	4	H	Sunderland	3-0	Beattie, McFadden, Cahill	33,186
19th Feb	5	H	Manchester United	0-2		38,664
2005-06						
7th Jan	3	A	Millwall	1-1	Osman	16,440
18th Jan	3 Replay	H	Millwall	1-0	Cahill	25,800
28th Jan	4	H	Chelsea	1-1	McFadden	29,742
8th Feb	4 Replay	A	Chelsea	1-4	Arteta (pen)	39,301

EVERTON GENERAL FA CUP STATISTICS

EVERTON PLAYERS SENT OFF IN FA CUP TIES

Name	Against	Date	Venue	Minutes
George Harrison	Barnsley	9th Jan 1915	H	32
Bobby Parker	Barnsley	9th Jan 1915	H	53
Jimmy Galt	QPR	20th Feb 1915	A	44
Hunter Hart	Bradford PA	17th Jan 1923	A	30
Archie Styles	West Bromwich Alb.	30th Jan 1974	A	75
Gary Jones	Altrincham	4th Jan 1975	H	40
Brian Kidd	Wigan Athletic	26th Jan 1980	H	81
Brian Kidd	West Ham United	12th Apr 1980	N	63
Kevin Ratcliffe	Manchester City	7th Mar 1981	H	85
Norman Whiteside	Oldham Athletic	21st Feb 1990	H	50
Barry Horne	Bolton Wanderers	8th Jan 1994	A	56
Marco Materazzi	Ipswich Town	23rd Jan 1999	H	48
Joe-Max Moore	Watford	6th Jan 2001	A	85

OPPOSITION PLAYERS SENT OFF IN FA CUP TIES V EVERTON

Name	For	Date	Venue	Minutes
Frank Barson	Barnsley	9th Jan 1915	H	32
Ambrose Fogarty	Sunderland	8th Jan 1958	H	92
Will Duff	Charlton Athletic	24th Jan 1959	A	89
John Hughes	Crystal Palace	15th Jan 1972	A	53
Willie Johnston	West Bromwich Alb.	30th Jan 1974	A	75
Leighton Phillips	Aston Villa	7th Jan 1978	H	87
Steve McCall	Ipswich Town	9th Mar 1985	H	72
Kevin Moran	Manchester United	18th May 1985	N	78
Jon Newsome	Norwich City	18th Feb 1995	H	56
Ian Culverhouse	Swindon Town	5th Jan 1997	H	1
Gary Elkins	Swindon Town	5th Jan 1997	H	75
Benito Carbone	Aston Villa	20th Feb 2000	H	90
Robert Page	Watford	6th Jan 2001	A	82

EVERTON FA CUP HAT-TRICKS

Name	Against	Date	Venue	Goals
Alfred Milward	Derby County	18th Jan 1890	H	3
Alexander Brady	Derby County	18th Jan 1890	H	3
Fred Geary	Derby County	18th Jan 1890	H	3
John Bell	Southport	2nd Feb 1895	A	3
Jimmy Settle	Southampton	4th Mar 1905	H	3
Hugh Bolton	Oldham Athletic	5th Feb 1908	H	4
Thomas Browell	Bury	8th Feb 1912	H	4
Thomas Browell	Stockport County	15th Jan 1913	H	3
Dixie Dean	Crystal Palace	24th Jan 1931	A	4
Dixie Dean	Southport	28th Feb 1931	H	4
Albert Geldard	Grimsby Town	12th Jan 1935	H	3
Jackie Coulter	Sunderland	30th Jan 1935	H	3
Tommy Lawton	Doncaster Rovers	21st Jan 1939	H	4
Graeme Sharp	Sheffield Wednesday	27th Jan 1988	A	3

OPPOSITION FA CUP HAT-TRICKS AGAINST EVERTON

Name	For	Date	Venue	Goals
Alf Edge	Stoke City	1st Feb 1890	A	3
Sam Marsh	Bolton Wanderers	22nd Feb 1908	A	3
Tommy Cook	Brighton & Hove Alb.	2nd Feb 1924	A	3
John Morrison	Tottenham Hotspur	22nd Feb 1937	A	3
Ron Wylie	Aston Villa	14th Feb 1959	H	3
Ian Storey-Moore	Nottingham Forest	8th Apr 1967	A	3

MOST EVERTON FA CUP APPEARANCES

Name	Years	Games
Neville Southall	1982-1997	70

MOST EVERTON FA CUP GOALS

Name	Years	Goals
Dixie Dean	1926-1937	28

EVERTON FA CUP OWN GOALS

Name	Against	Date	Venue	Time
William Balmer	Liverpool	30th Jan 1902	H	40
William Balmer	Tottenham Hotspur	6th Feb 1904	H	31
John Humphreys	Preston North End	5th Jan 1946	A	15
Mick Meagan	Blackburn Rovers	29th Jan 1958	H	f/h
Mick Meagan	Sunderland	15th Feb 1964	A	32
P. Van den Hauwe	Blackburn Rovers	25th Jan 1986	H	53

EVERTON'S BIGGEST FA CUP WIN

Against	Date	Venue	Score
Derby County	18th Jan 1890	H	11-2

EVERTON'S BIGGEST FA CUP DEFEAT

Against	Date	Venue	Score
Crystal Palace	7th Jan 1922	H	6-0

1	2	3	4	5	6	7	8	9	10	11	Used Subs
2003-04											
Martyn	Hibbert	Naysmith	Stubbs	Unsworth	Carsley	McFadden	Gravesen	Ferguson	Rooney	Kilbane	Jeffers/Yobo/Campbell
Martyn	Hibbert	Pistone	Stubbs	Unsworth	Nyarko	Gravesen	Rooney	Ferguson	Radzinski	Kilbane	Jeffers/Naysmith
Martyn	Hibbert	Naysmith	Unsworth	Pistone	Carsley	Nyarko	Gravesen	Rooney	Radzinski	Kilbane	Watson/Jeffers
2004-05											
Wright	Pistone	Naysmith	Stubbs	Yobo	Carsley	Osman	McFadden	Bent	Beattie	Kilbane	Ch'wick/Gravesen/Cahill
Wright	Pistone	Naysmith	Stubbs	Yobo	Carsley	Osman	McFadden	Beattie	Cahill	Kilbane	Weir/Chadwick/Bent
Martyn	Hibbert	Naysmith	Stubbs	Yobo	Carsley	Osman	Arteta	Bent	McFadden	Kilbane	Pistone/Weir
2005-06											
Wright	Hibbert	Valente	Ferrari	Weir	Neville	Arteta	Cahill	Bent	McFadden	Kilbane	Osman/Ferguson/Beattie
Martyn	Hibbert	Valente	Ferrari	Weir	Neville	Osman	Arteta	Beattie	Cahill	Kilbane	Kroldrup/McFadden
Martyn	Hibbert	Valente	Neville	Weir	Osman	Davies	Arteta	Ferguson	McFadden	Kilbane	Naysmith/Anichebe
Turner	Hibbert	Valente	Ferrari	Weir	Neville	Arteta	Cahill	Beattie	Osman	Kilbane	Davies/McFadden/Carsley

EVERTON GENERAL FA CUP STATISTICS

MOST EVERTON FINAL APPEARANCES

Name	Years
Kevin Ratcliffe	1984, 1985, 1986, 1989
Trevor Steven	1984, 1985, 1986, 1989
Graeme Sharp	1984, 1985, 1986, 1989
Neville Southall	1984, 1985, 1989, 1995

MOST EVERTON FINAL GOALS

Name	Goals	Years
Mike Trebilcock	2	1966
Stuart McCall	2	1989

YOUNGEST EVERTON PLAYER IN FA CUP FINAL

Name	Age	Year
Albert Geldard	19 yrs 18 days	1933

OLDEST EVERTON PLAYER IN FA CUP FINAL

Name	Age	Year
Neville Southall	35 yrs 246 days	1995

YOUNGEST EVERTON FA CUP FINAL SCORER

Name	Age	Year
Mike Trebilcock	21 years 166 days	1966

OLDEST EVERTON FA CUP FINAL SCORER

Name	Age	Year
Jimmy Dunn	32 yrs 155 days	1933

YOUNGEST EVERTON FA CUP SCORER

Name	Against	Date	Venue	Age
Tommy Lawton	Tottenham Hotspur	22nd Feb 1937	A	17 yrs 139 days

OLDEST EVERTON FA CUP PLAYER

Name	Against	Date	Venue	Age
Ted Sagar	Hull City	6th Jan 1951	A	40 yrs 333 days

YOUNGEST EVERTON FA CUP PLAYER

Name	Against	Date	Venue	Age
Wayne Rooney	Shrewsbury Town	4th Jan 2003	A	17 years 72 days

EVERTON PENALTIES IN THE FA CUP

Season	Date	Taker	Opponents	Venue	Time	Result
1892/93	18th Feb	Bob Kelso	Sheffield Wednesday	H	s/h	Scored
1895/96	15th Feb	Alfred Millward	Sheffield United	H	55	Scored
1902/03	21st Feb	Tom Booth	Manchester United	H	s/h	Scored
1904/05	2nd Feb	Harry Makepeace	Liverpool	A	81	Scored
1904/05	18th Feb	Harry Makepeace	Stoke City	A	s/h	Scored
1909/10	5th Feb	Jack Sharp	Arsenal	H	30	Scored
1909/10	31st Mar	Jack Sharp	Barnsley	N	41	Saved
1911/12	3rd Feb	John Maconnachie	Bury	H	56	Scored
1914/15	20th Feb	Bobby Parker	QPR	A	8	Woodwork
1921/22	7th Jan	Stan Fazackerley	Crystal Palace	H	82	Wide
1929/30	11th Jan	Dixie Dean	Carlisle United	A	52	Scored
1930/31	14th Feb	Tom Johnson	Grimsby Town	H	80	Scored
1935/36	11th Jan	Tommy White	Preston North End	H	71	Saved
1936/37	30th Jan	Cliff Britton	Sheffield Wednesday	H	37	Scored
1936/37	20th Feb	Dixie Dean	Tottenham Hotspur	H	71	Saved
1938/39	15th Feb	Billy Cook	Birmingham City	H	11	Scored
1945/46	9th Jan	Joe Mercer	Preston North End	H	29	Scored
1949/50	11th Feb	Eddie Wainwright	Tottenham Hotspur	H	4	Scored
1952/53	21st Mar	Tommy Clinton	Bolton Wanderers	N	44	Wide
1956/57	5th Jan	Jimmy Harris	Blackburn Rovers	H	60	Scored
1961/62	6th Jan	Roy Vernon	King's Lynn	H	50	Scored
1963/64	25th Jan	Roy Vernon	Leeds United	A	79	Scored
1964/65	30th Jan	Fred Pickering	Leeds United	A	65	Scored
1966/67	18th Feb	Alan Ball	Wolverhampton Wan.	H	78	Scored
1967/68	27th Apr	Johnny Morrissey	Leeds United	N	42	Scored
1969/70	3rd Jan	Alan Ball	Sheffield United	A	17	Scored
1974/75	7th Jan	Dave Clements	Altrincham	H	69	Scored
1977/78	7th Jan	Trevor Ross	Aston Villa	H	26	Scored
1979/80	16th Feb	Trevor Ross	Wrexham	H	67	Scored
1979/80	16th Apr	Brian Kidd	West Ham United	N	42	Scored
1980/81	7th Mar	Trevor Ross	Manchester City	H	48	Scored
1981/82	2nd Jan	Trevor Ross	West Ham United	A	78	Saved
1984/85	5th Jan	Graeme Sharp	Leeds United	A	39	Scored
1984/85	16th Feb	Kevin Sheedy	Telford United	H	71	Scored
1984/85	13th Mar	Graeme Sharp	Ipswich Town	A	76	Scored
1985/86	12th Mar	Trevor Steven	Luton Town	H	42	Saved
1988/89	7th Jan	Kevin Sheedy	West Bromwich Alb.	A	69	Scored
1988/89	28th Jan	Kevin Sheedy	Plymouth Argyle	A	78	Scored
1988/89	19th Mar	Graeme Sharp	Wimbledon	H	45	Saved
1989/00	21st Feb	Kevin Sheedy	Oldham Athletic	H	115	Scored
1991/92	26th Jan	Tony Cottee	Chelsea	A	80	Saved
1996/97	5th Jan	Andrei Kanchelskis	Swindon Town	H	2	Scored
1999/00	8th Jan	David Unsworth	Birmingham City	H	75	Scored
1999/00	8th Jan	David Unsworth	Birmingham City	H	90	Scored
2003/04	3rd Jan	Duncan Ferguson	Norwich City	H	38	Scored
2003/04	3rd Jan	Duncan Ferguson	Norwich City	H	70	Scored
2005/06	8th Feb	Mikel Arteta	Chelsea	A	72	Scored

EVERTON FA CUP APPEARANCES A-F

Name	Debut	Final	Start	Sub	Ttl	Gls
Abbott, Walter	27/1/1900	11/3/1908	34	0	34	5
Ablett, Gary	26/1/1992	27/1/1996	12	0	12	1
Adams, James	1/2/1896	29/2/1896	3	0	3	0
Alexandersson, Niclas	6/1/2001	4/1/2003	4	2	6	1
Amokachi, Daniel	9/4/1995	14/2/1996	2	3	5	3
Angus, Jack	17/1/1891	17/1/1891	1	0	1	0
Anichebe, Victor	28/1/2006	-	0	1	1	0
Arnold, Jim	8/1/1983	12/3/1983	5	0	5	0
Arridge, Smart	1/2/1896	27/2/1897	5	0	5	0
Arteta, Mikel	19/2/2005	-	5	0	5	1
Atkins, Ian	5/1/1985	5/1/1985	0	1	1	0
Atteveld, Ray	6/1/1990	27/2/1991	6	1	7	0
Bailey, John	5/1/1980	19/5/1984	22	0	22	0
Bain, David	21/2/1925	2/2/1927	5	0	5	0
Bakayoko, Ibrahima	2/1/1999	7/3/1999	1	2	3	2
Ball, Alan	28/1/1967	27/3/1971	21	0	21	5
Ball, Michael	4/1/1998	27/1/2001	7	1	8	0
Balmer, Robert	2/2/1905	14/1/1911	23	0	23	0
Balmer, William	29/1/1898	11/3/1908	38	0	38	0
Barlow, George	16/1/1909	31/3/1910	8	0	8	1
Barlow, Stuart	2/1/1993	12/3/1995	4	3	7	2
Barmby, Nick	5/1/1997	20/2/2000	12	0	12	3
Barrett, Earl	5/1/1997	25/1/1997	2	0	2	0
Beagrie, Peter	6/1/1990	19/1/1994	7	2	9	0
Beardsley, Peter	4/1/1992	12/1/1993	4	0	4	1
Beare, George	14/1/1911	10/1/1914	14	0	14	1
Beattie, James	8/1/2005	-	4	1	5	1
Belfitt, Rod	13/1/1973	3/2/1973	2	0	2	1
Bell, John	27/1/1894	7/3/1903	22	0	22	8
Bell, Lawrence	29/1/1898	11/2/1899	7	0	7	3
Bent, Marcus	8/1/2005	7/1/2006	3	1	4	0
Bentham, Stanley	11/1/1936	14/2/1948	15	0	15	0
Bernard, Mike	13/1/1973	1/2/1977	9	1	10	0
Berry, Arthur	14/1/1911	25/2/1911	2	0	2	0
Bilic, Slaven	2/1/1999	2/1/1999	1	0	1	0
Bingham, Billy	7/1/1961	16/3/1963	7	0	7	2
Birch, Kenneth	5/1/1957	29/1/1958	2	0	2	0
Blair, John	3/2/1921	3/2/1921	1	0	1	0
Blomqvist, Jesper	5/1/2002	10/3/2002	2	1	3	0
Blythe, Joe	27/1/1900	27/1/1900	1	0	1	0
Bocking, William	19/1/1932	19/1/1932	1	0	1	0
Bolton, Hugh	24/2/1906	11/3/1908	12	0	12	7
Booth, Tom	9/2/1901	10/3/1906	10	0	10	2
Bowman, Adam	25/1/1902	30/1/1902	2	0	2	0
Boyes, Wally	7/1/1937	9/1/1946	7	0	7	4
Boyle, Richard	21/1/1893	11/2/1899	21	0	21	1
Bracewell, Paul	5/1/1985	20/5/1989	19	2	21	0
Bradshaw, Frank	13/1/1912	10/1/1914	8	0	8	2
Bradshaw, George	2/3/1935	2/3/1935	1	0	1	0
Brady, Alexander	18/1/1890	3/2/1890	2	0	2	3
Bramwell, John	10/1/1959	14/2/1959	4	0	4	0
Branch, Michael	5/1/1997	23/1/1999	1	2	3	0
Brearley, John	7/2/1903	21/2/1903	2	0	2	1
Brewster, George	8/1/1921	5/3/1921	4	0	4	0
Briscoe, William	19/11/1887	19/11/1887	1	0	1	0
Britton, Cliff	14/1/1933	22/1/1938	19	0	19	1
Broad, James	10/1/1925	21/2/1925	3	0	3	0
Browell, Thomas	13/1/1912	8/3/1913	10	0	10	11
Brown, Sandy	4/1/1964	27/3/1971	16	8	24	0
Brown, William	10/1/1920	4/2/1925	9	0	9	0
Buckle, Ted	7/1/1950	21/3/1953	10	0	10	2
Buckley, Mick	13/1/1973	27/4/1977	7	0	7	1
Burnett, George	5/1/1946	25/3/1950	7	0	7	0
Burrows, David	7/1/1995	29/1/1995	2	0	2	0
Cadamarteri, Danny	4/1/1998	27/1/2001	6	3	9	0
Cahill, Tim	8/1/2005	-	4	1	5	2
Cain, Thomas	2/3/1895	2/3/1895	1	0	1	0
Caldwell, James	15/1/1913	8/3/1913	5	0	5	0
Cameron, John	1/2/1896	17/2/1898	6	0	6	2
Campbell, Kevin	11/12/1999	3/1/2004	9	1	10	3
Carsley, Lee	4/1/2003	-	6	1	7	0
Cassidy	15/10/1887	29/10/1887	2	0	2	0
Catterick, Harry	5/1/1946	25/3/1950	12	0	12	5
Chadwick, Edgar	18/1/1890	11/2/1899	30	0	30	13

Name	Debut	Final	Start	Sub	Ttl	Gls
Chadwick, Nick	10/3/2002	29/1/2005	0	3	3	1
Chadwick, Thomas	12/1/1907	12/1/1907	1	0	1	0
Chadwick, Wilf	13/1/1923	21/2/1925	7	0	7	5
Chedgzoy, Sam	9/1/1915	14/1/1926	21	0	21	3
Clark, Archie	19/1/1932	19/1/1932	1	0	1	0
Clark, Charles	7/3/1903	7/3/1903	1	0	1	0
Clarke, Peter	17/2/2002	4/1/2003	4	0	4	0
Clarke, Wayne	9/1/1988	31/1/1989	2	8	10	0
Cleland, Alec	23/1/1999	21/12/1999	2	0	2	0
Clements, Dave	5/1/1974	15/2/1975	6	0	6	2
Clennell, Joe	9/1/1915	10/1/1920	6	0	6	3
Clifford, Robert	16/1/1909	31/3/1910	8	0	8	0
Clinton, Thomas	12/1/1952	21/3/1953	7	0	7	1
Cock, Jack	12/1/1924	4/2/1925	3	0	3	2
Coggins, Billy	10/1/1931	14/3/1931	5	0	5	0
Coleman, John	16/1/1909	6/2/1909	2	0	2	1
Collins, Bobby	10/1/1959	17/2/1962	9	0	9	5
Collins, John	11/12/1999	20/2/2000	4	0	4	0
Connolly, John	13/1/1973	3/1/1976	3	1	4	0
Cook, Billy	14/1/1933	4/3/1939	24	0	24	1
Cook, Harry	3/2/1906	24/2/1906	2	0	2	0
Corrin, Thomas	6/2/1904	6/2/1904	1	0	1	0
Cottee, Tony	7/1/1989	19/1/1994	15	6	21	4
Coulter, Jackie	12/1/1935	20/2/1937	8	0	8	8
Crelley, Jack	21/2/1903	21/4/1906	11	0	11	0
Cresswell, Warney	14/1/1928	12/1/1935	16	0	16	0
Critchley, Ted	14/1/1928	13/1/1934	12	0	12	5
Crompton, Thomas	28/1/1899	28/1/1899	1	0	1	0
Crossley, Charlie	8/1/1921	5/3/1921	5	0	5	3
Cummins, George	10/1/1953	21/3/1953	5	0	5	0
Cunliffe, Jimmy	13/1/1934	22/1/1938	13	0	13	3
Curran, Terry	14/4/1984	9/3/1985	2	0	2	0
Dacourt, Olivier	2/1/1999	13/2/1999	2	0	2	0
D'Arcy, Francis	12/2/1969	12/2/1969	0	1	1	0
Darracott, Terry	15/1/1972	10/1/1979	12	0	12	0
Davidson, William	13/1/1912	5/2/1913	7	0	7	1
Davies, Arthur	7/2/1927	11/1/1930	3	0	3	0
Davies, Dai	4/1/1975	3/1/1976	5	0	5	0
Davies, Simon	28/1/2006	-	1	1	2	0
Davies, Stan	19/2/1921	5/3/1921	2	0	2	1
Dawson, Harold	6/2/1909	6/2/1909	1	0	1	0
Dean, Dixie	9/1/1926	22/2/1937	32	0	32	28
Dick, Alec	15/10/1887	19/11/1887	4	0	4	0
Divers, John	26/2/1898	19/3/1898	2	0	2	0
Dobson, George	15/10/1887	19/11/1887	4	0	4	0
Dobson, Martin	7/1/1975	10/1/1979	13	0	13	2
Dodds, Jock	11/1/1947	10/1/1948	3	0	3	1
Dominy, Arthur	8/1/1927	7/2/1927	4	0	4	1
Donnachie, Joe	12/1/1907	9/3/1907	2	0	2	0
Donovan, Don	12/1/1952	29/1/1958	8	0	8	0
Downs, Dicky	8/1/1921	5/3/1921	5	0	5	0
Doyle, Daniel	18/1/1890	17/1/1891	3	0	3	1
Dugdale, Gordon	24/1/1948	8/1/1949	5	0	5	0
Dunlop, Albert	5/1/1957	17/2/1962	15	0	15	0
Dunn, Jimmy	12/1/1929	13/1/1934	14	0	14	7
Dunne, Richard	5/1/1997	29/1/2000	8	0	8	0
Earp, John	16/1/1892	16/1/1892	1	0	1	0
Eastoe, Peter	26/1/1980	2/1/1982	12	0	12	6
Ebbrell, John	17/2/1990	14/2/1996	20	0	20	3
Eccles, George	27/1/1900	25/1/1902	4	0	4	0
Eglington, Tommy	11/1/1947	16/2/1957	34	0	34	6
Elliott, Jack	2/3/1895	2/3/1895	1	0	1	0
Elliott, Tom	5/1/1946	9/1/1946	2	0	2	1
Falder, David	7/1/1950	25/3/1950	5	0	5	0
Farmer, George	15/10/1887	19/11/1887	4	0	4	0
Farrell, Peter	11/1/1947	16/2/1957	31	0	31	4
Farrelly, Gareth	4/1/1998	4/1/1998	1	0	1	0
Fazackerley, Stanley	8/1/1921	7/1/1922	6	0	6	0
Fell, James	6/1/1962	6/1/1962	1	0	1	1
Ferguson, Duncan	7/1/1995	-	14	2	16	7
Fern, Tom	10/1/1914	7/1/1922	12	0	12	0
Ferrari, Matteo	7/1/2006	-	3	0	3	0
Fielding, Wally	5/1/1946	16/2/1957	30	0	30	5
Fleetwood, Tom	13/1/1912	17/1/1923	21	0	21	1

Name	Debut	Final	Start	Sub	Ttl	Gls
Fleming, George	12/11/1887	12/11/1887	1	0	1	0
Freeman, Bertie	16/1/1909	31/3/1910	8	0	8	4
Gabriel, Jimmy	7/1/1961	18/2/1967	25	0	25	2
Galt, Jimmy	9/1/1915	27/3/1915	4	0	4	2
Gascoigne, Paul	5/1/2002	10/3/2002	3	1	4	0
Gauld, Jimmy	5/1/1957	16/2/1957	3	0	3	1
Gault, William	10/1/1920	10/1/1920	1	0	1	0
Geary, Fred	18/1/1890	20/2/1895	7	0	7	8
Gee, Charlie	10/1/1931	22/2/1937	15	0	15	0
Gee, Ellis	11/2/1899	11/2/1899	1	0	1	0
Geldard, Albert	14/1/1933	8/1/1938	12	0	12	6
Gemmill, Scot	8/1/2000	4/1/2003	7	2	9	0
Gerrard, Paul	11/12/1999	8/1/2000	3	0	3	0
Gibson, Archie	15/10/1887	19/11/1887	4	0	4	0
Gidman, John	5/1/1980	11/3/1981	11	0	11	0
Gillick, Torry	11/1/1936	4/3/1939	12	0	12	4
Ginola, David	17/2/2002	26/2/2002	2	0	2	0
Goldie, Hugh	29/2/1896	29/2/1896	1	0	1	0
Goodlass, Ronnie	8/1/1977	27/4/1977	7	0	7	0
Gordon, Patrick	16/1/1892	20/3/1893	5	0	5	2
Goudie	15/10/1887	19/11/1887	4	0	4	0
Gough, Richard	8/1/2000	27/1/2001	3	1	4	0
Gourlay, James	14/1/1911	5/2/1913	4	0	4	1
Graham, Robert	1/2/1908	1/2/1908	1	0	1	0
Grant, Jackie	10/1/1948	6/1/1951	12	0	12	1
Grant, Tony	7/1/1996	7/3/1999	4	4	8	0
Gravesen, Thomas	6/1/2001	8/1/2005	6	2	8	0
Gray, Andy	6/1/1984	18/5/1985	14	1	15	3
Gray, Robert	27/1/1900	27/1/1900	1	0	1	0
Green, Colin	27/1/1962	17/2/1962	2	0	2	0
Greenhalgh, Norman	7/1/1939	25/1/1947	9	0	9	0
Greenyer, Alan	15/1/1913	29/1/1921	6	0	6	0
Griffiths, Tom	12/1/1929	11/1/1930	2	0	2	0
Hamilton, Bryan	3/1/1976	23/4/1977	2	2	4	0
Hannah, Andrew	18/1/1890	3/2/1890	2	0	2	0
Hardman, Harold	2/2/1905	11/3/1908	26	0	26	4
Hardy, Henry	9/1/1926	2/2/1927	5	0	5	0
Harland, Alfred	13/1/1923	31/1/1925	6	0	6	0
Harper, Alan	28/1/1984	12/1/1993	12	9	21	1
Harper, Joe	13/1/1973	27/1/1974	4	0	4	2
Harris, Brian	7/1/1956	14/5/1966	31	0	31	4
Harris, Jimmy	7/1/1956	9/1/1960	14	0	14	5
Harris, Val	1/2/1908	10/1/1914	24	0	24	1
Harrison, George	10/1/1914	13/1/1923	13	0	13	0
Hart, Hunter	13/1/1923	25/1/1930	11	0	11	0
Hartford, Asa	5/1/1980	11/3/1981	11	0	11	1
Hartley, Abe	27/1/1894	10/4/1897	11	0	11	4
Harvey, Colin	9/1/1965	5/2/1972	34	0	34	4
Heath, Adrian	8/1/1983	21/2/1988	24	5	29	6
Hedley, Jack	8/1/1949	25/3/1950	7	0	7	0
Henderson, William	7/2/1903	7/3/1903	2	0	2	0
Heslop, George	4/1/1964	4/1/1964	1	0	1	0
Hibbert, Tony	6/1/2002	-	9	0	9	0
Hickson, Dave	12/1/1952	14/2/1959	18	0	18	16
Higgins, Mike	15/10/1887	19/11/1887	4	0	4	0
Higgins, Mark	7/1/1978	12/3/1983	7	0	7	0
Higgins, William	8/1/1949	8/1/1949	1	0	1	1
Hill, Percy	13/1/1906	3/2/1906	2	0	2	0
Hillman, Jack	1/2/1896	29/2/1896	3	0	3	0
Hinchcliffe, Andy	5/1/1991	14/2/1996	12	2	14	1
Hodge, Martin	5/1/1980	24/1/1981	6	0	6	0
Hold, Oscar	6/1/1951	6/1/1951	1	0	1	0
Holmes, Paul	8/1/1994	8/1/1994	1	0	1	0
Holt, Johnny	18/1/1890	20/3/1893	27	0	27	1
Horne, Barry	2/1/1993	14/2/1996	11	1	12	0
Houston, John	22/2/1913	8/3/1913	2	0	2	0
Howarth, Robert	16/1/1892	20/3/1893	9	0	9	0
Hughes, Stephen	6/1/2001	27/1/2001	2	0	2	1
Humphreys, John	5/1/1946	14/2/1948	8	0	8	0
Hunt, Ernie	9/3/1968	9/3/1968	1	0	1	0
Hurst, John	28/1/1967	3/1/1976	30	2	32	4
Husband, Jimmy	28/1/1967	18/1/1972	22	0	22	10
Hutchison, Don	2/1/1999	20/2/2000	9	0	9	0
Irvine, Alan	19/2/1983	10/3/1984	8	0	8	2
Irvine, Bobby	7/1/1922	28/1/1928	15	0	15	3
Irving, David	4/1/1975	4/1/1975	1	0	1	0
Izat	15/10/1887	19/11/1887	4	0	4	0
Jackson, George	16/2/1935	25/1/1947	4	0	4	0
Jackson, Matthew	4/1/1992	14/2/1996	14	0	14	2
Jackson, Tommy	27/4/1968	3/1/1970	3	1	4	0
Jefferis, Frank	13/1/1912	10/1/1920	12	0	12	3
Jeffers, Francis	13/2/1999	4/2/2004	6	4	10	3
Johnson, David	13/2/1971	26/2/1972	5	0	5	2
Johnson, Tommy	10/1/1931	13/1/1934	13	0	13	8
Johnston, Maurice	4/1/1992	4/1/1992	1	0	1	0
Joliffe, Charles	15/10/1887	29/10/1887	2	0	2	0
Jones, David	8/1/1977	28/1/1978	5	0	5	1
Jones, Gary	26/2/1972	3/1/1976	7	2	9	1
Jones, Jack	26/1/1935	22/1/1938	10	0	10	0
Jones, Tommy E.	6/1/1951	7/1/1961	25	0	25	0
Jones, Tommy G.	8/1/1938	29/1/1949	10	0	10	1
Kanchelskis, Andrei	7/1/1996	25/1/1997	6	0	6	1
Kay, Tony	29/1/1963	15/2/1964	5	0	5	0
Kearton, Jason	12/1/1993	12/1/1993	1	0	1	0
Keeley, Jack	4/1/1958	29/1/1958	3	0	3	2
Kelly, Jerry	14/1/1928	28/1/1928	2	0	2	0
Kelso, Bob	16/1/1892	20/3/1893	14	0	14	0
Kendall, Howard	27/1/1968	2/1/1982	23	0	23	3
Kendall, John	4/2/1925	21/2/1925	2	0	2	0
Kenny, Billy (jnr)	2/1/1993	12/1/1993	2	0	2	0
Kenyon, Roger	30/3/1968	28/1/1978	15	1	16	2
Keown, Martin	10/1/1990	12/1/1993	12	1	13	0
Kerr, Jasper	29/1/1927	7/2/1927	3	0	3	0
Kidd, Brian	5/1/1980	12/4/1980	4	0	4	4
Kilbane, Kevin	3/1/2004	-	10	0	10	1
King, Andy	8/1/1977	18/2/1984	16	1	17	4
King, Francis	11/1/1936	11/1/1936	1	0	1	0
King, John	9/1/1960	9/1/1960	1	0	1	0
Kirby, George	26/1/1957	26/1/1957	1	0	1	0
Kirkwood, David	18/1/1890	17/1/1891	3	0	3	1
Kirsopp, William	9/1/1915	27/3/1915	5	0	5	1
Kirwan, John	28/1/1899	11/2/1899	2	0	2	0
Kitchen, George	25/1/1902	6/2/1904	3	0	3	0
Kroldrup, Per	18/1/2006	18/1/2006	0	1	1	0
Labone, Brian	9/1/1960	27/3/1971	45	0	45	0
Lacey, William	4/2/1911	24/2/1912	3	0	3	0
Latchford, Bob	4/1/1975	16/4/1980	17	1	18	10
Latta, Alex	18/1/1890	20/3/1893	12	0	12	1
Laverick, Bobby	9/1/1960	9/1/1960	1	0	1	0
Lawson, David	13/1/1973	27/4/1977	12	0	12	0
Lawton, Tommy	22/2/1937	4/3/1939	8	0	8	5
Lello, Cyril	29/1/1949	3/3/1956	17	0	17	0
Leyland, Harry	12/1/1952	18/2/1956	4	0	4	0
Li Tie	4/1/2003	4/1/2003	0	1	1	0
Lill, Michael	27/1/1962	17/2/1962	2	0	2	1
Limpar, Anders	7/1/1995	14/2/1996	7	3	10	1
Lindley, Maurice	8/1/1949	16/1/1952	3	0	3	0
Linderoth, Tobias	17/2/2002	10/3/2002	2	1	3	0
Lindsay, Jack	12/1/1952	20/2/1954	10	0	10	0
Lineker, Gary	5/1/1986	10/5/1986	6	0	6	5
Livingstone, Duggie	7/1/1922	2/2/1924	5	0	5	0
Lodge, Paul	2/1/1982	2/1/1982	1	0	1	0
Lyons, Mick	15/1/1972	2/1/1982	34	2	36	6
Maconnachie, John	16/1/1909	6/3/1915	25	0	25	1
Magner, Edward	14/1/1911	25/2/1911	3	0	3	1
Makepeace, Harry	21/2/1903	27/3/1915	52	0	52	7
Marshall, Cliff	25/1/1975	25/1/1975	1	0	1	0
Martin, George	25/1/1930	25/1/1930	1	0	1	1
Martyn, Nigel	3/1/2004	-	6	0	6	0
Materazzi, Marco	23/1/1999	7/3/1999	2	0	2	0
Maxwell, Alan	21/1/1893	20/3/1893	7	0	7	3
Mayers, Derek	26/1/1957	26/1/1957	1	0	1	0
McBain, Neil	12/1/1924	21/2/1925	6	0	6	0
McBride, Joe	5/1/1980	11/3/1981	6	0	6	1
McCall, Stuart	28/1/1989	11/3/1991	16	2	18	3
McClure, Joseph	10/1/1931	14/3/1931	5	0	5	0
McDermott, Tom	6/2/1904	29/3/1905	7	0	7	4
McDonagh, Jim	3/1/1981	11/3/1981	5	0	5	0

EVERTON FA CUP APPEARANCES M-V

Name	Debut	Final	Start	Sub	Ttl	Gls
McDonald, John	8/1/1921	2/2/1927	16	0	16	0
McDonald, Neil	18/2/1989	11/3/1991	17	0	17	0
McFadden, James	3/1/2004	-	6	2	8	3
McIlhatton, John	11/1/1947	29/1/1949	3	0	3	1
McInnes, Thomas	2/2/1895	15/2/1896	5	0	5	0
McIntosh, James	6/1/1951	6/1/1951	1	0	1	0
McKenzie, Duncan	8/1/1977	28/1/1978	7	1	8	5
McLaughlin, John	15/1/1972	7/1/1975	7	0	7	0
McLean, Duncan	17/1/1891	17/1/1891	1	0	1	0
McLeod, Kevin	3/1/2004	3/1/2004	0	1	1	0
McMahon, Steve	3/1/1981	12/3/1983	9	0	9	0
McNamara, Tony	12/1/1952	5/1/1957	2	0	2	0
McNaught, Ken	4/1/1975	27/4/1977	10	0	10	0
McPherson, Lachlan	25/1/1930	25/1/1930	1	0	1	0
Meagan, Mick	4/1/1958	15/2/1964	10	0	10	0
Meehan, Peter	13/2/1897	10/4/1897	4	0	4	0
Megson, Gary	16/2/1980	12/4/1980	3	0	3	1
Menham, Robert	30/1/1897	10/4/1897	5	0	5	0
Mercer, Joe	11/1/1936	9/1/1946	14	0	14	1
Miller, Willie	11/1/1936	11/1/1936	1	0	1	0
Milligan, Mike	11/3/1991	11/3/1991	1	0	1	0
Millington, Thomas	7/2/1927	7/2/1927	1	0	1	0
Milward, Alfred	18/1/1890	20/3/1893	23	0	23	11
Mimms, Bobby	5/4/1986	10/5/1986	2	0	2	0
Mitchell, Frank	27/3/1915	27/3/1915	1	0	1	0
Moffat, Harold	29/1/1927	29/1/1927	1	0	1	0
Molyneux, George	28/1/1899	11/2/1899	2	0	2	0
Moore, Eric	7/1/1950	3/3/1956	13	0	13	0
Moore, Joe-Max	11/12/1999	10/3/2002	3	6	9	2
Morrissey, John	15/1/1963	27/3/1971	29	0	29	3
Morton, Harry	8/1/1938	22/1/1938	2	0	2	0
Mountfield, Derek	6/1/1984	10/5/1986	17	0	17	2
Muir, William	29/1/1898	23/2/1901	10	0	10	0
Murray	15/10/1887	29/10/1887	2	0	2	0
Myhre, Thomas	4/1/1998	27/1/2001	9	0	9	0
Naysmith, Gary	6/1/2001	-	11	2	13	0
Neville, Phil	7/1/2006	-	4	0	4	0
Nevin, Pat	7/1/1989	26/1/1992	12	6	18	2
Newell, Mike	6/1/1990	11/3/1991	6	4	10	0
Newton, Henry	2/1/1971	26/2/1972	6	0	6	1
Newton, Keith	3/1/1970	27/3/1971	2	0	2	0
Nyarko, Alex	25/1/2004	4/2/2004	2	0	2	0
O'Donnell, John	9/1/1926	25/1/1930	9	0	9	0
O'Hara, Edward	28/1/1959	14/2/1959	2	0	2	0
O'Kane, John	23/1/1999	7/3/1999	1	2	3	0
O'Keefe, Eamonn	24/1/1981	2/1/1982	4	1	5	1
O'Neill, Jimmy	10/1/1953	3/3/1956	12	0	12	0
Oliver, Frank	24/2/1906	24/2/1906	1	0	1	0
Osman, Leon	8/1/2005	-	6	1	7	2
Oster, John	4/1/1998	7/3/1999	2	3	5	1
Page, John	10/1/1920	10/1/1920	1	0	1	0
Palmer, William	30/1/1915	30/1/1915	1	0	1	0
Parker, Alex	10/1/1959	16/3/1963	12	0	12	0
Parker, Bobby	10/1/1914	29/1/1921	8	0	8	3
Parker, John	12/1/1952	20/2/1954	9	0	9	7
Parker, Thomas	8/1/1927	8/1/1927	1	0	1	0
Parkinson, Joe	7/1/1995	25/1/1997	9	0	9	1
Parry, Charlie	18/1/1890	2/3/1895	8	0	8	0
Parry, Frank	10/1/1925	10/1/1925	1	0	1	0
Payne, Jimmy	16/2/1957	16/2/1957	1	0	1	0
Peacock, Joe	8/1/1921	29/1/1927	10	0	10	0
Pearson, Jim	4/1/1975	28/1/1978	9	0	9	2
Pejic, Mike	26/2/1977	28/1/1978	6	0	6	0
Pembridge, Mark	11/12/1999	26/2/2002	8	1	9	0
Phelan, Terry	25/1/1997	25/1/1997	1	0	1	0
Pickering, Fred	9/1/1965	5/4/1966	9	0	9	8
Pistone, Alessandro	10/3/2002	-	5	1	6	0
Pointon, Neil	5/1/1986	19/3/1989	16	2	18	0
Potts, Harold	6/1/1951	29/1/1955	4	0	4	1
Power, Paul	10/1/1987	21/2/1988	5	0	5	0
Proudfoot, John	28/1/1899	23/2/1901	5	0	5	1
Radosavijevic, Predrag	12/1/1993	12/1/1993	1	0	1	0
Radzinski, Tomasz	26/2/2002	4/2/2004	5	0	5	1
Raitt, David	13/1/1923	8/1/1927	9	0	9	0
Rankin, Andy	4/1/1964	27/3/1971	7	0	7	0
Rankin, Bruce	21/2/1903	21/2/1903	1	0	1	0
Rankin, George	6/1/1951	29/1/1955	3	0	3	0
Ratcliffe, Kevin	16/4/1980	11/3/1991	57	0	57	0
Rawlings, James	5/1/1946	9/1/1946	2	0	2	0
Rea, Ken	5/1/1957	8/1/1958	5	0	5	0
Reay, Harry	2/2/1895	2/2/1895	1	0	1	0
Reid, David	17/1/1923	21/2/1925	4	0	4	0
Reid, Peter	8/1/1983	11/1/1989	35	0	35	3
Richardson, Kevin	2/1/1982	5/4/1986	13	0	13	1
Rideout, Paul	2/1/1993	5/1/1997	9	1	10	3
Rigby, Arthur	11/1/1930	25/1/1930	2	0	2	0
Rioch, Bruce	8/1/1977	27/4/1977	7	0	7	1
Ritchie, Henry	12/1/1929	12/1/1929	1	0	1	0
Robertson, Hope	17/1/1891	16/1/1892	2	0	2	1
Robertson, John	30/1/1897	19/3/1898	6	0	6	0
Robinson, Neil	8/1/1977	8/1/1977	1	0	1	0
Robson, Thomas	11/1/1930	25/1/1930	2	0	2	0
Rooney, Walter	8/1/1927	14/1/1928	4	0	4	0
Rooney, Wayne	4/1/2003	4/2/2004	4	0	4	0
Roose, Leigh	2/2/1905	29/3/1905	6	0	6	0
Ross, Trevor	7/1/1978	2/1/1982	13	0	13	3
Rouse, Frederick	23/2/1907	23/2/1907	1	0	1	0
Royle, Joe	27/1/1968	30/1/1974	23	0	23	9
Sagar, Ted	25/1/1930	6/1/1951	32	0	32	0
Sanders, Alan	4/1/1958	14/2/1959	7	0	7	0
Saunders, George	11/1/1947	29/1/1949	7	0	7	0
Scott, Alex	4/1/1964	14/5/1966	17	0	17	2
Scott, Billy	13/1/1906	9/3/1912	38	0	38	0
Scott, Peter	15/1/1972	25/1/1975	5	0	5	1
Seargeant, Steve	25/1/1975	15/2/1975	2	0	2	0
Settle, Jimmy	27/1/1900	11/3/1908	32	0	32	13
Shackleton, Alan	9/1/1960	9/1/1960	1	0	1	0
Sharp, Bert	30/1/1902	30/1/1902	1	0	1	0
Sharp, Graeme	2/1/1982	11/3/1991	52	2	54	20
Sharp, Jack	27/1/1900	31/3/1910	42	0	42	12
Sheedy, Kevin	8/1/1983	17/2/1991	38	0	38	15
Short, Craig	17/1/1996	25/1/1997	4	0	4	0
Simonsen, Steve	5/1/2002	10/3/2002	5	0	5	0
Simpson, Robert	30/1/1915	27/3/1915	2	0	2	0
Smalley, Robert	12/11/1887	3/2/1890	4	0	4	0
Snodin, Ian	31/1/1987	19/1/1994	26	0	26	2
Southall, Neville	2/1/1982	25/1/1997	70	0	70	0
Southworth, Jack	27/1/1894	27/1/1894	1	0	1	0
Speed, Gary	5/1/1997	25/1/1997	2	0	2	1
Stanley, Garry	5/1/1980	7/3/1981	1	2	3	0
Stein, Jimmy	12/1/1929	13/1/1934	16	0	16	8
Steven, Trevor	14/4/1984	20/5/1989	33	0	33	4
Stevens, Dennis	15/1/1963	2/2/1965	10	0	10	1
Stevens, Gary	2/1/1982	21/2/1988	38	0	38	2
Stevenson, Alex	12/1/1935	8/1/1949	16	0	16	8
Stevenson, William	11/1/1908	8/3/1913	14	0	14	0
Stewart, Alex	21/1/1893	20/3/1893	7	0	7	0
Stewart, Billy	27/1/1894	19/3/1898	15	0	15	0
Storrier, David	2/3/1895	19/3/1898	10	0	10	0
Stuart, Graham	8/1/1994	25/1/1997	10	3	13	5
Stubbs, Alan	5/1/2002	-	11	0	11	1
Styles, Archie	13/1/1974	30/1/1974	4	0	4	0
Sutherland, John	5/1/1957	26/1/1957	2	0	2	0
Tal, Idan	6/1/2001	26/1/2002	0	3	3	0
Tansey, Jimmy	7/1/1956	8/1/1958	9	0	9	0
Taylor, Edward	14/1/1928	28/1/1928	2	0	2	0
Taylor, Jack	30/1/1897	31/3/1910	56	0	56	14
Telfer, George	27/1/1974	28/1/1978	4	4	8	1
Temple, Derek	29/1/1958	11/3/1967	21	0	21	8
Thomas, Dave	7/1/1978	10/1/1979	2	0	2	0
Thomas, Eddie	4/1/1958	14/2/1959	7	0	7	2
Thomas, Tony	4/1/1998	4/1/1998	1	0	1	0
Thompson, Robert	10/1/1914	27/3/1915	6	0	6	0
Thomsen, Claus	4/1/1998	4/1/1998	1	0	1	0
Thomson, George	6/1/1962	6/1/1962	1	0	1	0
Thomson, Jock	10/1/1931	15/2/1939	22	0	22	0
Tiler, Carl	4/1/1998	4/1/1998	1	0	1	0
Todd, Colin	10/1/1979	10/1/1979	1	0	1	0
Trebilcock, Mike	23/4/1966	14/5/1966	2	0	2	2
Trentham, Douglas	22/1/1938	22/1/1938	1	0	1	0
Troup, Alec	12/1/1924	28/1/1928	10	0	10	3
Turner, Iain	8/2/2006	-	1	0	1	0
Turner, Joseph	9/2/1901	23/2/1901	2	0	2	1
Tyrer, Alan	7/1/1961	7/1/1961	1	0	1	0
Unsworth, David	7/1/1995	4/2/2004	23	1	24	5
Valente, Nuno	7/1/2006	-	4	0	4	0

	Debut	Final	Start	Sub	Ttl	Gls
Van den Hauwe, Pat	5/1/1985	20/5/1989	30	0	30	1
Varadi, Imre	16/4/1980	11/3/1981	6	1	7	1
Vernon, Roy	7/1/1961	15/2/1964	12	0	12	7
Virr, Albert	10/1/1925	12/1/1929	9	0	9	1
Wainwright, Eddie	11/1/1947	3/3/1956	21	0	21	8
Wall, Alex	7/1/1922	7/1/1922	1	0	1	0
Walsh, Mick	10/1/1979	10/1/1979	1	0	1	0
Ward, Mark	4/1/1992	19/1/1994	4	0	4	0
Ward, Mitch	23/1/1999	13/2/1999	2	0	2	0
Wareing, William	15/1/1913	30/1/1915	5	0	5	2
Warzycha, Robert	4/1/1992	19/1/1994	1	3	4	0
Watson, Dave	10/1/1987	8/1/2000	47	1	48	5
Watson, Robert	15/10/1887	19/11/1887	4	0	4	0
Watson, Gordon	4/3/1939	14/2/1948	5	0	5	0
Watson, Steve	6/1/2001	4/2/2004	2	1	3	1
Weaver, Walter	10/1/1925	21/2/1925	4	0	4	0
Weir, David	7/3/1999	-	17	2	19	0
Weir, James	12/11/1887	19/11/1887	2	0	2	0
Weldon, Anthony	14/1/1928	12/1/1929	3	0	3	0
Weller, Louis	10/1/1920	5/3/1921	5	0	5	0
West, Gordon	15/1/1963	26/2/1972	40	0	40	0
White, Tommy	19/1/1932	11/1/1936	9	0	9	0
White, Walter	16/1/1909	31/3/1910	9	0	9	3
Whiteside, Norman	6/1/1990	21/2/1990	6	0	6	3
Whitley, Jack	7/2/1903	7/3/1903	3	0	3	0
Whittle, Alan	3/1/1970	26/2/1972	6	0	6	2
Wignall, Frank	9/1/1960	7/1/1961	2	0	2	0
Wilkinson, Jonathan	14/3/1931	14/3/1931	1	0	1	0
Wilkinson, Paul	5/1/1986	22/2/1987	3	0	3	1
Williams, Ben	11/1/1930	19/1/1932	8	0	8	0
Williams, Graham	10/1/1959	24/1/1959	2	0	2	0
Williams, Richard	16/1/1892	20/3/1893	12	0	12	0
Williams, William	29/1/1898	29/1/1898	1	0	1	0
Williams, William D.	13/1/1923	17/1/1923	2	0	2	0
Wilson, George	12/1/1907	25/3/1907	6	0	6	1
Wilson, Ian	9/1/1988	20/5/1989	3	2	5	0
Wilson, Ray	9/1/1965	12/2/1969	26	0	26	0
Wolstenholme, Sam	28/1/1899	6/2/1904	10	0	10	0
Wood, George	7/1/1978	8/3/1980	4	0	4	0
Wright, Billy	10/1/1979	11/3/1981	13	0	13	0
Wright, Richard	4/1/2003	-	4	0	4	0
Wright, Tommy	13/1/1965	3/2/1973	35	0	35	0
Wylie, Thomas	16/1/1892	16/1/1892	1	0	1	0
Xavier, Abel	11/12/1999	5/1/2002	4	0	4	0
Yobo, Joseph	3/1/2004	-	4	1	5	0
Young, Alex	6/1/1962	27/4/1968	25	2	27	4
Young, Alex 'Sandy'	25/1/1902	25/2/1911	39	0	39	15
Young, Robert	14/1/1911	25/2/1911	3	0	3	1

EVERTON'S COMPLETE FA CUP RECORD

Versus	P	W	D	L	F	A
Aldershot	1	1	0	0	4	1
Altrincham	2	1	1	0	3	1
Arsenal	3	2	0	1	10	4
Aston Villa	8	3	1	4	14	15
Barnsley	6	4	1	1	10	4
Bedford Town	1	1	0	0	3	0
Birmingham City	4	2	1	1	6	5
Blackburn Rovers	10	7	1	2	18	10
Bolton Wanderers	12	3	5	4	21	19
Bournemouth	1	1	0	0	5	0
Bradford City	5	3	0	2	6	6
Bradford Park Avenue	2	0	1	1	1	2
Brighton & Hove Albion	3	1	1	1	3	5
Bristol City	4	4	0	0	10	1
Bristol Rovers	2	2	0	0	5	0
Burnley	6	3	1	2	10	10
Burton Wanderers	1	1	0	0	5	2
Bury	4	3	1	0	13	2
Cardiff City	1	1	0	0	2	1
Carlisle United	2	2	0	0	6	2
Charlton Athletic	3	2	1	0	8	4
Chelsea	8	2	1	5	4	12
Chesterfield	1	1	0	0	3	0
Colchester United	1	1	0	0	5	0
Coventry City	4	4	0	0	9	1
Crewe Alexandra	2	1	1	0	2	1
Crystal Palace	7	4	2	1	20	11
Derby County	11	8	0	3	26	16
Doncaster Rovers	2	2	0	0	10	0
Exeter City	3	2	1	0	2	0
Fulham	7	0	3	4	5	9
Gillingham	3	1	2	0	3	0
Glossop North End	1	0	0	1	1	2
Grimsby Town	3	3	0	0	15	7
Hull City	6	1	3	2	8	10
Ipswich Town	6	5	1	0	11	6
Jarrow	1	1	0	0	3	1
King's Lynn	1	1	0	0	4	0
Leeds United	7	4	2	1	10	4
Leicester City	2	2	0	0	6	3
Leyton Orient	4	2	1	1	7	5
Liverpool	20	6	5	9	24	34
Luton Town	4	3	1	0	11	3
Manchester City	10	4	3	3	12	8
Manchester United	10	5	0	5	8	8
Middlesbrough	11	4	5	2	18	15
Millwall	4	1	1	2	2	4
Newcastle United	5	3	0	2	6	5
Newport County	2	1	1	0	3	2
Norwich City	3	3	0	0	9	1
Nottingham Forest	5	3	0	2	12	7
Notts County	2	2	0	0	4	2
Oldham Athletic	7	2	3	2	12	7
Plymouth Argyle	5	4	1	0	13	3
Poole Town	1	1	0	0	3	1
Port Vale	3	1	1	1	6	6
Portsmouth	1	1	0	0	5	0
Preston North End	9	4	3	2	16	11
Queens Park Rangers	2	2	0	0	4	1
Sheffield United	6	2	0	4	5	6
Sheffield Wednesday	19	9	5	5	35	26
Shrewsbury Town	3	2	0	1	6	3
Southampton	9	5	2	2	13	8
Southend United	3	3	0	0	8	3
Southport	3	3	0	0	13	1
Stockport County	4	3	1	0	11	5
Stoke City	8	5	1	2	16	6
Sunderland	14	7	3	4	28	16
Swansea City	1	1	0	0	3	0
Swindon Town	5	3	1	1	13	6
Telford United	1	1	0	0	3	0
Tottenham Hotspur	10	5	1	4	15	14
Tranmere Rovers	2	1	0	1	2	3
Walsall	1	1	0	0	2	1
Watford	2	2	0	0	4	1
West Bromwich Albion	9	4	2	3	11	7
West Ham United	9	4	1	4	12	12
Wigan Athletic	1	1	0	0	3	0
Wimbledon	4	1	1	2	3	5
Woking	1	1	0	0	3	0
Wolverhampton Wanderers	7	2	2	3	8	9
Wrexham	1	1	0	0	5	2
TOTAL	**388**	**209**	**76**	**103**	**705**	**434**

PENALTIES AGAINST EVERTON IN THE FA CUP

Season	Date	Taker	Opponents	Venue	Time	Result
1901/02	25th Jan	Tommy Robertson	Liverpool	A	44	Scored
1902/03	7th Mar	Alf Watkins	Millwall	A	s/h	Woodwork
1905/06	10th Mar	Harry Davies	Sheffield Wednesday	H	20	Saved
1905/06	10th Mar	Harry Davies	Sheffield Wednesday	H	s/h	Scored
1909/10	31st Mar	Tommy Boyle	Barnsley	N	39	Wide
1910/11	25th Feb	Steve Bloomer	Derby County	A	26	Scored
1945/46	9th Jan	Bill Shankly	Preston North End	H	117	Scored
1947/48	24th Jan	Johnny Hancocks	Wolverhampton Wan.	A	71	Saved
1947/48	14th Feb	Henry Freeman	Fulham	H	80	Wide
1958/59	28th Jan	Sam Lawrie	Charlton Athletic	H	73	Wide
1961/62	27th Jan	Bill Leivers	Manchester City	H	s/h	Saved
1962/63	16th Mar	Johnny Byrne	West Ham United	A	59	Scored
1976/77	27th Apr	Phil Neal	Liverpool	N	30	Scored
1978/79	10th Jan	Gary Rowell	Sunderland	A	20	Scored
1986/87	22nd Feb	Kevin Gage	Wimbledon	A	44	Saved
1989/90	17th Feb	Andy Ritchie	Oldham Athletic	A	56	Scored
1989/90	16th Mar	Ian Marshall	Oldham Athletic	A	93	Scored
1994/95	9th Apr	Jurgen Klinsmann	Tottenham Hotspur	N	62	Scored
2005/06	8th Feb	Frank Lampard	Chelsea	A	36	Scored